International Federation of Library Associations and Institutions
Fédération Internationale des Associations de Bibliothécaires et des Bibliothèques
Internationaler Verband der bibliothekarischen Vereine und Institutionen
Международная Федерация Библиотечных Ассоциаций и Учреждений
Federación Internacional de Asociaciones de Bibliotecarios y Bibliotecas

About IFLA   www.ifla.org

IFLA (The International Federation of Library Associations and Institutions) is the lead-
ing international body representing the interests of library and information services and
their users. It is the global voice of the library and information profession.

IFLA provides information specialists throughout the world with a forum for exchanging
ideas and promoting international cooperation, research, and development in all fields
of library activity and information service. IFLA is one of the means through which
libraries, information centres, and information professionals worldwide can formulate
their goals, exert their influence as a group, protect their interests, and find solutions to
global problems.

IFLA's aims, objectives, and professional programme can only be fulfilled with the cooperation and active involvement of its members and affiliates. Currently, over 1,700
associations, institutions and individuals, from widely divergent cultural backgrounds,
are working together to further the goals of the Federation and to promote librarianship
on a global level. Through its formal membership, IFLA directly or indirectly represents
some 500,000 library and information professionals worldwide.

IFLA pursues its aims through a variety of channels, including the publication of a major
journal, as well as guidelines, reports and monographs on a wide range of topics. IFLA
organizes workshops and seminars around the world to enhance professional practice
and increase awareness of the growing importance of libraries in the digital age. All this
is done in collaboration with a number of other non-governmental organizations, funding
bodies and international agencies such as UNESCO and WIPO. IFLANET, the Federation's website, is a prime source of information about IFLA, its policies and activities:
www.ifla.org

Library and information professionals gather annually at the IFLA World Library and
Information Congress, held in August each year in cities around the world.

IFLA was founded in Edinburgh, Scotland, in 1927 at an international conference of
national library directors. IFLA was registered in the Netherlands in 1971. The Koninklijke Bibliotheek (Royal Library), the national library of the Netherlands, in The Hague,
generously provides the facilities for our headquarters. Regional offices are located in
Rio de Janeiro, Brazil; Dakar, Senegal; and Singapore.

IFLA Publications 127

Measuring Quality

Performance Measurement in Libraries

2nd revised edition

Roswitha Poll
Peter te Boekhorst

K · G · Saur München 2007

IFLA Publications
edited by Sjoerd Koopman

Bibliographic information published by the Deutsche Nationalibliothek
The Deutsche Nationalbibliothek lists this publication in the Deutsche Nationalbibliografie; detailed bibliographic data is available in the Internet at http://dnb.d-nb.de.

⊗

Printed on permanent paper
The paper used in this publication meets the minimum requirements of American National Standard – Permanence of Paper for Publications and Documents in Libraries and Archives ANSI/NISO Z39.48-1992 (R1997)

Printed in the Federal Republic of Germany by Strauss GmbH, Mörlenbach

ISBN 978-3-598-22033-3
ISSN 0344-6891 (IFLA Publications)

CONTENTS

6

PREFACE

It is now more than ten years since "Measuring Quality" was first published. We have been gratified indeed to see that the book has not only been translated into five other languages, but has also been widely used, as frequent citations and lists of performance indicators in different countries show.

In the ten years since this handbook appeared, there have been rapid and extensive changes as well in scholarly communication as in the services of libraries. Libraries are increasingly offering their services in electronic and web-based form. Therefore performance measurement must include indicators for electronic resources and services and should – if possible – combine traditional and new forms of service in the assessment. The first edition contained only two very simple indicators for electronic library services. The new edition offers seven indicators especially intended for electronic services; a great part of the other indicators combine the quality assessment of both traditional and electronic services.

There are other issues beside electronic services that gained in relevance since the first edition:

- **The demand for cost-effectiveness**: Libraries today are experiencing growing problems when organising their work and offering their services within the given budget and resources. In addition, there is a general demand for transparency as to costs and quality in all areas, especially in the public sector. The new edition offers six indicators dealing with costs or expenditure ratios and seven indicators for measuring the effectiveness of processes.

- **The library as working place and meeting point**: Contrary to all expectations, the importance of the library as physical place has in most cases not decreased. The possibility of "hybrid" use, combining print and electronic media, and a growing tendency to work in groups are reasons for attracting users to the library. Libraries have taken up these issues by offering group working areas and information commons. The library's activities in cultural life (exhibitions and other events with a literary, cultural or educational intent) add to the relevance of the library as physical place.

  The topic "library as a physical place" is represented by six indicators in the new edition.

- **The library's teaching role**: The dramatic change in information resources entails problems in information seeking. "Information overload"

7

has become a serious problem in research, and academic teachers are complaining about the "Google mentality" of students who do not proceed beyond a quick search on the web. The difficulty today is how to find and select relevant information. Libraries have taken up the new task of teaching information literacy, often in cooperation with faculties.

The new edition presents three indicators for the library's information and teaching services.

- **The library's functions for external users**: Most libraries offer services to external users, users not belonging to the population the library has been set up to serve. But the services delivered to external users have seldom been included in quality assessment, though they may add up to a considerable part of a library's expenses and activities.

  The new edition shows one indicator for the topic.

- **The importance of staff**: In times of ongoing changes in the information world, the quality of library services is more than ever dependant on employees whose professional qualification and engagement can cope with the change.

  The new edition includes two indicators for this topic.

Of the 17 indicators in the first edition, 6 have been deleted, either because they proved too difficult in practice and therefore were not often used (e.g. expert checklists for collection assessment, success rate of subject searches) or because they have been replaced by more up-to-date indicators including electronic services.

This handbook is intended as practical instrument for the evaluation of library services. While the first edition aimed only at academic libraries, the perspective has now been widened to include public libraries. That does not mean that the book will not be of use for other types of libraries. Special libraries serving research will be able to use most of the indicators. General research libraries without a specified clientele cannot use the "per capita" indicators that compare resources and usage to the population to be served. National libraries could apply part of the handbook, but they will need an additional set of indicators that reflect their special tasks of collecting, cataloguing and preserving the national documentary heritage.

Libraries vary as to mission and goals, collections and services, size and type of population. Therefore not all performance indicators in this book will be applicable in every library. The collection is not meant to be prescriptive. Libraries should choose the indicators best adapted to their needs, and local circumstances might make it necessary to modify the methods of data collection. In most cases, it will be necessary to repeat the measuring process after some time in order to note changes and to monitor the effect of organisational steps taken after the first measuring.

The handbook shows a set of 40 indicators that were selected according to the following criteria:

- To cover the full range of resources and services generally offered in academic and public libraries
- To consider traditional services as well as new electronic services and, if possible, to combine them in "merged" indicators
- To select indicators that have been tested and documented, at least in a similar form to what is described here
- To cover the different aspects of service quality as described in the Balanced Scorecard, including indicators for the aspect of development and potentials

The Balanced Scorecard is a management strategy developed for the commercial sector[1], with the four perspectives: users, finances, processes, learning and development. It was adapted to libraries in several projects.[2]

As in the first edition, the authors have tried to limit the number of indicators. But evaluation in libraries can serve different purposes and can aim at different target groups. "It is difficult to produce a core set for all stakeholders, for all purposes, and for all frequencies. An annual core set for accountants looks different from a core set for the library manager to check productivity or for a Li-

---

[1] Kaplan, R. S. and Norton, D. P. (1996), The Balanced Scorecard: translating strategy into action, Harvard Business School Press, Boston, Mass.

[2] see e.g. Ceynowa, K. and Coners, A. (2002), Balanced Scorecard für wissenschaftliche Bibliotheken, *Zeitschrift für Bibliothekswesen und Bibliographie, Sonderheft* 82, Klostermann, Frankfurt a.M.; Krarup, K. (2004), Balanced scorecard at the Royal Library, Copenhagen, LIBER Quarterly 14,1, pp.37-57, available at: http://liber.library.uu.nl/ ; Pienaar, H. and Penzhorn, C. (2000), Using the balanced scorecard to facilitate strategic management at an academic information service, *Libri* 50,3, pp.202-209, available at: http://www.librijournal.org/pdf/2000-3pp202-209.pdf; Poll, R. (2001), Performance, processes and costs: managing service quality with the balanced scorecard, *Library Trends* 49,4, pp.709-718; University of Virginia Library, Balanced scorecard at UVa Library, available at: http://www.lib.virginia.edu/bsc/index.html

brary Committee to see how use and users have changed over the last five years. Reasonably large bundles of indicators seem unavoidable..."[3]

Another reason for a large set of indicators is that there may be several well-tested indicators for the same service that answer different aspects of the same question.

Example: How intensively is the collection used?
Indicators:
- collection turnover
- loans per capita
- percentage of stock not used

Each indicator gives a somewhat different picture and might serve different purposes of the evaluating library.

Trying to consider all stakeholder groups, all purposes of measuring and all aspects of the Balanced Scorecard, it did not seem possible to restrict the handbook to only 15 or 20 indicators.

For the selection of indicators, the following sources have been consulted:
- The existing literature on performance measurement, especially reports on practical use of certain indicators
- The benchmarking projects, where groups of libraries join in using a specified set of performance indicators
- The International Standard for library performance indicators that is being revised at the moment[4]

It proved especially helpful that the authors cooperated in the national and international groups for benchmarking and standardization.

Experience of libraries when using the first edition showed, that in spite of detailed descriptions libraries had problems using the different methods and calculating and interpreting the results of the measuring process. The new edition tries to give more help as to the calculation of costs and as to possible actions based on the results of measuring.

---

[3] Sumsion, J. (1999), Popularity ratings, core sets and classification of performance indicators, *Proceedings of the 3rd Northumbria International Conference on Performance Measurement in Libraries and Information Service,* University of Northumbria, Newcastle upon Tyne, p. 249.
[4] ISO DIS 11620 (2006), Information and documentation – Library performance indicators, International Organization for Standardization, Geneva

In many cases it will be difficult to know whether the results of an indicator are "good" or "bad". Where results of libraries using the same indicator were available, they have been added to the individual indicators in order to give help in rating the own score. For example, if a library reaches a shelving accuracy of 85%, seeing that between 92 to 99% are the usual score will allow to rank the own results.

The detailed description of measuring techniques (sampling, surveying) in the first edition has been omitted as there is now a sufficient number of handbooks available for these methods.

The first edition of the handbook offered a comprehensive bibliography of the literature dealing with performance measurement. As performance measures are now established and standardized, the new edition presents only a short bibliography of the most important literature, but more sources and additional reading have been added to the individual indicators.

Measures for the outcome or impact of library services on users and on society have not yet been included in this handbook, as methods and possible "indicators" are still being tested in projects. But because of the growing importance of this issue a chapter has been added showing an overview of possible methods for assessing impact and outcome.

Acknowledgements

The authors are grateful for the manifold information gained in contacts with experts in the German and international groups concerned with library assessment and benchmarking. The working groups of ISO TC 46 SC 8 "Quality – statistics and performance evaluation" have been especially helpful in discussing the indicators.

All links cited in this book have been checked in June 2007.

1. The role of performance indicators in quality management

1.1 Quality in library and information services

To achieve high quality in their products and services is essential not only for commercial firms, but also for all non-commercial institutions. Quality will have a different aspect in every institution, but there is a broad consensus in management literature about a general definition of quality. The most frequently cited definition is:

Quality is fitness for purpose

In the ISO 9000 standard quality is described as "the consistent conformance of a product or service to a given set of standards or expectations".[5]

In most definitions quality is defined in relation to the customer or user: "...the key issue is that quality becomes a meaningful concept only when it is indissolubly linked to the aim of total customer satisfaction".[6]

Quality of a product or service defined in relation to the customer must not necessarily mean the highest grade possible. A product of a simpler grade may have high quality because it meets the needs and expectations of its target customer group. Quality for one customer or customer group does not always mean quality for another customer or group

Example: Bicycles
For the normal cyclist, a bicycle should be:
- Solidly built
- Easy to use
- Cheap

For the racing cyclist, it should have:
- Highest possible durability
- Minimum weight
- High-end components

The price will not be as important as for the normal cyclist.

Quality in library and information services can have many aspects. Peter Brophy, starting from the general management literature, has adapted a set of qual-

---

[5] ISO 9000 (2005), Quality management systems, fundamentals and vocabulary, International Organization for Standardization, Geneva
[6] Brophy, P. and Coulling, K. (1996), Quality management for information and library managers, Aslib Gower, Aldershot, p. 6

13

ity attributes to libraries.[7] The following table relies for the most part on Brophy's set and shows the quality criteria with typical examples of their appliance to library services.

Criteria of library quality		Example
Performance	A service meets its most basic purpose	Making key information resources available on demand
Features	Secondary characteristics which add to the service but are beyond the essential core	Alerting services
Reliability	Consistency of the service's performance in use	No broken Web links
Conformance	The service meets the agreed standard	Dublin Core
Durability	Sustainability of the service over a period of time	Document delivery within 2 days
Currency	Up-to-dateness of information	Online catalogue
Serviceability	Level of help available to users	Complaint service
Aesthetics	Visual attractiveness	Physical library, website
Usability/Accessability	Ease of access and use	Opening hours, website structure
Assurance/Competence/Credibility	Good experience with staff's knowledgability	Correct reference answers
Courtesy/Responsiveness/Empathy	Accessibility, flexibility and friendliness of staff	Reference service
Communication	Clear explanation of services and options in language free of jargon	Website, signposting in the library
Speed	Quick delivery of services	Interlibrary lending
Variety of services offered	May clash with quality, if the resources are not sufficient for maintaining quality in all services	Comprehensive collection, reference service in walk-in, mail and chat form
Perceived quality	The user's view of the service	User satisfaction

---

[7] Brophy, P. (2004), The quality of libraries, in Die effektive Bibliothek, Roswitha Poll zum 65. Geburtstag, Saur, München, pp. 30-46.

1.2 The stakeholders' view

Stakeholders are all groups that have an interest in the functioning of an institution. For a library, this will normally be:

- The users (actual and potential users)
- The funding institutions (a university, a community, a commercial firm, etc.)
- Library staff
- Library managers

Additional stakeholders may be staff representatives and a library board or controlling committee.

The perception of library quality will differ in the stakeholder groups. Users see library quality according to their experience with the services they use. They will not care for the efficiency of background processes, but for the effective delivery of services. The funding or parent institution will be interested in the library's benefit to the institution and in the library's cost-effectiveness. Staff, on the other hand, will rate the library's quality by their working conditions, by adequate offers for further education, and by an efficient organisation.

Users	• Access to information worldwide
	• Delivery of information to the desktop
	• Speed and accuracy of delivery
	• Good in-library working conditions
	• Responsiveness of staff
	• Reliability of services
Financing authorities	• Cost-effectiveness
	• Clear planning, effective organisation
	• Positive outcome on users
	• Benefits for the institution's goals
	• Effective cooperation with other institutions
	• High reputation of the library
Staff	• Good working conditions
	• Clear planning, straight processes
	• Systematic staff development
	• High reputation of the library

Not all of the issues named here are indeed criteria of library quality. A good reputation for instance is rather an effect of quality services, but it is important for maintaining quality.

Two studies are especially informative when assessing stakeholder perceptions of library quality: The New Zealand University Libraries Effectiveness

Study[8] and a project at Glasgow Caledonian University[9]. Both studies offered an extensive list of possible performance indicators to different stakeholder groups and asked respondents to rate the usefulness of the indicators for judging the effectiveness of a university library. The stakeholder groups in New Zealand were

- resource allocators,
- senior library staff,
- other library staff,
- academic staff,
- graduate students,
- undergraduates,

with a subdivision of academics and students into seven subjects like chemistry or law. The Glasgow project replaced "resource allocators" by "university senior management team" and subdivided graduate and undergraduate students in part-time and full-time and academics into research and teaching.

Both projects found that the university management was mostly interested in issues concerning staff performance and user satisfaction like "competence of library management", "helpfulness, courtesy of staff" and "match of open hours to user needs", but also in financial issues like the amount and flexibility of the library budget and the cost-efficiency of the library.

Library staff also showed a strong focus on management issues and on helpfulness and courtesy of staff. "Other library staff", being directly involved in user services, showed a higher identification with user needs than senior staff.

The user groups showed differing priorities. Academics ranked indicators of expert assistance and document delivery very high, but showed also an interest in library management and library financing. Student groups placed the emphasis on their immediate needs. The availability of seats or of multiple copies of titles in high demand, longer opening hours and adequate equipment, but also helpfulness of staff, especially at the reference desk, ranged high.

The existing performance indicators have been devised, tested, and selected by librarians. That means that they reflect the librarian's picture of the ideal library. "In other words, the measures we use tell us, presumably, what it is we

---

[8] Cullen, R. and Calvert, P. J. (1995), Stakeholder perceptions of university library effectiveness, *The Journal of Academic Librarianship* 21,6, pp. 438-448

[9] Crawford, J., Pickering, H. and McLelland, D. (1998), The stakeholder approach to the construction of performance measures, *Journal of Librarianship and Information Science* 30,2, pp. 87-112

value in libraries."[10] The view of the funding institutions, of the users or the general public might not be the same.

The best way for combining the different views will be for libraries to

- assess what their users (or non-users) expect from the services they use (or do not use because of bad experience),
- ask the funding institution's opinion about what the library should do and how it should perform in order to support the institution's goals,
- try to find measures that assess quality in the sense of stakeholder groups.

1.3 The model of quality management

Managing a library's quality requires that the special tasks of the library in question are clearly defined. A definition of the library's mission – in consensus with the authorities – should precede all other steps.

The International Standard ISO 11620 defines "mission" as:

"Statement approved by the authorities formulating the organisation's goals and its choices in services and products development"

Stating a library's mission means formally describing the framework within which the library is to move. The mission statement should specify the primary user group whom the library intends to serve and what kind of fundamental services the library intends to offer. It should consider the mission and goals of the parent institution or community and – as far as possible – not only the present needs of its population, but also predictable future demand.

The mission of a library could be summarized as follows:

To select, organize and provide access to information for users, in the first place for the primary user group, and to further information literacy by help and training services.

The German benchmarking project BIX[11] developed a mission statement for academic libraries that defined the following tasks (shortened version):

- **Mediating information use by**
    - building a collection that supports learning, teaching and research,
    - guiding to the existing literature and information worldwide via portals

---

[10] Cullen, R. (1998), Measure for measure: a post modern critique of performance measurement in libraries and information services, IATUL Proceedings 8, available at: http://iatul.org/conferences/pastconferences/1998proceedings.asp
[11] BIX. Der Bibliotheksindex, available at: http://www.bix-bibliotheksindex.de/

and bibliographic databases,
- organizing quick delivery or online access for documents not available locally.

- **Producing and preserving information by**
  - offering an infrastructure for electronic publishing,
  - archiving and preserving print and electronic information in the library's parent institution,
  - indexing, digitizing and promoting its collections for local, national and international use.

- **Supporting teaching and learning by**
  - offering a place for individual and group work with adequate technical facilities,
  - supporting online and multimedia teaching and learning and remote access,
  - furthering information literacy via teaching modules and help services.

- **Managing the services effectively by**
  - developing and maintaining innovative technology,
  - using adequate management methods for effectiveness and efficiency,
  - furthering staff competences by staff training and development,
  - cooperating locally, nationally and internationally.

The mission of public libraries is summarized in the IFLA/UNESO public library manifesto of 1994[12] that defines as "key missions":

1. creating and strengthening reading habits in children from an early age;
2. supporting both individual and self conducted education as well as formal education at all levels;
3. providing opportunities for personal creative development;
4. stimulating the imagination and creativity of children and young people;
5. promoting awareness of cultural heritage, appreciation of the arts, scientific achievements and innovations;
6. providing access to cultural expressions of all performing arts;
7. fostering inter-cultural dialogue and favouring cultural diversity;
8. supporting the oral tradition;
9. ensuring access for citizens to all sorts of community information;

---

[12] IFLA/UNESCO Public Library Manifesto 1994, available at http://www.ifla.org/VII/s8/unesco/eng.htm

10. providing adequate information services to local enterprises, associations and interest groups;
11. facilitating the development of information and computer literacy skills;
12. supporting and participating in literacy activities and programmes for all age groups, and initiating such activities if necessary.

For each individual library's mission statement it will be necessary to add the special tasks of that library, e.g. legal deposit right, archiving functions, tasks in cooperative programs, or services for special user groups.

Based on the definition of the mission and the general tasks, long- and short-time goals can be fixed and resources (funds, space, staff time) can be allocated to the activities that are necessary for attaining the goals. This includes defining the quality that should be reached in the delivery of services. The goals should be realistic, achievable within a given time, and the results should be measurable and comparable over time.

If the general goal is for instance to inform users by comprehensive and current online catalogues, the short-time objectives might be

- to eliminate backlogs within a certain period,
- to include separate catalogues for special collections in the online catalogue.

After some time, it will be necessary to control whether the goals and the desired quality have been attained. This will probably lead to re-planning and to redefining goals for the next period.

A simple model of quality management could show like this:

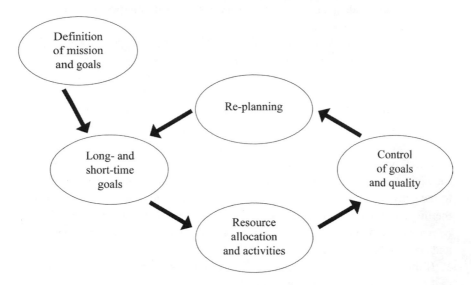

Quality management is a recurrent process, a continual revision of goals, processes, and evaluation. "Effective planning is impossible without an evaluation component, and evaluation has little practical utility unless the findings are integrated into the planning process."[13]

1.4 Performance measurement in the context of quality management

There is today a general demand for transparency, accountability, and quality assurance in non-commercial institutions. For libraries, it will generally be the funding institution that wants to see "value for money" and asks not only for data of input and output, but also for evidence of effective and cost-efficient delivery of services and products. The library must be able to show how well it is performing, but also what resources are needed for maintaining or raising its level of quality. Quality assessment is "...a political weapon in acquiring resources and securing the library's place in the organisation."[14] It can help to make libraries "visible" to the financing authorities and to the public.

---

[13] Hernon, P. and Altman, E. (1996), Service quality in academic libraries, Ablex Publ., Norwood, NJ, p. 16

[14] Brophy, P. and Coulling, K. (1996), Quality management for information and library managers, Aslib Gower, Aldershot, p. 157

Quality planning needs a measuring instrument to assess whether a library comes up to its goals. Such an instrument is performance measurement.

Measuring performance means collecting statistical and other data that describe the performance of the library and analysing these data in order to evaluate the performance. Or, in other words: Comparing what a library is doing (performance) with what it is meant to do (mission) and what it wants to achieve (goals).

Performance or quality indicators (also called performance measures) have been developed and applied by libraries since several decades and have been published in handbooks and standards. The International Standard ISO 11620 defines a performance indicator as "numerical, symbolic or verbal expression, derived from library statistics and data used to characterize the performance of a library". Performance indicators include both simple counts and ratios between counts.

The criteria for performance indicators are established in the International Standard 11620. Performance indicators should be

- **informative** = helpful for identifying problems and possible actions to be taken,
- **reliable** = producing the same results when used under the same circumstances,
- **valid** = measuring what they are intended to measure,
- **appropriate** = compatible with the library's procedures and working environment,
- **practical** = easy to use and understand, applicable with a reasonable amount of effort in terms of staff time, staff qualifications, operational costs and users' time and patience,
- **comparable** = allowing comparison of results between libraries of similar mission, structure and clientele.

It could be added that indicators should address only factors that can be controlled or at least influenced by the library.

Performance indicators measure on the one side the **effectiveness** in delivering services to users and on the other side the **cost-effectiveness**, the efficient use of existing resources. Quality would then mean that a service is "good" as well as "cheap".

The reasons for measuring performance are manifold. For library management, quality assessment will support the improvement of services and products and will help to demonstrate the library's effectiveness to funding institutions and the public. An additional "outcome" of the measurement process will be that staff will get a better overview of the different aspects of services, of the goals to be achieved and the ways to reach them. There will be awareness of the way the library functions. "The key purpose of performance measurement, sometimes forgotten, is to influence people – their behaviour and their decision-making".[15]

1.5 The choice of indicators

The first step for a library will be to choose a set of performance indicators that corresponds to its mission and goals. The indicators should also refer to the mission and goals of the library's parent institution and show the library's support for the institution's goals.

Not all libraries will be allowed to choose those performance indicators that they think most appropriate. If there is an evaluation program for libraries organized by government or other authorities, or if the library's parent institution engages in a specified evaluation program, the evaluation processes and measures will be prescriptive. It may therefore be expedient for libraries to take the initiative and present methods by which they want to demonstrate their effectiveness. If groups of libraries use a joint evaluation system, e.g. a benchmarking system on a national scale, this might help to avoid measures imposed on them by external institutions.

Different libraries will have different missions. Even in libraries in higher education that apparently have the same goals, there will be differences as to
- the structure of the clientele,
- the research subjects of the institution,
- the level of research and teaching,
- special tasks like a collection of rare material.

There is no objective standard for library "goodness", though standards have been developed for different types of libraries. The concept of quality may be different for each library, and measures must be selected according to that concept and the special tasks. In addition, the library's mission and tasks may change over time, e.g. by
- certain subjects being deleted from or added to the curriculum,
- new tasks like teaching information literacy being added,
- other libraries taking over tasks of the library.

---

[15] Winkworth, I. (1998), Making performance measurement influential, *Proceedings of the 2nd Northumbria International Conference on Performance Measurement in Libraries and Information Services,* Information North, Newcastle upon Tyne, p. 93

Generally, a set of indicators should be chosen that allow an overall view of the library, including traditional and electronic services, and that show the interaction of the different services.

Normally, libraries will not start measuring performance by systematically using all indicators described in a handbook or standard. Rather, the library will first be interested in using only a few indicators for specified services, because

- users complain about specific services,
- staff suggests that a particular service might be improved,
- library statistics point to decreasing use of certain services,
- the introduction of new technology or budget restraints imply organisational changes.

In such cases, the choice of indicators will be determined by the results that the library wants to obtain from the evaluation. But isolated evaluation of only one service or aspect might lead to wrong perceptions.

Example:
- The processing speed of media is measured and proved to be high.
- But: Both the availability of required media and the overall collection use are low.

Apparently the wrong titles are purchased – but processed efficiently.

Performance indicators evaluate different services or activities of a library, but there may be interdependencies. Trying to achieve a higher score for one indicator may affect the score of another indicator.

Example:
A high percentage of library funds spent on acquisitions can mean lower expenditure for staff and therewith a lower rate of "staff per capita".

The library will have to decide on priorities, but the results of indicators can support such decisions.

1.6 Staff involvement

After choosing the appropriate indicators for the individual library, it is important to involve staff in the measurement project, especially those persons that are actually responsible for the service that is evaluated. Staff members could suggest possible problems bound up with the measurement process or could help to adapt the method to the specific circumstances of the library.

It should be made quite clear that performance indicators measure the quality of the library's services, not the performance of individual persons. Data about staff performance like in indicator C.9 "Employee productivity in media processing" in this handbook should be summarized.

Yet, staff may be concerned about the implications of the measuring process. They feel that the efficiency of their department may be questioned, and that there might be organisational changes starting from the results that can affect their individual area of responsibility.

It is necessary, therefore, to

- reach consensus with staff about the mission and goals of the library,
- inform staff representatives at an early stage of the planning,
- give constant feedback to all staff members affected by a measuring process or the results,
- discuss and analyze results with staff,
- develop strategies for improvement together with staff,
- ensure data protection,
- establish transparency about the reasons for measuring and the expected gains.

1.7 Using the results

It is crucial that the results of the measuring process find their way into the organisation and procedures of the library. Too often, performance measurement seems to be an end in itself, the results being stored without practical effects.

Above all, the staff members must be informed about the results of the often tedious measuring procedures. A short summary illustrated with diagrams and stating the conclusions drawn from the project and the actions to be taken will be interesting to all staff, even if they are not directly affected by the measures. This will also help to overcome possible reservations in regard to performance measurement.

If the indicator has been used before by the library, it will be informative to compare with former results in order to evaluate the effect of activities taken after the first measuring. It will also be useful to identify changes in the library's working environment that occurred in the meantime and that might have affected the results of the second measuring.

The interpretation of the results should – if possible – include comparison with scores of the same indicator obtained in other libraries of similar structure and clientele. "In using performance measures for planning and evaluation one needs to know how one library compares with another in order to determine what the figures 'should be', and whether particular figures are 'high' or 'low'.

This is particularly important when dealing with the library's public and providers of finance."[16] Such comparisons should consider special goals and conditions of a library that may make it impossible to obtain the same results as other libraries. For example, a library whose mission includes archival functions cannot have the same results in the indicator "Collection use" as a library that can weed its collection regularly. The rating whether a score is "good enough" for the library will depend on the library's mission and goals, that is on what services the library has to offer, and what range of services is adequate to its clientele. But comparison with other libraries will help to get a broader view of the library's own results.

Using a performance indicator will not directly show what activities could be taken in order to achieve higher effectiveness or efficiency for the service that was evaluated. There is not always a clear-cut correlation between cause and effect. "...the reason that the term 'performance indicator' is generally preferred to 'performance measure' is that interpretation is always necessary. The figures produced are indicative of a situation which may need to be investigated or monitored."[17]

Insufficient scores of indicators can be due to manifold issues:
- Inadequate knowledge of the population's needs
- Lack of staff skills
- Insufficient staffing for a service
- Insufficient promotion of the services
- Users' lack of competences or of knowledge about the library's services and procedures
- Other libraries nearby supplying services to the library's clientele
- Inefficient workflows
- Insufficient degree of automation
- Inadequate buildings
- Legal regulations that do not allow flexible use of resources
- Low priority of the service that was evaluated in the library's policy

Not all of these issues can be influenced by the library.

Libraries would probably see insufficient resources as first reason for poor performance. But additional resources will not lead to higher quality, if management issues are not considered at the same time, and in many cases better performance can be reached without additional resources.

---

[16] Revill, D. (1990), Performance measures for academic libraries, in Kent, E. (Ed.), Encyclopedia of Library and Information Science, Vol.45, Suppl.10, Dekker, New York, Basel, p. 322
[17] Brophy, P. (2005), The academic library, 2nd edition, Facet, London, p. 189

Actions to be taken in case of bad results relate in the first place to organisational changes. In close collaboration with the staff directly involved in the services that were evaluated, workflows and procedures should be reconsidered. Staff will probably be able to name training issues, additional equipment, or changes in the organisational structure that would help them to perform better. The experience of performance measurement will awake sensibility for possible improvements in the library's services.

In most cases, organisational changes should not be addressed after the first use of an indicator. It will be useful to repeat the measurement after some time in order to make sure that the time of measurement or special conditions during the measuring process have not influenced the score.

While the results of performance measurement will in the first place be used for management decisions in the library, they will also be extremely useful when reporting to authorities or applying for funding. If a library uses standardized indicators or joins in a benchmarking project, this will make the results more convincing for the funding institutions.

The results should also be presented to the library's population or clientele. Especially the users who have actively taken part in a study, e.g. via questionnaires, have a right to know the outcome of the study. Results should be published even if they are worse than expected. In that case special emphasis should be placed on the initiatives to improve the situation. If the scores are good, the presentation of the results will be an effective public relations tool for the library.

All stakeholder groups – library staff, the library's parent organisation or funding authority, the library's clientele – should be acquainted not only with the results of performance measurement, but also with the actions taken in consequence of the results and with the improvements achieved by such actions. "Measurement is a political activity."[18]

1.8 The present state of performance measurement

In the literature about quality assessment in libraries, there have been frequent complaints about a lack of reports on practical use of performance indicators opposed to a broad theoretical discussion on the merits or problems of performance measurement. Though this situation has become somewhat better in the last

---

[18] Cullen, R. (1998), Measure for measure: a post modern critique of performance measurement in libraries and information services, *IATUL Proceedings* 8, available at: http://iatul.org/conferences/pastconferences/1998proceedings.asp

ten years, there is still a majority of articles concerned with the theory of quality assessment, asking for better and more qualitative measures or for new topics to be addressed in measuring. But while there is already a demand for a "new generation" of performance indicators[19], including indicators of impact and outcome, there seems to be still a lack of knowledge about how to choose and use indicators for the evaluation of library services.

Yet evidently the usefulness of performance measurement has by now been recognized worldwide. Though there are few reports about the use of special indicators, this could mean that some indicators (e.g. availability or collection use) are so well established that libraries do not publish the results every time they use them.

That quality measures have been accepted as an important management instrument is probably not least due to the Northumbria International Conference on Performance Measurement in Libraries and Information Services, which since 1995 every two years assembles experts of quality management worldwide. This conference and its journal[20] have certainly acted as communication centre for projects on development and use of performance indicators and have supported the promotion of quality measurement in theory and practice.

The proceedings of the Northumbria conference clearly show the development of quality assessment in the last ten years and the growing interest for topics like

- user-orientation as focal point,
- assessment of stakeholder views,
- qualitative measures as a necessary complement to quantitative measures (though qualitative measures must be made quantifiable in order to be convincing),
- impact and outcome measures as a step beyond input and output measures.

Use of performance indicators has proceeded from individual libraries using certain indicators for their specific problems to joint benchmarking projects of library groups on a regional or even national scale.[21] There are quite a number of

---

[19] see e.g. Brophy, P. (2002), Performance measures for 21st century libraries, *Proceedings of the 4th Northumbria International Conference on Performance Measurement in Libraries and Information Services,* Association of Research Libraries, Washington DC, pp. 1-7

[20] Performance Measurement and Metrics, Vol.1 (2000) ff.

[21] Poll, R. (2007), Benchmarking with quality indicators: national projects, *Performance Measurement and Metrics* 8,1, pp. 41-53

projects now where groups of libraries have found consensus on a set of indicators that they use regularly, some already since several years. Examples are:

BIX –Library Index[22]
German public and academic libraries (two separate sets of indicators)
Public libraries 1999 ff., academic libraries 2002 ff.

CASL (Council of Australian State Libraries) [23]
Public libraries
1998 ff.

Swedish Quality Handbook[24]
All types of libraries
3-years project 2001-2004; continuation not decided

HELMS (UK Higher Education Library Management Statistics) [25]
Academic libraries
1997/98 ff.

Benchmarking of the Netherlands University Libraries[26]
University libraries
1999 ff.

Norwegian indicators[27]
Academic and public libraries
New project starting 2007

The problem for such joint projects is to reach consensus on a list of performance indicators that consider the goals and special tasks of each participating library. Libraries often restrict themselves to "measuring the measurable". When discussing a possible set of indicators in a group of libraries, the main question

---

[22] BIX. Der Bibliotheksindex, available at: http://www.bix-bibliotheksindex.de/
[23] Australian Public Libraries Comparative Report 1998-2004, available at: http://www.nsla.org.au/publications/statistics/2004/pdf/NSLA.Statistics-20040701-Australian.Public.Library.Comparative.Report.1998.2004.pdf
[24] Edgren, J. et.al. (2005), Quality handbook, performance indicators for library activities, The Swedish Library Association's Special Interest Group for Quality Management and Statistics, available at: http://www.biblioteksforeningen.org/sg/kvalitet/handbook_eng.html
[25] UK Higher Education Library Management Statistics 2003-2004 (2005), Sconul, London
[26] http://www.ukb.nl/benchmark.htm; see also Laeven, H. and Smit, A. (2003), A project to benchmark university libraries in The Netherlands, *Library Management* 24, 6/7, pp. 291-304
[27] Forslag til indikatorer for fag- og folkebibliotek (2007), version 4.0, ABM-utvikling, Oslo, available at: http://www.abm-utvikling.no/bibliotek/statistikk-for-bibliotek/indikatorer-for-fag-og-folkebibliotek

is always whether the data could be taken from existing (national) library statistics, and what time would be needed for the measuring process. But some important questions cannot be addressed by taking only data from the automated system, a turnstile, or the institutional member statistics and nearly all joint library projects mentioned before have also used indicators that require additional data collection.

It is interesting to see that though the projects differ in the sets of indicators they deem most important, yet they address the same topics, and most indicators are taken form existing handbooks or the ISO standard 11620, so that results become comparable between library groups and countries. Using such standardized methods does not only allow benchmarking, but will give the individual library more confidence in its measuring process and will add reliability to the data when reporting to funding institutions.

2. Indicators of impact or outcome

2.1 Impact/outcome of libraries

Libraries have always been able to calculate the input into their services (funding, staff, collections, space, equipment) and the output of those services (loans, visits, downloads, reference transactions, etc). Measures have also been developed for assessing the quality of library services and the cost-efficiency of the library's performance. Performance measurement evaluates whether a library is effective and efficient in delivering its services.

But quantity of use and quality of performance do not yet prove that users benefited from their interaction with a library. Measuring impact or outcome means going a step further and trying to assess the effect of services on users and on society. "Impact" and "outcome" are often used synonymously in the professional literature, but "outcome" is also used for the output/usage of library services (e.g. a user reading a book), while "impact" is also seen as the broader term, denoting changes in users (e.g. the user gaining knowledge).[28]

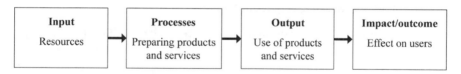

Input	Processes	Output	Impact/outcome
Resources	Preparing products and services	Use of products and services	Effect on users

Outcome or impact means that there is a change in a user's skills, knowledge, or behaviour.

> "Outcomes are the results of library use as affecting the individual user."[29]

> "Outcomes are the ways in which library users are changed as a result of their contact with the library's resources and programs."[30]

What changes can a library effect in users? Using library services can further

---

[28] Brophy, P. (2005), The academic library, 2nd edition, Facet, London, p. 189

[29] Revill, D. (1990), Performance measures for academic libraries, in Kent, E. (Ed.), Encyclopedia of Library and Information Science, Dekker, New York, Basel, Vol.45, Suppl.10, p.316

[30] ACRL. Association of College and Research Libraries. Task Force on Academic Library Outcomes Assessment Report. June 27 1998, available at: http://www.ala.org/ala/acrl/acrlpubs/whitepapers/taskforceacademic.htm

- knowledge,
- information literacy,
- democracy (access to information for all),
- higher academic or professional success,
- social inclusion (e.g. of elderly people or immigrants),
- lifelong learning,
- individual well-being.

Short-term effects even of a single library visit may be that users find relevant information, can solve a problem, save time in their work, gain searching skills and self-reliance in using information.

Long-term effects of using library services could be permanently higher information literacy, higher academic or professional success, changes in attitudes and motivation (e.g. motivation to read), and changes in information behaviour (e.g. using a broader variety of information resources).

The changes could be seen as a pyramid, going from cognitive impacts (knowledge acquisition) to changes in attitudes and opinions and lastly to changes in behaviour.

2.2 Methods for assessing impact/outcome

For several years, projects worldwide have tried to find methods for proving an outcome of library services.[31] The main problem for such methods is that influences on an individual are manifold and that therefore it is difficult to trace changes and improvements in users back to the library. Nevertheless, there are quite a number of possible methods that have already yielded interesting results. They can be roughly differentiated into quantitative and qualitative methods.[32]

Qualitative ("soft") measures, developed in social science, try to assess outcomes by evaluating users' experiences and opinions. Methods used are:
- Surveys (print, telephone, or online)
- Interviews
- Focus groups, discussion groups
- Users' self-assessment of skills and competences gained

---

[31] An overview of ongoing research is given in: Poll, R., Bibliography "Impact and outcome of libraries", available at: http://www.ulb.uni-muenster.de/outcome

[32] Poll, R. and Payne, P. (2006), Impact measures for libraries and information services, *Library High Tech* 24,2, pp. 547-562, available at: http://conference.ub.uni-bielefeld.de/2006/proceedings/payne_poll_final_web.pdf

The methods have not only been used with actual library users, but also with non-users and the general public in order to gain estimates of potential outcomes of libraries.

In surveys, interviews or discussion groups, users and non-users are asked for

- direct benefit from using library services,
- potential benefits from using libraries or a specified library,
- indirect (potential) benefit of a library's existence, (e.g. free access to information, cultural life in the community, children's literacy, social inclusion),
- potential value of libraries for future users (e.g. preservation of the national documentary heritage).

Users' self-assessment of their benefits has proved less reliable, as users tend to over-estimate the competences gained.

Qualitative methods have been frequently used in public libraries in order to show their social impact and local importance.[33] Such qualitative methods will deliver a rich fund of "stories" that show what users think about actual or potential benefits of libraries. This "anecdotal evidence" helps to elucidate and corroborate the results of quantitative measuring, but it should be organized and made quantifiable to be convincing. The Museums, Libraries and Archives Council, London, cites such quantified results in a conspicuous place on its website, e.g.:

"70% of children believe that a library is one of the best places to learn, outside school." [34]

It should always be kept in mind that results gained by qualitative methods will have a subjective bias. They show the "perceived benefit", but do not prove benefit. They should therefore be compared with results of quantitative methods or with statistics of library usage in order to validate the results.

Quantitative methods try to obtain tangible data for a change in user competences or behaviour or to find correlations between library use and a person's academic or professional success. The following methods have been used:

---

[33] Bohme, S. and Spiller, D. (Ed.) (1999), Perspectives of public library use 2. A compendium of survey information, Library & Information Statistics Unit (LISU), Loughborough; Debono, B. (2002), Assessing the social impact of public libraries : what the literature is saying, *Australasian Public Libraries and Information Services* 15,2, pp. 80-95; Linley, R. and Usherwood, B. (1998), New measures for the new library: a social audit of public libraries, *British Library Research and Innovation Centre Report* 89, British Library Board, London
[34] MLA. Museums, Libraries and Archives Council, available at: http://www.mla.gov.uk/

- Tests that assess user skills before and after a library training lesson or the use of library services
- Performance monitoring/data mining
- Unobtrusive observation of users
- Analysis of citations in course work or research publications over years
- Comparison of success data with data of library use

Tests for assessing changes in users' skills and competences are today widely applied in libraries, especially for evaluating the learning outcome of a library's information literacy training. Such tests can be used before and after a training session or a series of training sessions in order to show differences in the competence of finding and evaluating relevant information. Tests for measuring training impact will be compulsory when a library's information literacy modules are included in the curriculum of its institution.[35]

Performance monitoring, data mining and unobtrusive observation have been used for tracing users' searching procedures, their search terms, and their use of help functions. These methods can show successes, failures and problems. When the study is repeated regularly, results may trace quantifiable changes in the searching skills of users.

Analysis of bibliographies in users' papers, especially in doctoral dissertations, has been used for two different purposes:

1. To assess the importance of the local library for research and study: The citations in research papers are compared with the local collection (including electronic resources licensed by the library). The results show how far the materials cited in the papers have been (or could have been) accessed via the local library and thus whether the local library offers sufficient material for research.[36]

---

[35] For literature on the outcome of information literacy training see: Poll, R., Bibliography "Impact and outcome of libraries", Part 3, available at: http://www.ulb.uni-muenster.de/out come

[36] Ahtola, A. A. (2002), How to evaluate and measure the impact of the library's collection on the learning outcome? *68th IFLA Council and General Conference*, available at: http://www.ifla.org/VII/s2/conf/ahtola.pdf; Kayß, M. and Poll, R. (2006), Unterstützen Bibliotheksbestände die Forschung? Zitatanalyse in Dissertationen, *B.I.T. online* 2006,2, available at: http://www.b-i-t-online.de/archiv/2006-02-idx.html; Smith, E. T. (2003), Assessing collection usefulness: an investigation of library ownership of the resources graduate students use, *College & Research Libraries* 64, pp. 344-355

2. To show whether there are changes over time or after library training sessions as to the accuracy of citations, the currency of cited titles, the type of resources used or the number of electronic resources cited.[37]

It would of course be most interesting to funding institutions to know whether library services positively influence the academic or professional success of users. For assessing such influence, data as to the frequency of library use and the type of services used are set in relation to data about the same persons' success. This method has especially been used for students' success, described by data like

- duration of studies,
- grades in exams,
- student persistence (retention),
- employment rates after exams.

A number of projects worldwide have tried to find a correlation between the use of library services and the success of users.[38] Problems occur when data protection rules forbid the use of personal data, but even comparing groups of users has yielded valid results in some cases.[39]

2.3 Assessing the financial value of libraries

In the frame of outcome assessment, libraries have also tried to "measure" their economic value. The funding that is necessary for libraries (collections, buildings, equipment, and especially staff) constitutes a considerable factor in the budget of universities or communities, and funding institutions and the taxpayers will want to see whether investment in libraries yields "value for money".

Libraries have tried to answer this question, including the actual and the potential economic benefit as well for single users as for the general public. As most library services have no equivalent on the common market and therefore

---

[37] Emmons, M. and Martin, W. (2002), Engaging conversation: evaluating the contribution of library instruction to the quality of student research, *College and Research Libraries* 63, pp. 545-560; Tunón, J. and Brydges, B. (2006), Improving the quality of university libraries through citation mining and analysis using two new dissertation bibliometric assessment tools, *World Library and Information Congress: 71th IFLA General Conference and Council*, available at: http://www.ifla.org/IV/ifla71/papers/078e-Tunon_Brydges.pdf

[38] see: Poll, R., Bibliography "Impact and outcome of libraries", Part 4, available at: http://www.ulb.uni-muenster.de/outcome

[39] de Jager, K. (2002), Impacts and outcomes: searching for the most elusive indicators of academic library performance, *Proceedings of the 4th Northumbria International Conference on Performance Measurement in Libraries and Information Services*, Washington DC, Association of Research Libraries , pp. 291-297

no "market prices" for services can be determined, two other ways have been tried for assessing the economic value of libraries:

- Assessing time costs ("replacement value of a client's time")
- Using the contingent valuation method

Measuring time costs starts from the assumption: When users invest time and effort in order to use library services the financial value that they - or their institution - place on that use must be at least as high as their "sacrifice" of time. The time costs of library usage are calculated by multiplying the time users spend on library services with the average salary costs of the population served by that library. The problems of this method are that in many cases it will not be possible to calculate average salaries, e. g. for students, and that the time costs of library usage might as well be seen as just another cost factor, not as a financial value achieved by the library.

More promising is the contingent valuation method that has been developed for assessing the financial value of non-profit organisations and services, especially for projects in health care, environmental protection, education or culture.[40] Persons that would be directly or potentially interested in a specified organisation or its services are asked to rate the value of the organisation or service in financial terms, expressed by their "willingness-to-pay" or "willingness-to-accept". For assessing the financial value of libraries, the questions could be:

- Willingness-to-pay: What would you pay for maintaining this library/this particular library service?
- Willingness-to-accept: Which sum would you accept as an equivalent if this library/this particular library service were given up?

Usually, the interviewees are given options between sums they would pay (e.g. in higher taxes) or accept (e.g. in lower taxes). The problem of this method is that people are asked to financially rate services or institutions that they never thought of in terms of money. The contingent valuation method has already been frequently applied for public libraries.[41] The British Library used this method

---

[40] see e. g. Mitchell, R. C. and Carson, R. T. (1993), Using surveys to value public goods, the contingent valuation method, Resources for the Future, Washington

[41] Aabø, S. (2005), The value of public libraries in Norway, *Bibliotekforum* 6, pp. 38-40; Holt, G. E., Elliott, D. and Moore, A. (1999), Placing a value on public library services, *Public Libraries* 38, pp. 89-108; Morris, A., Hawkins, M. and Sumsion, J. (2001), The economic analysis of public libraries, *Library and Information Commission Research Report* 89, British Library, London

with the impressive result that for every £1 of public funding that the British Library receives each year, £4.4 are generated for the national economy.[42]

2.4 Impact/outcome assessment and performance measurement

Performance measures assess the quality of library services, either by quantitative data or by users' perception of the quality. Assessing impact or outcome tries to find out whether library services have an identifiable effect on users.

It might be assumed that services with good quality (speed, reliability, user-orientation) will have more positive impact on users than services with poor performance. If outcome assessment shows that the outcomes that the library intends to achieve are not reached, performance measurement can help to identify problems or failures in the service delivery that may lead to minimally positive or even negative outcome on users.

Information literacy training is a good example for showing relations between impact and performance assessment. If attendants of training sessions do not show higher skills in tests after the training, the library could use satisfaction surveys in order to find reasons for poor impact. It could also use indicator B.10 "Attendances at training lessons per capita" to see whether the lessons attract a sufficient part of the population.

Another example is the relation between library use and academic success of users. If the results of such comparison show that students with high success have not used library services frequently, again satisfaction surveys will help to detect reasons for non-use of certain services. The library might then apply specified indicators for measuring the quality of those services in order to see whether insufficient service delivery has influenced the use of services and thus impeded possible positive outcomes on users.

2.5 Projects of outcome assessment

A number of projects worldwide are trying to find methods, measures, and tools for assessing impact/outcome of libraries and information services.

- The eVALUEd Project, based within the evidence base at the University of Central England, was set up to develop a transferable model for e-

---

[42] Pung, C., Clarke, A. and Patten, L. (2004), Measuring the economic impact of the British Library, *New Review of Academic Librarianship* 10,1, pp. 79-102

library evaluation in higher education. The project produced a toolkit for evaluating electronic information services[43].

- IMLS (Institute of Museum and Library Services) fosters outcome-based evaluation of projects.[44]

- The New Measures Initiative of ARL (Association of Research Libraries) includes several outcome-related programs[45]:
  - Learning Outcomes
  - Higher Education Outcomes Research Review
  - MINES (Measuring the Impact of Networked Electronic Services)

- IBEC, a joint research initiative of the Information School of the University of Washington and the University of Michigan School of Information has developed a toolkit for assessing the impact of information in communities.[46]

- SCONUL (Society of College, National and University Libraries) and LIRG (Library and Information Research Group) have started an impact initiative. [47]

---

[43] available at: http://www.evalued.uce.ac.uk/index.htm
[44] available at: http://www.imls.gov/index.shtm
[45] available at: http://www.arl.org/stats/initiatives/index.shtml
[46] available at: http://ibec.ischool.washington.edu/default1024.aspx?cat=Home&b=y
[47] available at: http://www.sconul.ac.uk/groups/performance_improvement/impact2.html

3. Overview of the indicators

The set of indicators used in this handbook has many sources and has developed over time. The 17 indicators in the first edition, considering only academic libraries, were based on the existing literature, on the results of IFLA sessions in 1989 and 1990, and on practical tests undertaken by the authors. These indicators were partly adopted by the project EQLIPSE (1995-1998), a European Commission funded research project for quality management and performance measurement in libraries,[48] and also by the ISO group that edited the first international standard on performance measurement in libraries.[49] The authors of this handbook cooperated in both projects.

Up to 1998, performance measurement had mainly considered the traditional library services. The next step was again initiated by a project of the European Commission: EQUINOX (1998-2000)[50], where nearly the same partners as in EQLIPSE tested performance indicators for electronic library resources and services. The result was a list of 14 indicators that greatly influenced international quality measurement in libraries, especially the ISO Technical Report for performance measures in electronic library services.[51]

In 1999, a German project for controlling in academic libraries was funded by the German Research Foundation and chaired by the University Library Münster. This project adapted the Balanced Scorecard, developed for the commercial sector by Kaplan and Norton, for the use in libraries. The performance indicators used in the project relied only partly on the work done before, as new indicators had to be developed in order to cover all perspectives of the Balanced Scorecard, especially the perspective "potentials and development". The project resulted in a handbook in 2002.[52]

---

[48] EQLIPSE. Evaluation and quality in library performance: system for Europe, 1995-1997, available at: http://www.cerlim.ac.uk/projects/eqlipse/
[49] ISO 11620 (1998), Information and documentation – Library performance indicators
[50] EQUINOX. Library performance measurement and quality management system, 1998-2000, available at: http://equinox.dcu.ie/
[51] ISO TR 20983 (2003), Information and documentation – Performance indicators for electronic library services
[52] Ceynowa, K. and Coners, A. (2002), Balanced Scorecard für wissenschaftliche Bibliotheken, *Zeitschrift für Bibliohekswesen und Bibliographie*, Sonderheft 82, Klostermann, Frankfurt a.M.

Many ideas and indicators of this controlling handbook were then taken over by the German benchmarking project BIX.[53] BIX had been started for public libraries in 1999 by the Bertelsmann Foundation in cooperation with the German Library Association. Data are collected and published annually. In 2002, the project was widened to academic libraries. The 17 indicators used for academic libraries are grouped in the perspectives of the Balanced Scorecard.

In 2004, work started on the revision of the International Standard ISO 11620. The goal was to combine performance indicators for traditional and electronic library services, if possible in "merged" indicators. The German example led to the adoption of the Balanced Scorecard and of the newly developed indicators for potentials and development. The ISO standard will probably be published later in 2007.

Thus, influences on this handbook have been manifold, going to and fro from the national to the international level, and there was a broad selection of indicators to choose from. And yet, the authors decided to develop and test two new indicators, as some crucial aspects seemed to be missing: One indicator for the quality of the library website, another for the overall cost per case of usage, including traditional forms of use (loans, in-house use) as well as downloads.

In order to avoid naming the general sources at each indicator, a list of the indicators with the main sources was added as Annex 2.

---

[53] BIX. Der Bibliotheksindex, available at: http://www.bix-bibliotheksindex.de/

4. Description of the indicators

Each indicator is presented in the standard format described below.

4.1 Name

Each indicator has a unique, descriptive name.

4.2 Background

The background statement describes the present state and importance of the service, activity or aspect the indicator is meant to measure.

The statement shows what is regarded as quality in the service, activity or aspect in libraries and what measures/indicators have as yet been used for assessing quality.

4.3 Definition

The definition describes the data that are necessary for the indicator and their relation.

Definitions of the data elements used rely for the most part on ISO 2789.[54] If terms are used in a specified sense in the frame of an indicator, the special definition is given.

Unambiguous terms used in the customary sense are not defined.

4.4 Aims of the indicator

Explains what the indicator is meant to measure in relation to the library's goals.

Describes what types of services or activities would benefit most from using the indicator and limitations in the application of the indicator.

Explains under what circumstances comparison of results with other libraries may be possible.

---

[54] ISO 2789 (2006) Information and documentation – International library statistics, International Organisation for Standardization, Geneva

4.5 Method(s)

The method statement describes the way of collecting the data and of calculating the results.

If more than one method has proved effective for the same purpose, several methods are described.

If possible, the descriptions of methods indicate the effort necessary for preparation, data collection and analysis of results.

4.6 Interpretation and use of results

The interpretation statement discusses what the results may point to, especially reasons for low effectiveness. It points to difficulties and to circumstances that could affect the results.

The statement names possible reactions to the results in order to achieve better results and explains what other indicators might be useful in the same context.

The interpretation statement may include information about the variability to be expected, such as seasonal variations or variations in time of day.

4.7 Examples and further reading

References are supplied to document the source of the indicator or of similar indicators.

If possible, examples are given of results when using this or a similar indicator, in order to show the range of scores that may be possible and to help libraries in interpreting their own results.

5. List of indicators

The definitions in the indicators follow for the most part the International Standard ISO 2789 (2006) Information and documentation – International library statistics.

The description of methods in the indicators relies partly on the newest draft of the International Standard ISO DIS 11620 (2006) Information and documentation – Library performance indicators.

The indicators are presented in the perspectives of the Balanced Scorecard and within those along the service areas. The Balanced Scorecard as defined for commercial institutions had originally four perspectives: users, finances, processes, and learning and development. Here, as in the standard 11620 and the German project BIX, these perspectives are adapted to libraries as follows:

- Resources, infrastructure
- Use
- Efficiency
- Potentials and development

Using the structure of the Balanced Scorecard helps to consider all relevant management issues and to establish a "balance" between user-orientation and cost-effectiveness, effective organisation and the ability to cope with future developments

A. Resources, infrastructure: What services does the library offer?

The aspect "Resources/infrastructure" is represented by 10 indicators. The library's attractiveness as place for learning and research is defined by the size of the user area, the availability of user workplaces and by the opening hours. The quality of the collection is measured by the acquisitions expenditure per capita, by a comparison of giving and taking in interlibrary lending and by the availability of requested media (Indicators A.5, A.6, and A.8). Staff resources and website quality are each represented by one indicator.

Library as place for learning and research	A.1. User area per capita
	A.2. Seats per capita
	A.3. Opening hours compared to demand
Collections	A.4. Expenditure on information provision per capita

	A.5. Availability of required titles
	A.6. Percentage of rejected sessions
	A.7. Ratio of requests received to requests sent out in interlibrary lending
	A.8. Immediate availability
Staff	A.9. Staff per capita
Website	A.10. Direct access from the homepage

B. Use: How are the services accepted?

This perspective is represented by 12 indicators. Market penetration, user satisfaction and the number of visits are used as general indicators for user-oriented services. Seat occupancy is the indicator for the library as place. The attractiveness of the physical collection is evaluated by using loan data (Indicators B.6, B.7 and B.8), that of the electronic collection by using downloads.

The adequacy of the library's information services is measured against attendances at user training and reference questions per capita. Attendances are also used as criterion for the attractiveness of events.

There is one indicator especially addressing the issue of external users.

General	B.1. Market penetration
	B.2. User satisfaction
	B.3. Library visits per capita
Library as place for learning and re-search	B.4. Seat occupancy rate
Collections	B.5. Number of content units downloaded per capita
	B.6. Collection use (turnover)
	B.7. Percentage of stock not used
	B.8. Loans per capita
	B.9. Percentage of loans to external users
Information services	B.10. Attendances at training lessons per capita
	B.11. Reference questions per capita
Cultural activities	B.12. Attendances at events per capita

C. Efficiency: Are the services offered cost-effectively?

The perspective "efficiency" includes both indicators measuring cost-effectiveness and indicators for the quality of processes.

The library's operating expenditure is set in relation to users, visits and total collection use. Acquisitions costs are compared to staff costs in order to assess whether a sufficient part of the budget is spent on the collection. The efficiency of collection building is calculated as cost per download and cost per document processed.

The efficiency of processes is evaluated as to speed (of acquisition, media processing, lending and interlibrary loan) and correctness (of shelving and of reference answers).

General	C.1. Cost per user
	C.2. Cost per visit
	C.3. Cost per use
	C.4. Ratio of acquisitions costs to staff costs
Collection costs	C.5. Cost per document processed
	C.6. Cost per download
Processes - speed	C.7. Acquisition speed
	C.8. Media processing speed
	C.9. Employee productivity in media processing
	C.10. Lending speed
	C.11. Interlibrary loan speed
Processes - reliability	C.12. Reference fill rate
	C.13. Shelving accuracy

D. Potentials and development: Are there sufficient potentials for future development?

This perspective is especially important in times of constant change, as it assesses the library's ability to cope with such change. It has not been easy to find performance indicators for this aspect, as is shown by the small number.

The potential for development is measured on the one hand against the library's input in electronic services (expenditure on the electronic collection, percentage of staff in electronic services), on the other hand against the library's success in gaining funding from its institution and external sources or by income generation.

The most relevant indicator for potentials and development is certainly the library's input into staff training.

Electronic services	D.1. Percentage of acquisitions expenditure spent on the electronic collection
	D.2. Percentage of library staff providing and developing electronic services
Staff development	D.3. Attendances at training lessons per staff member
Budget	D.4. Percentage of library means received by special grants or income generation
	D.5. Percentage of institutional means allocated to the library

A. Resources, infrastructure

A.1 User area per capita

Background

"Institutions today are asking for and retrieving much greater accountability for the use of their library space. They need to know how it enhances the institution's educational mission and at what cost." (Library as place, 2005, p.8)

With more and more information being accessible from the desktop, funding institutions tend to economize on library buildings; libraries seem to need less space in future. In spite of such predictions, libraries remain important as places for research, learning, reading, or attending cultural events. "The variety and combination of resources, services, spaces, and activities renders the library a destination of academic adventure and serendipitous discovery." (Demas, 2005, p.28)

While formerly the planning of library buildings focussed on the space for collections and the library's technical services, today planning involves the knowledge of user activities in a library. Space for user activities, including areas for meeting and recreation, has become an important issue for the library's success in performing its tasks.

Technological changes and users' growing familiarity with electronic services will affect the planning of user areas in libraries. A Delphi study for health sciences libraries in 2005 sees the following developments for user areas in libraries: "Our experts believe that by 2010, most users will primarily come to a health sciences library not for access to information, but for time-saving or value-added information services and for places to collaborate and study....To attract users, it will be common for health sciences libraries to provide access to food services, within or adjacent to the library. Learning commons will become commonplace as well, as users need help with both the use of information and the tools to access it. Libraries will continue to include both enclosed group study areas and open areas designed for quiet study to satisfy user needs for both group work and privacy." (Logan and Starr, 2005, p.321)

Definition of the indicator

The library's net user area per 1.000 members of the library's population to be served.

User area in the sense of this indicator includes reading and working areas for users, special study places, space for lending, reference and user training services, open-access storage areas, space for exhibitions and events, and all other space designed for user services, including halls, stairways, lobbies and functional rooms.

Areas not usually available to users are excluded.

The population to be served is the number of persons to whom the library is commissioned to provide its services. For public libraries, this will normally be the population of the community (or part of the community); for academic libraries, this will normally be the total of students and academic staff in the institution.

Aims of the indicator

The indicator assesses the adequacy of user space to the library's population and therewith the priority given to user services by the library and the funding institution. It is relevant for all libraries with a defined population to be served.

Comparison between libraries of similar mission, structure and clientele is possible, if special conditions (e.g. a new building, special tasks of the library) are considered.

Method

The user area is calculated in square meters.

The members of the population to be served are counted as persons, not as FTE (full time equivalent). Thus, part-time students or staff in academic institutions will be counted each as one person.

The user area in square meters is set in relation to the number of persons in the population to be served, divided by 1.000.

Interpretation and use of results

A higher score will normally be considered as better. The indicator can be influenced by studying, reading, and meeting facilities that are offered by the library's parent institution outside the library premises, or by another institution near the library.

If the user area per capita seems insufficient compared with other libraries, the library could of course apply for building funds. It might be useful for such appliances to show results of user satisfaction surveys, if users complain of inadequate space for learning, lack of quiet areas or group learning areas.

But building projects take a long time. A shorter way could be to look into the space for the background services and see whether some of that space might be dispensed with and converted into user area. For example, libraries converting their catalogues have used the space of the former card catalogues for user workplaces.

Another solution could be to merge a service with that of other institutions, e.g. the institution's IT centre, in order to find space for new user services like information commons.

Libraries have also cooperated with commercial firms to find funding for a building annex combining e.g. a bookshop and a reading room.

Examples and further reading

The indicator as described above is used in the German benchmarking project BIX (BIX. Der Bibliotheksindex). In 2005, BIX showed the following results (BIX, 2006):

	User area in sqm per 1.000 capita	mean	maximum	minimum
Public Libraries	Communities under 15.000 inhabitants	50,5	121.7	20,3
	Communities from 15.000 to 30.000 inhabitants	35,0	85,3	7,9
	Communities from 30.000 to 50.000 inhabitants	27,5	58,4	6,9
	Communities from 50.000 to 100.000 inhabitants	26,3	44,6	9,2
	Communities over 100.000 inhabitants	23,6	52,3	5,9
Academic Libraries	Universities of applied sciences	359,3	676,3	97,1
	Universities: One-tier systems	832,7	2490,8	286,7
	Universities: Two-tier systems (only the central library considered)	322,1	807,5	37,8

The results demonstrate that comparison is only meaningful between libraries with a similar mission and population. Public libraries offer significantly less user space, as their users usually do not work in the library. Public libraries in smaller communities reach better scores with this indicator, as there will be a certain basic user space (e.g. for the lending area), which will not be much less in a small community.

Academic libraries have to offer large areas for learning and working. In two-tier systems with separate institute libraries, it will be nearly impossible to separate user space in the institute libraries from other functions. Therefore in BIX only the space in the central library of two-tier systems is considered.

It is easier to compare the library's total space to the population. This is for instance done in the SCONUL statistics (Creaser, 2006). SCONUL, Society of College, National and University Libraries, UK measures "traditional floor space per FTE student" in square meters. Space for "non-traditional" library services, such as binderies or reprographics, is excluded. Results did not vary much between 1994-95 and 2004-05, but showed an average between 0,82 and 0,90 m^2 floor space per full-time equivalent student.

The statistics of CAUL (Council of Australian University Libraries) count the library's total floor space in m^2 and total persons in the population, including students, academic and non-academic staff. Comparing these data in the online statistics shows a mean value of 0.67 m^2 per person (CAUL online statistics).

A study in Polish academic libraries calculated total library space per member of the population and found for 2003 a median score of 0,27 m^2 for university libraries and 0,15 m^2 for technical university libraries (Derfert-Wolf, Górski and Marcinek, 2005).

Comparing the total library space to the population could be misleading, as the space for special tasks of the library (storage space for rare collections or legal deposit, rooms for training students in librarianship etc.) might influence the score. And if funding institutions doubt the library's need for space, a performance indicator especially considering the user area may be more convincing.

BIX. Der Bibliotheksindex, available at: http://www.bix-bibliotheksindex.de/

BIX. Der Bibliotheksindex (2006), *B.I.T. online,* Sonderheft 2006

CAUL online statistics, Council of Australian University Libraries, available at: http://www.anu.edu.au/caul/stats/

Creaser, C. (2006), SCONUL library statistics: trends 1994-95 to 2004-05, LISU, Loughborough University

Demas, S. (2005), From the ashes of Alexandria: what's happening in the college library?, in Library as place: rethinking roles, rethinking space, Council on Library and Information Resources, Washington D.C., pp. 25-40, available at: http://www.clir.org/pubs/reports/pub129/pub129.pdf

Derfert-Wolf, L., Górski, M. and Marcinek, M. (2005), Quality of academic libraries – funding bodies, librarians and users, *World Library and Information Congress, 71th IFLA General Conference and Council,* available at: http://www.ifla.org/IV/ifla71/papers/080e-Derfert-Wolf.pdf#search=%22Derfert-Wolf%22

Library as place: rethinking roles, rethinking space (2005), Council on Library and Information Resources, Washington D.C., available at: http://www.clir.org/pubs/reports/pub129/pub129.pdf

Logan, L. and Starr, S. (2005), Library as place: results of a Delphi study, *Journal of the Medical Library Association* 93,3, pp. 315-326, available at: http://www.pubmedcentral.nih.gov/articlerender.fcgi?artid=1175798

A.2 Seats per capita

Background

Libraries are highly esteemed places for reading, learning and working. Though in some libraries physical library visits are decreasing, due to a high number of the library's services and resources being available for remote use, the growing tendency of group work in libraries or of users working with their own material in libraries and the advantage of using both print and electronic resources together with help and training services make the library attractive as a place to meet and study.

Especially in institutions of higher education, the library is the physical place where students meet for studying singly or in groups. Therefore a sufficient number of working places with adequate equipment will be one of the most important issues for user satisfaction.

In public libraries, where users primarily need seats for a shorter time of reading and browsing, the number of seats for the population to be served will be significantly lower than in academic libraries, where users might need a seat for the whole day.

In order to know whether the number of seats provided is adequate to the population to be served, libraries can calculate the ratio of seats per member of the population and benchmark the result with other libraries of similar structure and mission.

Definition of the indicator

The number of user seats provided for reading or working in the library per 1.000 members of the library's population to be served

The definition includes seats with or without equipment, seats in carrels, in seminar and study rooms and in the audiovisual and children's departments of the library.

Seats in halls, lecture and auditory theatres intended for audiences of special events are excluded. The definition also excludes informal seating, e.g. floor space on which users may sit.

The population to be served is the number of persons to whom the library is commissioned to provide its services. For public libraries, this will normally be the population of the community (or part of the community); for academic libraries, this will normally be the total of students and academic staff in the institution.

Aims of the indicator

The indicator assesses the adequacy of seats in the library provided to the library's population and therewith the priority given to the library's role as physical place for reading, learning and working.

The indicator is relevant for all libraries to be served that offer reading and working facilities to a defined population to be served. It will be most relevant for libraries in institutions of higher education.

Comparison between libraries of similar mission, structure and clientele is possible.

The indicator does not measure the usage of the provided seats (see Indicator B. 4 "Seat occupancy rate").

Method

Count the number of seats provided for reading and working in the library.

In a library system with branch, departmental or institute libraries, seats in those libraries should be included.

The members of the population to be served are counted as persons, not as FTE (full time equivalent). Thus, part-time students or staff in academic institutions will be counted each as one person.

The number of seats provided for reading and working in the library is set in relation to the number of persons in the population to be served, divided by 1.000.

Interpretation and use of results

A higher score will normally be considered as better.

The indicator can be influenced by studying, reading, and meeting facilities that are offered by the library's institution outside the library premises, or by another institution near the library.

If the number of seats seems inadequate compared to other libraries, or if the occupancy rate of seats demonstrates such inadequacy, the library should try to find space for offering more seats. Longer opening hours may contribute to a better distribution of users needing seats over the day/week, so that even with the same number of seats there will be lower seat occupancy.

Examples and further reading

Many national library statistics count the number of user seats provided by the library, some count also the number of persons in the population to be served, some only the number of registered users.

The statistics of CAUL, Council of Australian University Libraries, show for 2005 the following result (CAUL online statistics):

- Total seats per total population, including students, academic and non-academic staff (persons) = median value 0.1007

For higher education libraries in the UK the statistics show the "seat hours per week per FTE student" (Creaser, 2005):

- Seat hours per week per FTE student = 8.4

If average opening hours per week are calculated as 70, seats per student would be 0.12, which corresponds to the CAUL data.

The statistics of the Finnish research libraries (Finnish research library statistics database) count:

- Seats per capita (population to be served) x 1.000

The result for 2006 is 203,6 per 1.000 capita = 0,20 seats per member of the population.

A survey in five Bavarian university libraries counted seats per 1.000 members of the population to be served (similar to the Finnish statistics); the result was 137.6 = 0.1376 per member of the population (Kennzahlen für Hochschulbibliotheken, 2003).

CAUL online statistics, Council of Australian University Libraries, available at: http://www.anu.edu.au/caul/stats/

Creaser, C., Maynard, S. and White, S. (2005), LISU annual library statistics 2005, featuring trend analysis of UK public and academic libraries 1994 – 2004, LISU, Loughborough University, available at: http://www.lboro.ac.uk/departments/dils/lisu/downloads/als05.pdf

Finnish research library statistics database, Helsinki University Library, available at: https://yhteistilasto.lib.helsinki.fi/language.do?action=change&choose_language=3

Kennzahlen für Hochschulbibliotheken in Bayern (2003), Unpublished document

A.3 Opening hours compared to demand

Background

The hours the library is open to users have always been regarded as the main criterion for the accessibility of library services. Though many services and resources are today offered for remote access, the physical library with its user space and collections remains important as place for meeting, studying and learning. "Match of opening hours with user needs" was the library effectiveness measure that ranked highest or second highest in the New Zealand university libraries effectiveness study (Cullen and Calvert, 1995). Opening hours are counted in most national library statistics and are also used as performance indicator in quality assessment and benchmarking projects.

Longer opening hours are generally seen as better service, and in most cases this will be true. But if a library wants to assess the adequacy of its opening times, it will be most informative to compare them with users' wishes and needs. "Never accept an assertion that more hours will increase use – or even that they will make lots of users happy. Check first, with user conversations or focus groups … to find out which users are using a particular library when." (Holt, 2005, p.89) The ACRL Standards do not ask for the longest opening hours possible, but for user-friendly opening times: "Hours of access to the library should be reasonable and convenient for its users." (ACRL, 2004) Longer opening times, e.g. after 10 p.m. in the evening, might be unnecessary from the users' point of view, if most users have left the campus by then.

An important issue is to have the same opening hours on all weekdays and – if possible – in all library departments. It is confusing for users if they have to remember different hours for different days and services.

There is always a discrepancy between users' wishes and the library's ability to fulfil these wishes because of restrictions in finances and staff time. The point is to find the right balance between wishes and financial capabilities. Assessing demand in regard to opening hours will help to find such balance within given resources.

Definition of the indicator

The present number and time of a library's opening hours compared to the number and time of opening hours as desired by users.

Opening hours are the hours in a normal week when the main services of the library (e.g. reference and loan services, reading rooms) are available to users.

Aims of the indicator

To assess the correspondence of a library's present opening hours with users' demand.

The indicator is applicable to all libraries.

Comparison between libraries will only be possible as to the general satisfaction with present opening times.

The indicator will be especially informative if it is applied separately for user groups (e.g. undergraduates, graduates, and academic staff).

Methods

1. A survey is handed out to a random sample of users when entering or leaving the library. Data collection should be spread equally over the day and throughout the week to make sure that users preferring morning or evening time or certain days for their visits are not over-represented. The advantage of this method is that there will be in most cases a quick and ready response and that users can make comments when returning the survey. The disadvantage is that potential users that cannot visit the library because of the existing opening times will not be represented.

2. An online survey is put on the library's website at certain times, again with an equal spread over times of the day and week. The advantage is that potential users are considered. The disadvantage is that actual heavy users might be under-represented.

Both surveys should ask for satisfaction with the present opening times and should give the option to name additional times the library should be open. The survey could be added to a comprehensive survey of user satisfaction with the library's services.

Example of a survey:
How would you rate your satisfaction with the present opening times of the library?

very unsatisfactory	☐
unsatisfactory	☐
moderately satisfactory	☐
satisfactory	☐
very satisfactory	☐

Please specify the hours other than the present opening hours you would like the library to be open, by placing an "O" in the appropriate box. The present opening hours are already represented by an "X".

	Mon	Tue	Wed	Thu	Fri	Sat	Sun
0 - 7							
7 - 8							
8 - 9	X	X	X	X	X		
9 - 10	X	X	X	X	X		
10 - 11	X	X	X	X	X	X	
11 - 12	X	X	X	X	X	X	
12 - 13	X	X	X	X	X	X	
13 -14	X	X	X	X	X	X	
14 - 15	X	X	X	X	X	X	
15 - 16	X	X	X	X	X	X	
16 - 17	X	X	X	X	X	X	
17 - 18	X	X	X	X	X	X	
18 - 19	X	X	X	X	X	X	
19 - 20	X	X	X	X	X		
20 - 21	X	X	X	X	X		
21 - 22	X	X	X	X	X		
22 - 23							
23 - 24							

In case the library can only offer further opening hours (e.g. Sunday opening) in exchange for opening hours on other days, users could be asked what present opening hours they would be willing to sacrifice in exchange for hours they prefer.

Many libraries have different opening hours during academic term or vacation. In these cases it would be advisable to have separate surveys during term and vacation time.

Branch libraries or departments such as the loan department or the children's library may have opening hours that differ from the general opening hours. If the library wants to assess the adequacy of such special opening times, it would be best to hand out special surveys to visitors of the individual branch library or department.

Interpretation and use of results

The library should react, if a high percentage of respondents is dissatisfied with present opening hours and asks for extended hours or a different distribution of opening hours over the day/week. This may be difficult, especially if users ask for extended times on weekends or during the night. A possible solution might be to open the library without offering full service, so that non-professional staff could run the library during these times. What services should be offered during additional opening hours should depend on users' needs. The easiest solution would be to offer only study space, if studying is the main reason for users' visits, e.g. during late hours (Engel, Womack and Ellis, 2002). Many libraries when enlarging their opening hours offer only study space, the open access collections, and lending service; reference service might not be available during such times

The survey results should be compared to actual usage data (number of library visits, loans, or reference questions over the day/week). This would help to assess – what the indicator does not measure - whether existing opening times are too liberal and the supply exceeds demand.

Evaluating usage statistics might also help to draw the line between "reasonable" and "unreasonable" demand. In order to know what is "reasonable", the library could offer extended opening hours on trial, e.g. for a test period of two or three months. For a decision on permanent longer opening times it will be useful to assess the number of visits during the test opening and the status of the users visiting the library in that time. It might be that the additional hours attract new user groups or users not belonging to the library's population to be served. It could also be helpful to make use of other libraries' experience with longer opening hours, if the libraries are in a similar situation (e.g. central campus or spread over town).

In addition to the questions referring to satisfaction and demand, users could also be asked to estimate how frequently they visit the library at certain times of the day or certain days of the week. This might help to judge the urgency of the demand for extended hours.

Examples and further reading

An example for the indicator as described above is the joint user survey of 15 German university libraries in 2001 that applied the same survey methodology and collected the data under comparable conditions (Follmer, Guschker and Mundt, 2002; Mundt, 2003). Users were asked to rate their satisfaction with a service and also the importance of the service to them. Opening hours were one of the survey topics. A regression analysis was applied in order to determine the contribution of each factor to the overall satisfaction of each user. Opening hours had a high influence on general satisfaction with the library (14 %). Most libraries had opening times from 8.00 to 22.00 on weekdays, and users seemed content with this; there was not much demand for a 24-hours service. But in libraries with only morning opening on Saturday, there was a clear demand for afternoon opening. Sunday opening was generally not much in demand. Long opening hours on weekday evenings had a higher influence on satisfaction than extended opening hours on weekends. Libraries offering different opening hours for individual departments or services faced lower satisfaction than those offering the same opening hours for all services.

In the project EQLIPSE (EQLIPSE, 1995-1997) that tested data collection for a large set of performance indicators, "opening hours compared to demand" was assessed in two ways:

- Using a survey in short interviews with users and recording their answers
- Offering four options for possible extended opening times:
  - Sunday opening
  - later Saturday opening
  - later weekday opening
  - satisfied with present opening hours

The Swedish Quality Handbook project used the indicator as described above, but added a formula for calculating the relation between the present opening hours and those desired by the respondents (Edgren et. al., 2005):

A/B

A = the number of present opening hours

B = the number of hours which the users state that they need (present hours + additional hours)

If a library is open 60 hours per week and users ask for 10 hours more, the score would be 60:70 = 0.86.

Users could also be asked for the reasons of preferring certain hours, e.g. late hours, for their visits (Curry, 2003, p.12). This can show the importance of additional opening times for certain user groups, e.g. users with a full timetable who would prefer to visit the library in late evening.

Don Revill describes a method for assessing not the additional demand, but the effectiveness of the present opening hours (Revill, 1983). The indicator, named "effective user hours", assesses the total number of hours spent by users in the library during a sampling period and divides them by the number of hours open during the same period. This method would serve for evaluating whether the existing opening times are sufficiently used, but does not measure whether additional times are needed.

ACRL, Association of College & Research Libraries (2004), Standards for libraries of higher education, available at: http://www.ala.org/ala/acrl/acrlstandards/standardslibraries.htm

Cullen, R. J. and Calvert, P.J. (1995), Stakeholder perceptions of university library effectiveness, *Journal of Academic Librarianship* 21,6, pp. 438-448

Curry, A. (2003), Opening hours: the contest between diminishing resources and a 24/7 world, *Journal of Academic Librarianship* 27,6, pp. 375-385

Edgren, J. et.al. (2005), Quality handbook, performance indicators for library activities, The Swedish Library Association's Special Interest Group for Quality Management and Statistics, available at:
http://www.biblioteksforeningen.org/sg/kvalitet/handbook_eng.html

Engel, D., Womack, K. and Ellis, U. (2002), Opening a library 24 hours, *Journal of Library Administration* 36,4, pp.95-108

EQLIPSE. Evaluation and quality in library performance: system for Europe (1995-1997), available at: http://www.cerlim.ac.uk/projects/eqlipse/

Follmer, R., Guschker, S. and Mundt, S. (2002), Gemeinsame Nutzerbefragung der nordrhein-westfälischen Universitätsbibliotheken – methodisches Vorgehen und Erfahrungen, *Bibliotheksdienst* 36,1, pp. 20-33, available at:
http://bibliotheksdienst.zlb.de/2002/02_01_02.pdf

Holt, G. (2005), "Library myths", *The Bottom Line* 18,2 , pp. 87-91

Mundt, S. (2003), Benchmarking user satisfaction in academic libraries – a case study, *Library and Information Research* 27 (87), pp. 29-37, available at:
http://www.lirg.org.uk/lir/pdf/article87_mundt.pdf

Revill, D H. (1983), Some examples and types of performance measures, in Blagden, J. (ed.), Do we really need libraries: Proceedings of the first joint Library Association Cranfield Institute of Technology conference on performance assessment, Cranfield Press, Cranfield, pp. 59-66

A.4 Expenditure on information provision per capita

Background

Libraries provide a wide range of services, but "the provision of materials for readers' use is the single most important role" (Scientific publications, 2004). Against the background of stagnant library budgets and rising prices, the amount of money spent on information provision per member of the population is a crucial indicator when assessing a library's effort to cope with one of its main tasks.

The indicator is helpful in benchmarking procedures, but the calculation of the expenditure may differ between libraries. It is indisputable to include expenditure on books, periodicals, and electronic resources of various kinds as well as binding costs, but the money spent on document delivery is arguable. Some libraries meet document delivery costs for their users instead of buying books and periodicals, either as a deliberate shift from holdings to access or for saving costs.

Definition of the indicator

The expenditure on information provision per member of the library's population to be served during a year.

Expenditure on information provision in the sense of this indicator means the total expenditure for traditional and electronic media, including licenses, pay-per-view costs and expenditure on binding.

Electronic document delivery costs are included if the library covers the document delivery costs for its users.

Expenditure on infrastructure, such as hardware, software or networking, and on digitisation of documents is excluded.

The population to be served is the number of persons to whom the library is commissioned to provide its services. For public libraries, this will normally be the population of the community (or part of the community); for academic libraries, this will normally be the total of students and academic staff in the institution.

Aims of the indicator

The indicator assesses the adequacy of the expenditure on information provision per member of the population and describes in monetary terms the benefit of collection building for the individual user.

The indicator is relevant for all libraries with a defined population to be served.

Comparison of results between libraries with similar mission, structure and clientele is possible, if differences in collection policies are taken into account and if the expenditure is calculated in the same way.

Method

For a clearly defined budget period (usually a year) the library's expenditure on acquisition and licensing (including binding and pay-per-view) is determined. In the context of electronic resources the library's involvement in consortia and other over-all contracts should be taken into account: only the library's own share in the contractual expenses should be counted.

Libraries paying the document delivery charges for their users should add the amount to the expenditure on information provision.

The members of the population to be served are counted as persons, not as FTE (full time equivalent). Thus, part-time students or staff in academic institutions will be counted each as one person.

The total expenditure on information provision during a year is divided by the number of persons in the population to be served.

Interpretation and use of results

A higher score will be considered as good, but the indicator should be seen in the context of the library's goals. It will be especially useful to compare results over time.

Budget cuts and changes in the size of the population will affect the indicator.

Benchmarking effort on the basis of this indicator should consider that special funding, e.g. for special collections supporting information provision on a national scale or for library consortia purchasing databases and other electronic resources will influence the scores.

Examples and further reading

In Great Britain the university libraries' expenditure on information provision per capita has increased considerably in the period between 1994-95 and 2004-05. The new universities recorded a rise from 60.33 £ to 71.23 £, whereas the old universities saw a rise from 97.98 £ to 131.72 £ – an increase by almost 26% (Creaser, 2006, pp.123-127).

In 2005 academic libraries taking part in the German benchmarking project BIX (BIX. Der Bibliotheksindex) recorded an average expenditure on information provision per capita of 123.96 €. Separated according to categories the figures were as follows (BIX, 2006):

	mean	minimum	maximum
University libraries (one-tier systems):	195.30 €	69.15 €	662.05 €
University libraries (two-tier systems):	106.67 €	31.22 €	260.60 €
Universities of applied sciences:	50.81 €	16.93 €	124.59 €

In two-tier systems with many departmental libraries, only the expenditure of the central library was considered in BIX.

The statistics of CAUL, Council of Australian University Libraries, report for 2005 a mean "acquisitions expenditure per population member" of 268.60 AUD which would be about 169.69 € (CAUL online statistics). The figure is higher than the German mean for academic libraries and lower than what old universities in Great Britain spent in the same period (ca. 196,14 €).

For public libraries the score will be lower. In 2006 the Finnish public libraries spent 7.01 € for "library materials per inhabitant" (Finnish public library statistics).

The public libraries in British Columbia, Canada, spent 4,9 CAD = ca. 3,4 € for library materials per "population of the service area" in 2003 (British Columbia public library statistics, 2004).

BIX. Der Bibliotheksindex, available at: http://www.bix-bibliotheksindex.de/

BIX. Der Bibliotheksindex (2006), *B.I.T. online* Sonderheft 2006

British Columbia public library statistics (2004), Ministry of Education, Victoria, British Columbia, available at: http://www.bced.gov.bc.ca/pls/bcplstats_2004.pdf

CAUL online statistics, Council of Australian University Libraries, available at: http://www.anu.edu.au/caul/stats/

Creaser, C., Maynard, S. and White, S. (2006), LISU annual library statistics 2006, featuring trend analysis of UK public and academic libraries 1995 – 2005, LISU, Loughborough University, available at:
http://www.lboro.ac.uk/departments/dils/lisu/downloads/als06.pdf

Finnish public library statistics, Culture and Media Division of the Ministry of Education, available at: http://tilastot.kirjastot.fi/Default.aspx?&langId=en

Scientific publications: free for all? (2004), *House of Commons, Science and Technology, 10th report*, Vol.2, Appendix 135, available at:
http://www.publications.parliament.uk/pa/cm200304/cmselect/cmsctech/399/399we160.htm

A.5 Availability of required titles

Background

"Availability" is a classic among performance indicators in both public and academic libraries. As such it has been often described in the wake of Buckland's landmark *Book Availability and the Library User* (1975) and Kantor's groundbreaking study (Kantor, 1984) and – even more important – has been practically applied in different library settings all over the world (Nisonger, 2007). Despite the librarians' best efforts the complaints can still be heard: "But the good books are still never available when I need them." (Gregory, 2003, p. 283)

The two main aspects of availability are mirrored in the two questions users ask when looking for information in the library's collection:

- Is the document (book, journal article, E-book) I am looking for in the collection?
- If yes, is it available for me?

While the former deals with the quality of the library collection in terms of its fit to users' information needs the latter examines the extent to which titles in the collection are actually available and is therefore a primary measure of demand satisfaction.

Consequently, the ISO standard 11620 distinguishes two indicators to measure the two aspects of availability. This is understandable from a theoretical point of view. However, for practical reasons in most cases where the indicator is used the two aspects are combined in the data collection procedure.

In this sense the availability of required titles as described here is the more comprehensive indicator. It checks both how far the collection fits the requirements of the users and to what degree the titles in demand are actually available.

The indicator also sheds a light on the reasons why the library's collection does not match the requirements of the user. It is multidimensional in that it not only monitors whether the users get what they ask for but also carefully records the various stages of the process in which the user tries to align his short-term information needs with the momentary state of the collection. Ignoring any incident of user failure like inaccurate bibliographic references or inability to locate books in the OPAC or on the shelf, the indicator brings to light where the library is to blame, because it produced incorrect catalogue information, misshelved the book, or failed to buy a sufficient number of spare copies. In the context of electronically available documents the range of reasons for failures widens considerably, from a dead link to an outdated browser version.

In the run of the data collection procedure the indicator pinpoints a variety of reasons preventing the user from receiving the information asked for. Therefore, the indicator is extremely helpful in identifying weaknesses in a core aspect of the library's service provision.

Definition of the indicator

The percentage of titles requested by users that are directly available to the users.

Available in the sense of this indicator means both that the title is included in the library's collection and that it is actually available at the time of the request for consultation in the form of loan, in-library use, or downloading. Non-availability because of user failures is excluded.

"Titles" in the sense of this indicator covers not only books, but also individual articles and all kinds of electronic documents.

The indicator measures the success of known-item searches and does not consider subject searches.

Aims of the indicator

The indicator quantifies the degree of congruence between supply and demand at the core of library services. Firstly, the indicator assesses to what extent the library collection contains what is demanded by the users. Secondly, the indicator assesses to what extent the titles demanded by the users are actually available to them. A third aim is a by-product of the data collection procedure: the detailed analysis of reasons why user and requested title do not come together.

The indicator is relevant for all libraries.

Comparison between libraries of similar mission, structure and clientele is possible.

Method

A sample of users looking for specific items in the collection is asked to fill out a form with the title(s) they were seeking. Users should also note whether their search was successful, as this will help the librarian's follow-up of the title.

Duplicate titles are removed from the sample. The titles are then checked on the catalogue and the automated system to see

- whether the title is included in the collection,
- whether, if it is included, it is available at the moment.

In addition to the catalogue and system check, the titles are then checked on the shelves. This is important to see whether items have been misshelved.

If titles are not found by users because of user failure - e.g. wrong search in the catalogue, item not found on the shelves - but are identified as available in the follow-up, these titles are counted as available. The indicator is meant to measure the library's, not the user's failure.

Titles ordered by the library but not yet received are counted as not included in the collection.

Non-availability of titles owned by the library can be due to many reasons:

- The documents are momentarily involved in processing procedures such as cataloguing, binding, reshelving etc.
- The documents are on loan, momentarily used by others in the library etc.
- The documents have been stolen, misshelved etc.
- Electronic documents cannot be accessed because the computer system is down, the number of simultaneous users is exceeded, or the link is dead.

The different reasons for non-availability should be noted separately.

Example:

In a sample of 400 titles requested by users

- 50 have not (yet) been acquired by the library,
- 120 are on loan,
- 45 are not in their right position on the shelves,
- 15 are in processing procedures (accounted for in the library's system),
- 10 electronic documents were not accessible at the moment of request (this information can only be obtained from the user who was doing the search).

Thus, 240 titles all in all were not available. Availability for the sample would then be 40%.

The size of the sample as well as the sample period should be carefully chosen. Because of the time-consuming nature of the data collection process it is not possible to repeat it at small intervals. A comparison over time is, however, very useful to determine the ups and downs in one of the key areas of library service provision.

Interpretation and use of results

High availability will of course be seen as good.

If the percentage of available titles falls below a certain value - which will vary considerably between public and academic libraries - the library could take various measures:

- Adjust its collection policy to user needs by closely analysing loan statistics and interlibrary loans (see indicators B.6 "Collection use", B.7 "Percentage of stock not used", A.7 "Ratio of requests received to requests sent out in interlibrary lending").
- Order multiple copies of titles in heavy demand
- Review the workflow of the processing department if required titles are in the library but not yet on the shelf
- Reduce loan periods to accelerate turnaround time for a copy
- Reduce the number of misshelved items by systematic shelf reading (see indicator C.13 "Shelving accuracy")
- Restrict the number of renewals by the same person.

All activities that support the users in their effort to locate an item in the collection – e.g. explaining the shelf-location system in user training, improved sign-posting – will help to avoid non-availability by failures on the part of the users.

Examples and further reading

An overview of availability studies in the last 20 to 25 years is given by Nisonger (2007).

Nisonger found that the mean availability rates for known-item searches by actual users range between 61.3 and 63.1 percent, depending on the calculation method. But several studies have found higher availability scores.

The following table differentiates between the availability of requested items in the collection and the direct availability of requested items to the user. The examples show that while usually ca. 90% or even more of the requested items could be found in the collection, the direct availability to the user ranged only between 42 to 81 percent. In the examples shown here, user failure was included in the percentage of non-availability.

Library	Year	Availability in the collection %	Direct availability %
Universitäts- und Landesbibliothek Münster (te Boekhorst, 1992)	1991	81	42
King Fahd University of Petrol & Minerals Library (Chaudry and Ashoor, 1994)	1993	93	63
University of Southern Queensland (Watson, 1998)	1996	88	54
University of New South Wales (UNSW, 2004)	2004	97	63
University of Wollongong Library (James, 2005)	2005	96	77
La Trobe University Library (2005)	2005	98	81
Griffith University Library (2005)	2005	92	69

CAUL, Council of Australian University Libraries, uses the indicator "availability" with a clear differentiation of reasons for non-availability (CAUL performance indicators):

- Not owned
- User error - not found in catalogue
- Owned at other location
- User error - failure to identify location
- On loan
- User error - failure to identify status
- Missing
- User error - on shelf
- Other

One of the libraries using the CAUL indicator noted also the staff time needed for assessing availability (La Trobe University Library, 2005). For three campuses, staff time needed was

- 82,7 hours for local planning,
- 70,25 hours for form distribution,
- 47,25 hours for checking and coding.

The example shows that an availability study must not be extremely time-consuming.

All examples named before are from academic libraries. For public libraries, goals for the availability of requested items are sometimes included in standards. The best value guidance for library authorities in England names as goal for "Percentage of library users reporting success in obtaining a specific book" a percentage of 65% (Watson, 2001).

Buckland, M. K. (1975), Book availability and the library user, New York, Pergamon

CAUL performance indicators, materials availability, available at:
http://www.anu.edu.au/caul/best-practice/PerfInd.html

Chaudhry, A. S. and Ashoor, S. (1994), Comprehensive materials availability studies in academic libraries, *Journal of Academic Librarianship* 20,5/6, pp. 300-305

Gregory, D. J. and Pedersen, W. A. (2003), Book availability revisited: turnaround time for recalls versus interlibrary loans, *College & Research Libraries* 64/4, pp. 283-299.

Griffith University Library (2005), Materials availability survey 2005, available at: http://www.griffith.edu.au/ins/publications/reports/availability_survey2005/content01.html

James, K. (2005), University of Wollongong Library - materials availability - CAUL survey results 2005 - Did they find it? available at:
http://www.library.uow.edu.au/about/news/survey/pdfs/matavail2005.pdf

Kantor, P. B. (1984), Objective performance measures for academic and research libraries, Association of Research Libraries, Washington, D.C.

La Trobe University Library (2005), Materials availability survey 2005, available at:
http://www.lib.latrobe.edu.au/about/surveys/materialavailability2005.pdf

Nisonger, T. E. (2007), A review and analysis of library availability studies, *Library Resources & Technical Services* 51,1, pp. 30-49

te Boekhorst, P. (1992), Methoden der Leistungsmessung in Bibliotheken, *Bibliothek, Forschung und Praxis* 16,2, pp. 153-161

UNSW, University of New South Wales (2004), Materials availability performance, available at: http://info.library.unsw.edu.au/libadmin/about/materials.html

Watson, A. et al. (2001), Best returns. Best value guidance for library authorities in England, 2nd ed., Exhibit 6, available at: http://www.la-hq.org.uk/directory/prof_issues/exhibit6.html

Watson, T. K. (1998), How to plan and manage library performance measurement projects through continuous improvement practice: USQ library experience, *Proceedings of the 2nd Northumbria International Conference on Performance Measurement in Libraries and Information Services,* Information North, Newcastle upon Tyne, pp.239-259

A.6 Percentage of rejected sessions

Background

The availability of documents they want to read or consult is an important issue for library users. This indicator covers a special aspect of availability in the electronic environment. Over the years more and more information suppliers have based their pricing models for expensive databases on the number of concurrent users. This leaves the library with the problem to even out the discrepancy between its budgetary restrictions and the demand for unhindered access to information on the part of the user. In this regard the indicator is an indispensable tool to fine tune the users' needs and the library's financial resources in regard to the number of access licences for databases.

Turnaways (rejected sessions) have been firmly established in various standards of network library services such as the international standard ISO 2789, the International Coalition of Library Consortia (ICOLC, 2006) and Release 2 of the COUNTER code of practice for journals and databases (COUNTER, 2005). Unfortunately, not all information suppliers are able to provide usage statistics according to the COUNTER standard.

Definition of the indicator

The percentage of rejected sessions of the total attempted sessions for each licensed database during a specified time period.

A session is defined as successful request of a database, a rejected session as unsuccessful request of a database by exceeding the simultaneous user limit. Sessions by library staff and for user training should be included in the counts. Sessions rejected because of incorrect passwords or user ID's are not included.

Aims of the indicator

The indicator assesses whether the number of licenses for a database is sufficient for user demand. The indicator could be compared to the number of copies available for print documents in high demand.

Since especially the expensive databases have prices graduated according to the number of simultaneous users, the ratio of attempted sessions to rejected sessions helps to balance the users' demand for unlimited access to information and the restrictions of the library budget.

The indicator is relevant for libraries with licensed databases in high demand.

Comparisons for individual databases may be possible between libraries with a similar clientele.

Method

Starting point for the data collection is a list of all electronic resources where the number of simultaneous accesses is limited. For each item on the list the number of total attempted sessions and the number of unsuccessful requests are recorded. The information will basically be gained from two sources:

- The usage statistics for online databases as provided by the database supplier
- Data drawn from the statistics packages which are integral part of most servers that control the access to local databases

For each electronic service the percentage of rejected sessions must be calculated and interpreted separately.

It is necessary to bear in mind that the data recorded by library suppliers are not always comparable, since not all vendors adhere closely to the recommended standards such as COUNTER.

Interpretation and use of results

A high figure is a clear indication that the present number of concurrent users allowed to access the database simultaneously is too low. Depending on the price and the level of gradation additional licences should be bought. An extremely low figure or the total absence of rejected accesses points to a surplus of licences for concurrent usage. Depending on the gradation level the number of licences could be reduced.

Examples and further reading

The indicator was introduced in the project EQUINOX: Library performance measurement and quality management system (EQUINOX, 2000).

A detailed description of the data collection procedure and its pitfalls is to be found on the E-metrics instructional system of the Information Use Management and Policy Institute (2005).

A particular kind of turnaways is counted in usage statistics for e-journal packages. In this context a turnaway is an unsuccessful attempt to access an e-journal title offered by the publisher but not subscribed to by the institution the user belongs to. For huge aggregator databases containing journals with and without full text the count of unsuccessful attempts at accessing certain re-stricted titles provides valuable information about what titles are requested by the users and should be subscribed to in the future. To extend the definition of the indicator in this direction might be useful.

Counter (2005), Release 2 of the COUNTER code of practice for journals and databases (Published April 2005), available at:
http://www.projectcounter.org/r2/Appendix_A_Glossary.pdf

Equinox. Library performance measurement and quality management system (2000), available at: http://equinox.dcu.ie/index.html

Information Use Management and Policy Institute (2005), E-metrics instructional system: librarian education in network statistics, Florida State University, available at:
http://www.ii.fsu.edu/emis/

ICOLC, International Coalition of Library Consortia (2006), Revised guidelines for statistical measures of usage of web-based information resources, available at:
http://www.library.yale.edu/consortia/webstats06.htm

A.7 Ratio of requests received to requests sent out in interlibrary lending

Background

Resource sharing is more important than ever if libraries want to maintain a high service level in spite of stagnating budgets. Rising costs for journal subscriptions and additional resources needed for information technology have seriously affected the budget of libraries worldwide. At the same time, there are an ever increasing number of new publications, and with easy access to online bibliographies users tend to consult more publications than ever. It is impossible for any library to satisfy all user needs via its own collection. Interlibrary lending or document delivery is a matter of give and take in the library community, where every library has to play its role according to its capacities. The balance between giving and taking can be seen as an indicator for the comprehensiveness and adequacy of the library's collection for its population, but also for the library's role in resource sharing and for the relevance of its collection to the scientific community.

Definition of the indicator

The number of requests received in interlibrary lending (ILL) divided by the number of requests sent out.

Requests received: The number of requests for materials received from other libraries or directly from their users during a specified period of time (usually a year).

Requests sent out: The number of requests for materials sent by a library to other libraries on behalf of its users within a specified period of time (usually a year). Requests made by the library's users directly to other libraries are included if the number can be obtained from the cooperative automated system.

Aims of the indicator

The indicator assesses whether the library's collection is adequate and sufficient for the needs of the library's population. A large number of titles requested from other libraries are a clear indication that either the acquisitions budget is insufficient or the collection policy is not based on the needs of the local users.

On the other side, the number of requests received shows the importance of the library's collection for the scientific community and the library's role in resource sharing.

The indicator is relevant for all libraries participating in interlibrary lending and document delivery services. It will be most useful for academic libraries.

Comparison between libraries of similar size, structure and mission will be possible, if the request allocation procedures of cooperative systems are taken into account.

Method

Establish the number of requests received and requests sent out in interlibrary lending during a year.

Requests made by users directly to other libraries should be included if the cooperative automated system for the interlending procedures can deliver these data.

The number of requests received is divided by the number of requests sent out to obtain the ratio for the indicator.

It might be useful to count requests for books and articles separately to get more detailed information about possible shortcomings in the collection.

Interpretation and use of results

A higher score will generally be considered as good, as it shows the relevance and comprehensiveness of the library's collection. The results of the indicator can also be used for promoting the library's importance and role.

But a high score also indicates high workload for the library and might lead to the library's trying to be less frequented by requests in a cooperative system.

A low score points to the collection not being adequate to the population to be served, as many items have to be borrowed from other libraries. The following measures could be taken:

- Check outgoing requests for recent publications and buy them
- Analyse outgoing requests to see what subjects are in highest demand and reallocate the budget accordingly
- Revise existing collection building policies
- Ask users to suggest new titles for the collection

The indicator should be seen in relation to the library's mission and goals. Libraries commissioned to collect and preserve the national or regional documentary heritage or libraries with large special collections may see it as their goal to serve as last resort for materials in their collections. Libraries primarily serving the actual needs of a specified population may consider it sufficient if they can serve such needs to some extent by quick delivery from other libraries.

Today, interlibrary lending and document delivery are increasingly organized in cooperative automated systems, where self-initiated user requests may go directly to a supplying library. The location of the requested item has either been verified in the online catalogues, or link resolvers lead from a citation in a database to a catalogue search and an interlibrary lending or document delivery request. If such systems have automated procedures for the allocation of requests to libraries, this will greatly influence the amount of requests received by a library.

Examples and further reading

The indicator as described here is used in the benchmarking project of the university libraries in the Netherlands, but with a differentiation between book and article requests (Laeven and Smit, 2003). In 2004, the ratio of ILL book requests received to ILL book requests made by each library ranged between 0,52 and 10,83, with an average of 3,28 in 12 libraries (UKB, 2004). The ratio of ILL article requests received to ILL article requests made by each library ranged between 0,52 and 9,54, with an average of 2,72.

The online statistics of the Australian university libraries allow comparing "total documents delivered" to "total documents received" (CAUL online statistics). The mean value for 2005 was 1,885, the median was 0,647.

The Finnish university library statistics allow comparing "given distance loans and copies" to "received distance loans and copies" (Finnish research library statistics database). In 2005, the value was 0,9.

The statistics of the Association of Research Libraries compare total interlibrary lending to total interlibrary borrowing (ARL statistics). The median score for 2005 was 1,37.

An Australian benchmarking study surveyed all types of libraries as to interlibrary lending (National Resource Sharing Working Group, 2001). There was an overall ratio of 1,22 for supplying to requesting, but the results showed considerable differences between library types:

- University libraries did the most requesting, but supplied a similar number.
- Public libraries requested only little more than they supplied.
- National/state libraries supplied significantly more than they requested.

- Special libraries, on average, requested more than they supplied.

The Finnish public library statistics show for 2005 a total of 357.996 given interlibrary loans and 354.317 received interlibrary loans, which is a ratio of 1,01 (Finnish public library statistics).

ARL statistics interactive edition, available at: http://fisher.lib.virginia.edu/arl/index.html

CAUL online statistics, Council of Australian University Libraries, available at: http://www.anu.edu.au/caul/stats/

Finnish public library statistics, Culture and Media Division of the Ministry of Education, available at: http://tilastot.kirjastot.fi/Default.aspx?&langId=en

Finnish research library statistics database, Helsinki University Library, available at: https://yhteistilasto.lib.helsinki.fi/language.do?action=change&choose_language=3

Laeven, H. and Smit, A. (2003), A project to benchmark university libraries in the Netherlands, *Library Management* 24, 6/7, pp. 291-304.

National Resource Sharing Working Group (2001), Interlibrary loan and document delivery benchmarking study, National Library of Australia, available at: http://www.nla.gov.au/initiatives/nrswg/illdd_rpt.pdf (last visit 16/09/06)

UKB (2004), Benchmarking, Samenwerkingsverband van de Nederlandse universiteitsbibliotheken en de Koninklijke Bibliotheek, results only available to participants

A.8 Immediate availability

Background

Measuring the availability of required titles in the collection as described in indicator A.5 is both complicated and time-consuming, as it means following up users' actual requests. It will be easier to use data out of the regular library statistics to assess whether a user's loan request can be met immediately. For the evaluation of the Copenhagen Business School Library in 1992, a simple indicator was used comparing the data of "loans made directly from the shelves" with loans made in connection with reservations or interlibrary loans (Cotta-Schønberg and Line, 1994, p.60). This indicator was adopted in the German benchmarking initiative for academic libraries in 2002 and called "immediate availability" (BIX. Der Bibliotheksindex). The idea behind the indicator is to simplify the data collection procedure considerably while determining as closely as possible the users' chance of immediately receiving requested items.

Definition of the indicator

The percentage of immediate loans of total loans during a specified period, usually a year.

Loans in the sense of this indicator are lending transactions of physical items to one user. This includes on-site loans (loans within the library) and copies supplied in place of original documents.

Immediate loans in the sense of this indicator are loans where users receive the requested item directly, either by the user fetching the item from open access shelves or the library delivering the item from closed shelves. Renewals are excluded.

Total loans in the sense of this indicator include all loans, whether immediate or via reservations, and interlibrary loans. Renewals are excluded.

Aims of the indicator

The indicator assesses the probability that a user's loan request will be fulfilled immediately.

It can be seen as a stopgap for all libraries that shrink from conducting the availability study as described in indicator A.5 but are looking for a figure indicating the library's potential to satisfy the loan requests of its users.

The indicator is relevant for all libraries with a loan collection.

The indicator is ideal for benchmarking purposes, since the data elements it is made up of are usually part of the annual library statistics. Comparison between libraries should consider the libraries' mission and clientele.

Method

The data elements involved, namely number of loans, number of reservations, number of interlibrary loans received by the library, are easily obtained from the annual library statistics.

For the number of immediate loans, calculate the number of all loans during a specified time, usually a year, and deduct the number of reservations in the same time period.

For the number of total loans, the interlibrary loans received by the library are added to the number of all loans during a specified time, usually a year.

It is essential that for both immediate and total loans the number of renewals is not counted. Interlibrary lending requests sent to other libraries as well as document delivery transactions are not considered.

The immediate availability is then calculated as the percentage of immediate loans of total loans.

Interpretation and use of results

A high score will be considered as good. It shows the probability of the user's obtaining the requested items directly.

Values between 80 and 90% are to be expected regardless of the type of library (see table below). This is considerably higher than the results for direct availability in availability studies following up samples of titles required by users. The indicator "immediate availability" disregards cases when users trying to borrow an item do not transact a reservation if the item is on loan. The disappointed user just walking away is not considered.

In case that immediate availability seems too low, the library might take the following measures:

- Adjust its collection policy to user needs by closely analysing loan statistics and interlibrary loans (see indicators B.6 "Collection use", B.7 "Percentage of stock not used", A.7 "Ratio of requests received to requests sent out in interlibrary lending").

- Invest in multiple copies of titles in heavy demand
- Review the workflow of the processing department if required titles are in the library but not yet on the shelf
- Reduce loan periods to accelerate turnaround time for a copy
- Reduce the number of misshelved items by systematic shelf reading (see indicator C.13 "Shelving accuracy")
- Restrict the number of renewals by the same person.

The indicator should be seen in relation to the library's goals. "On the other hand, it is not the aim of the library to ensure that needed books should be available to all users immediately, and a direct availability rate of 80 per cent is not considered unacceptable" (Cotta-Schønberg and Line, 1994, p.60).

Examples and further reading

When the indicator was first used in the evaluation of the Copenhagen Business School Library, "direct loans" were compared to "delayed loans" (loans via reservation or interlibrary lending). The results for 3 years were (Cotta-Schønberg and Line, 1994, p.60):

	1991 %	1992 %	1993 %
Direct loans	84	79	78
Delayed loans	16	21	22

From the beginning of the BIX benchmarking project "immediate availability" was used as main indicator for the quality of the collection.

BIX-results 2006-2007 for indicator "immediate availability"

Immediate availability	2006	2007
mean	85,1	84,34
standard deviation	6,9	7,47
min	72,8	70,67
max	99,2	99,01
Polytechnics		
mean	89,2	87,88
standard deviation	5,5	5,97
min	77,5	75,33
max	98,8	97,76
University libraries (one-tier)		

mean	83,2	84,62
standard deviation	7,0	7,88
min	73,5	70,94
max	99,2	99,01
University libraries (two-tier)		
mean	82,7	79,10
standard deviation	6,3	5,55
min	72,8	70,67
max	94,6	90,99

The possibility to obtain requested items quickly ranks high in users' wishes. In the New Zealand university libraries effectiveness study "proportion of items wanted by user finally obtained" was ranked in the top 10 indicators by academic staff, and "provision of multiple copies of items in high use" was seen as number one indicator by undergraduate students (Cullen and Calvert, 1995, pp. 443-44).

BIX. Der Bibliotheksindex, available at: http://www.bix-bibliotheksindex.de/

BIX. Der Bibliotheksindex (2006), *B.I.T. online* Sonderheft 2006

Cotta-Schønberg, M. and Line, M. B. (1994), Evaluation of academic libraries: with special reference to the Copenhagen Business School Library, *Journal of Librarianship and Information Science* 26,2, pp. 55-69

Cullen, R. J. and Calvert, P.J. (1995), Stakeholder perceptions of university library effectiveness, *Journal of Academic Librarianship* 21,6, pp. 438-448

A.9 Staff per capita

Background

What number and qualification of staff is adequate for a specific library's tasks?

This question has always been debated between funding institutions and libraries. Library associations as well as funding institutions have tried to find models for calculating "necessary" staff.

Such models start in most cases from statistics describing a library's regular and special tasks:

- Number of acquired media per year
- Number of current journal subscriptions
- Number of loans
- Number of users (active, registered or potential users)
- Opening hours
- Number of service points (control desks, reference points, issue desks etc.)
- Number of rare materials in the collection

A certain percentage is then added for administrative tasks, the information technology department etc.

Recently, such a model has been published by the German Higher Education Information System HIS (Vogel and Cordes, 2005, pp.77-82). The model starts from average production times for a product or service where such products and services can be quantified, e.g. 20 minutes for one acquired medium or 3 minutes for one loan. Staff for control or reference desks is calculated by the number of such points. Percentages are then added for other activities, e.g. 6-10% for administration.

The problem in such models is always to find reliable data for production times, as production times will be influenced by the kind of material acquired or the specific services the library offers. The best way would be to use time-logging in a number of libraries of similar structure and clientele in order to get reliable data (Ceynowa and Coners, 2003, pp.78-84).

Other projects have tried to answer the question the other way round: How much can one FTE staff achieve on average in one year (how many loans, how many media processed)? This is easier, as the number of processed media or of loans is counted anyway in the library's statistics, but it is necessary to estimate the number of persons and the percentage of their working time involved in the specified activities like lending or media processing (see Indicator C.9 "Employee productivity in media processing"). Again, time-logging might be necessary to assess what percentage of an employee's time is spent on the different activities.

The calculation of "necessary" staff based on production times or products per FTE person takes a long time, and the results might soon be outdated by changes in library services and workflows. Therefore, other models simply compare the number of employees to the population to be served in order to get an estimate of whether the number of employees seems to be adequate. This method is used in the indicator described here.

Definition of the indicator

The number of library staff members in FTE per 1.000 members of the library's population to be served.

Library staff for this indicator means total staff, including project staff, temporary staff, voluntaries, student assistants etc.

The population to be served is the number of persons to whom the library is commissioned to provide its services. For public libraries, this will normally be the population of the community (or part of the community); for academic libraries, this will normally be the total of students and academic staff in the institution.

Aims of the indicator

The indicator assesses the adequacy of the number of library employees to the library's population. It is relevant for all libraries with a defined population to be served.

Comparison between libraries of similar structure, mission and clientele is possible.

Method

Staff members are calculated in FTE (full time equivalent).

The members of the population to be served are counted as persons, not as FTE (full time equivalent). Thus, part-time students or staff in academic institutions will be counted each as one person.

The number of staff members in FTE is set in relation to the number of persons in the population to be served, divided by 1.000.

Interpretation and use of results

A higher score will normally be considered as better. But the results should be seen in relation to the library's mission and goals. Special tasks like preserving a rare collection may make more staff necessary than in other libraries with a similar population size.

If the results of the indicator seem too low compared to other libraries, it will not always be possible for the library to provide more staff. A special budget for staff expenditure or a fixed position chart for staff minimizes the library's ability to recruit more staff. The library could apply for extra funding, e.g. for student assistants, or recruit volunteers for certain tasks. If the library has a global budget (lump sum), it will be possible to spend more resources on staff.

If the library has a high percentage of professional librarians in all services, it may also be possible to test producing some services with a higher percentage of non-professionals. In the long range, staff costs might be saved and used for hiring additional staff, e.g. for new services.

If the indicator is used together with indicators of staff efficiency and service quality, it will be easier to decide whether the number of staff is sufficient for the needs of the population.

Examples and further reading

The indicator as described above is used in the German benchmarking project BIX (BIX. Der Bibliotheksindex). In 2005, BIX showed the following results (BIX, 2006):

Staff in FTE per 1.000 capita		mean	maximum	minimum
Public Libraries	Communities under 15.000 inhabitants	0,26	0,43	0,14
	Communities from 15.000 to 30.000 inhabitants	0,20	0,47	0,09
	Communities from 30.000 to 50.000 inhabitants	0,20	0,38	0,08
	Communities from 50.000 to 100.000 inhabitants	0,21	0,50	0,10
	Communities over 100.000 inhabitants	0,24	0,40	0,10

Academic Librar-	Universities of applied sciences	2,7	4,7	1,3
ies				
	Universities: One-tier systems	7,2	15,3	2,2
	Universities: Two-tier systems (only the central library considered)	5,1	11,0	2,1

The BIX results show that comparison is only meaningful between libraries with a similar mission and population. Public libraries offer significantly less staff compared to their population than academic libraries, but the BIX results for public libraries in small and large communities are similar, ranging from 0,20 to 0,26. For public libraries in British Columbia, Canada, the average number of FTE staff per 1.000 members of the population was somewhat higher (Ministry of education, British Columbia):

- 2003 = 0,50
- 2004 = 0,51

Academic libraries have to provide staff for information in specialized areas, for electronic services, teaching, interlibrary lending and partly also for activities like preservation and digitizing. In two-tier systems with separate institute libraries, many persons involved in library services of institutes will also have other functions. Therefore in BIX only the staff in the central library is considered.

The annual library statistics compiled by LISU at Loughborough University (Creaser, Maynard and White, 2005) show the following data for academic libraries 2003/04:

- Old universities:
  Total library staff (FTE) = 5.870
  Total population (FTE, students and academic staff) = 932.700
  That would mean 6.29 staff per 1.000 capita.
- New universities:
  Total library staff (FTE) = 3.409
  Total population (FTE, students and academic staff) = 711.800
  That would mean 4.79 staff per 1.000 capita.
- Higher education colleges:
  Total library staff (FTE) = 960
  Total population (FTE, students and academic staff) = 185.900
  That would mean 5.16 staff per 1.000 capita.

The statistics of the Council of Australian University Libraries count total positions of library staff and total persons in the population (CAUL online statistics).

Comparing these data shows a mean value of 6.7 staff positions per 1.000 persons in the population.

The data taken from BIX, LISU and CAUL suggest that "staff per 1.000 capita" ranges somewhere between 5 and 7 in academic libraries.

Other projects have compared the number of users to the number of staff members in order to assess the workload of staff. The statistics of SCONUL, Society of College, National and University Libraries, UK measure "FTE students per FTE professional staff" (Creaser, 2006). Data from 1994-95 to 2004-05 show an increase from 372 to 451 students per professional staff member.

A study in Polish academic libraries calculated users per library staff member and found for 2003 a median score of 339,33 users per staff member in university libraries and 403,89 in technical university libraries (Derfert-Wolf, Górski and Marcinek, 2005).

A study in the United States evaluated data of 1.380 academic institutions as to library staffing (Applegate, 2007). The ratio of FTE students to librarians (professional librarians) was:

- For libraries in public institutions an average between 466 and 574 students per librarian
- For libraries in private institutions an average between 223 and 423 students per librarian

Librarians in large libraries served fewer students than those in medium or small libraries.

Applegate, R. (2007), Charting academic library staffing: Data from national surveys, *College & Research Libraries 68,1*, pp. 59 - 68

BIX. Der Bibliotheksindex available at: http://www.bix-bibliotheksindex.de/

BIX. Der Bibliotheksindex (2006), *B.I.T. online* Sonderheft 2006

CAUL online statistics, Council of Australian University Libraries, available at: http://www.anu.edu.au/caul/stats/

Ceynowa, K. and Coners, A. (2003), Cost management for university libraries, Saur, München

Creaser, C. (2006), SCONUL library statistics: trends 1994-95 to 2004-05, LISU, Loughborough University

Creaser, C., Maynard, S. and White, S. (2005), LISU annual library statistics 2005, featuring trend analysis of UK public and academic libraries 1994 – 2004, LISU, Loughborough University, available at: http://www.lboro.ac.uk/departments/dils/lisu/downloads/als05.pdf

Derfert-Wolf, L., Górski, M. and Marcinek, M. (2005), Quality of academic libraries – funding bodies, librarians and users, *World Library and Information Congress, 71th IFLA General Conference and Council,* available at: http://www.ifla.org/IV/ifla71/papers/080e-Derfert-Wolf.pdf#search=%22Derfert-Wolf%22

British Columbia public library statistics (2004), Ministry of education, Victoria, British Columbia, available at: http://www.bced.gov.bc.ca/pls/bcplstats_2004.pdf

Vogel, B. and Cordes, S. (2005), Bibliotheken an Universitäten und Fachhochschulen, Organisation und Ressourcenplanung, HIS, Hannover, pp. 77-82

A.10 Direct access from the homepage

Background

Most libraries today make their services accessible via a website. The library website may be the library's own domain, or it may be within the institution's/community's domain.

The quality of a library website can have different aspects:

- Contents
- Language
- Structure
- Design
- Navigation
- Accessibility

Taken together these aspects describe the usability of the website. Usability is generally defined as "the extent to which a product can be used by specified users to achieve specified goals with effectiveness, efficiency and satisfaction in a specified context of use" (ISO 9241-11, 1998). Extensive information about how to evaluate websites can be found on the websites of Jacob Nielsen, an authority on website design (useit.com), and Ursula Schulz (Schulz, 2006).

The usability of a website can be assessed with different methods:

1. **Evaluation without user participation:**
   - Heuristic evaluation: A small group of experts evaluates the website, based on the principles of usability. Nielsen provides a list of 10 "heuristics" (Nielsen, 1994).
   - Cognitive walk-through: Experts construct a "user scenario" and perform tasks of an imaginary user.

2. **Evaluation with user participation:**
   - Web surveys: Surveys ask for user satisfaction with the website, purposes of a search, problems in searching, etc.
   - Focus groups: The website is discussed with a small group of website users who talk about their experiences and problems.
   - Group tests: Groups work on specified tasks, moderated by an expert.
   - Thinking aloud: A test user's verbalizing his or her thoughts when searching is recorded on tape.

- Observation: Users perform a set of tasks and are observed either by video or by an observing person.
- Transaction logs: Evaluation of data as to frequency of use, most-used pages, ways of searching, etc.

There is a broad range of literature about the usability of library websites, especially about usability tests that concentrate on the three issues effectiveness, efficiency, and satisfaction. In most cases, evaluation of the website starts with an expert review, followed by usability testing involving website users. A bibliography of usability testing for library websites has been published by Letnikova (2003). Another bibliography can be found on the website of North Carolina State University Libraries (Library usability bibliography).

When designing a library website, the most important issue is to consider the special needs, competences and behaviour of the library's population to be served. What users generally want when accessing a website is either to find a specific information (the opening times of the library, the way to get a user card) or to perform a specific activity (a catalogue search, a renewal). The library should identify what kind of information is most often needed and which are the most-used services and collections in order to give direct and quick access to those topics. "One of the most successful design strategies ... is the placement of direct links on the homepage to a very small number of high-priority operations" (Nielsen and Loranger, 2006, p.210).

The homepage is the most important part of the website. "A company's homepage is its face to the world and the starting point for most user visits" (Nielsen, 2002). Normal users spend only about 35 seconds looking at the homepage, expert users about 25 seconds (Nielsen and Loranger, 2006, p.30). During this time, they should be able to recognize whether the site is interesting for them and how they can get to the information they are seeking. Users generally scan the page instead of reading consecutively. They will scan the headings until they suppose they find what they are seeking, and they will follow the line of minimum effort. "After all, the main goal of a homepage is to guide users somewhere else ..." (Nielsen and Loranger, 2006, p.32).

If the homepage does not correspond to users' needs and terminology, they will either leave quickly, or they may spend much time by "clicking the wrong link and being lost forever in the wrong part of the site" or "scouring a site for a term that the site doesn't use and doesn't cross-reference" (Nielsen, 2006). The need to keep information on the homepage short and concise can lead to misunderstandings. "The brevity of some home pages places a semantic burden on the chosen vocabulary" (Spivey, 2000, p.151). An overview of library terminology and its problems in usability tests is given by Kupersmith (2006). A study about students' recognition of the terms librarians use in teaching was conducted in California State University in 2000/2001 (Hutcherson, 2004).

The design and contents of the homepage will be decisive for the success of the website visit. "Minimize the number of clicks users must make…Most users come to a library site wanting to do research, and the shorter their paths, the happier they are" (Jasek, 2004). Therefore, speed of information access via the homepage was chosen as indicator for website quality. It is an indicator that is applicable for every library homepage, easy to use, and with an informative content that enables the library to directly take steps for improving access via the homepage

Definition of the indicator

The availability of the most frequently used resources and services via the homepage of the library's website, measured by the number of clicks (key strokes) necessary to find the topics and the comprehensibility of the terms used.

The homepage is the page which serves as the visual unit that is displayed when accessing the library's website. It may appear after the redirection through an entry page.

Aims of the indicator

To assess whether the homepage leads directly or very quickly, with adequate terminology, to the most frequently needed information and the most-used services and thus serves as an efficient sign-posting.

The indicator is applicable to all libraries with a library-owned website.

Comparison will be possible between libraries of similar mission and clientele, if a standardized set of topics is used.

The indicator does not evaluate the design or navigation options of the website or the overall contents of the website.

Method

The method used is a kind of cognitive walk-through. A small group of experts simulates user behaviour when seeking for specified information via the homepage.

The first step is to define the services and information that are most important for the library's clientele. This includes the decision what terms would be comprehensible to the library's clientele when describing the services and information topics on the homepage. This decision should be based on tests with users.

The two sets of main topics for academic and public libraries described here should be seen as prototypes that should be adapted to the special situation of a library or of a group of libraries. Additional issues could be added according to the library's mission and clientele.

The lists were defined after searching 50 websites each for public and academic libraries in Australia, Germany, UK, and the United States. The search showed that the most-used services may differ between regions or countries, but that libraries with similar mission show common traits in their websites. Instruments for searching the website like search functions, FAQ (frequently asked questions), sitemap, or A – Z have not been included in the lists, as the question is whether the main topics can be found directly, not via search functions. Customising of websites (e.g. MyLibrary) is not considered either.

For academic libraries, the set might include the following topics:

15 main topics	Possible terms for locating the service/information
Address of the library	Address, location, visit us; possible general headings: about us, contacts
Way to the library	Way to the library, how to reach us, map to library; possible general headings: contacts, visiting the library, directions
Opening times	Opening times, library hours
Online catalogue	Catalogue/s, OPAC, search (with explanation); possible general headings: How to find…, finding information
Lending service	Circulation, lending, loan service, borrowing, how to get a book; possible general heading: use
User card	User card, library card, registering, membership, how to join; possible general headings: circulation, borrowing, lending, loan service, use
User account	Loans record, borrowing record, renewals, check loans, library record, view my record; possible general headings: circulation, borrowing, lending, loan service, use
ILL & document delivery	Interlibrary loan, document delivery, ILL, document supply, borrow from other libraries; possible general headings: borrowing, how to get a book, how to get an article
Reference service	Reference, e-reference, reference questions, enquiries, ask a librarian, ask us; possible general heading: information services,

	help
Electronic journals (general term, not the single journal)	Electronic journals, E-journals; possible general headings: electronic collection, electronic resources, digital resources, online resources, journals, find a journal or article
Databases (general term, not the single database)	Databases; possible general headings: electronic collection, electronic resources, digital resources, online resources, find an article
Access to research subjects	Subject areas, subject guides, subject resources, library resources by faculty; browse by subject
User training	Training, user training, teaching, library tours, research skills training, information skills training, tutorials; possible general heading: help
News, events	News, forum, events

For public libraries, the set might include the following topics:

15 main topics	Possible terms for locating the service/information
Address of the library	Address, location, visit us; possible general headings: about us, contacts
Way to the library	Way to the library, how to reach us, map to library; possible general headings: contacts, visiting the library, directions
Opening times	Opening times, library hours
Online catalogue	Catalogue/s, OPAC, search (with explanation); possible general headings: How to find…, finding information
Lending service	Circulation, lending, loan service, borrowing, how to get a book; possible general heading: use
User card	User card, library card, registering, membership, how to join; possible general headings: circulation, borrowing, lending, loan service, use
User account	Loans record, borrowing record, renewals, check loans, library record, view my record, my password; possible general headings: circulation, borrowing, lending, loan service, use
Electronic collection	Electronic collection, digital collection, electronic resources, databases, e-journals; possible general headings: digital library, electronic library
Link collection	Internet resources, Internet links, web links, recommended websites, reference links
Reference service	Reference, e-reference, reference questions, enquiries, ask a librarian, ask us; possible general heading: information services, help
Fees	Fees, charges; possible general headings: circulation, borrowing, lending, loan service, use
Services for children and juveniles	Children, kids, teens, children and young, youth services, young people
Branch libraries	Branch libraries, branches, locations, local libraries

Community services	Our community, about (name of community), town of (name of community), local links, local history, local studies
News, events	News, forum, events, cultural programs, exhibitions, calendar, what's on

As a second step, the experts should test the homepage as to the speed of finding the topics and the adequacy of the terminology for the library's clientele. The rating could be like this:

Service/resource		Clicks	Points
	Topic directly on the homepage (e.g. address, opening times, search box for the catalogue)	0	10
	adequate term on the homepage	1	8
	adequate term on the homepage	2	6
	adequate term on the homepage	3	4
	adequate term on the homepage	> 3	0
	ambiguous term on the homepage	1	2
	ambiguous term on the homepage	> 1	0

It is irrelevant for the rating whether the topics appear on the homepage in systematic order or in a "quick links" list.

Terms named "possible general headings" in the two lists that lead to the requested topic are considered as adequate, but the number of necessary clicks should be counted.

"Direct access from the homepage" is then calculated by dividing the total number of points by the number of topics on the list.

There may be several possibilities for finding a requested topic via the homepage. For instance, information about the reference service might be searchable via the broader terms "help" or "information services". In such cases, the quickest way should be counted.

Interpretation and use of results

A high score would be seen as good. The following actions could be taken in order to achieve a better score:
- Put links to the most-used services directly on the homepage.
- Change library jargon into user-friendly language. Task-based links like "find books", "find articles", or "check loans" have proved to be easier to understand than terms like "databases", "e-journals", or "library record" (Kupersmith, 2007). Users probably would not click on a link if they do

93

not know what the term means. But extremely "popular" language should also be avoided, as it may irritate users.

- Avoid abbreviations the users are not familiar with. "ILL" was misunderstood as meaning "Illinois" in a survey (VandeCreek, 2005).
- Use a consistent set of terms, e.g. not "periodicals" beside "e-journals".
- Evaluate frequently asked questions and place the topics on the homepage. If a question occurs frequently (e.g. "How to look into my account" or "Where can I find articles"), it is more useful to have a link on the homepage than to refer the user to "FAQ".

If the library sees that it takes too many clicks to find its main services, or that the services are not clearly labelled, the indicator could be followed up by a user survey or a usability test in order to find more details about the usability of the homepage.

Users' searching ways are not predictable. There may be differences between the searching ways and the terminology of new users and advanced users. Some users may prefer access to resources by format (books, journals), others may prefer a subject-oriented search (medicine, linguistics). The terminology and the links on the homepage should always consider several search options and differences in the needs and experience of user groups. "A library website requires an interface that can accommodate the different needs, scholarly disciplines and capabilities of the many and varied users within its institution" (Raward, 2001). A good solution would be to offer options for different user groups on the homepage, for instance:

- first-time visitors
- external users
- children, juveniles
- seniors
- first-year students
- graduates
- faculty
- disabled persons

The problem in offering quick access to the main services via the homepage for all user groups will be that on the one side the homepage should offer all relevant information, on the other side it must not be overloaded and confusing. This can be a tightrope walk between conflicting wishes. If, based on the results of this indicator, the library wants to place additional topics on the homepage, the existing topics should be examined and possibly weeded. Surveys show that there is often too much general information about the library, e.g. its history, organisation, and mission, placed prominently on the homepage, information that would not matter to users performing a quick search. Information on the homepage should be limited to the necessary.

Examples and further reading

The number of clicks necessary to find an information, starting from the homepage, was counted in a project of the School of Communication, Information, and Library Studies, Rutgers, The State University of New Jersey, US (Jeng, 2005, p.104). Students were given specified tasks, and the study measured as well the time needed as the keystrokes, clicks, or movements necessary for completing the task. As the tasks included finding certain journal or encyclopedia articles, students on average needed between 2 to 4 minutes and between 7 to 13 clicks.

The "minimum number of moves" to complete a task was also counted in a usability study at Louisiana State University Libraries, US (Robins and Kelsey, 2002). The study differentiated between "correct" and "incorrect" moves, where 65% were rated as correct moves. An interesting result was that for most of the assigned tasks the project staff identified more than one way to navigate to the desired information. "In some cases, it was possible to navigate various paths from the libraries' home page to the desired page and still complete the task in the minimum number of moves."

A usability study at the e-library at Iowa State University, US, with 14 participants and "think out loud" method differentiated between participants following "expected paths" (paths anticipated by the research team) and participants finding information in their own way (Report on the 2004 usability study, 2005). The success rate of the participants following expected paths was 42%, while the average overall success rate was 81%. The average number of clicks by participants following expected paths was 2.75 – 3, while the average number of clicks by participants following their own paths was 5.5. Users evidently were more successful with their own ways, but needed more clicks.

A usability test in the University of Hull, UK, graded the test results by the number of attempts made to find a specific resource or information (Holland, 2005). The categories were:
- Grade 1 – Found the information or resource straight away (the volunteer performed a correct series of clicks to locate the answer).
- Grade 2 – Found the link after two or three false starts.

- Grade 3 – Found the information or resource they needed after more than three attempts.
- Grade 4 – The volunteer was unable to find the information.

49% of the participants found the information at the first attempt. Library jargon was found to be the main barrier.

A study at the University of Wollongong, Australia, tried to find the most commonly used services in order to give them prominent placement on the homepage (Norris and Freeman, 2005). They found that the most frequent searches concerned:

- database search (more topic than article searches)
- catalogue search (more item than topic searches)
- journal search
- circulation record

A study evaluating 41 websites of academic health sciences libraries offers a list of "obligatory" homepage links for health library websites (Brower, 2004):

- bibliographic databases, listed by title
- e-books
- e-journals
- hours of operation
- instruction or tutorials
- news, events
- descriptions of services

A study of university library websites in four English speaking countries (Australia, Canada, the UK and the US) found that the visual display of information was similar across all countries, but that there were differences in the content supplied (Still, 2001). "These are no doubt tied to the educational environment, such as the prevalence of exam papers in some countries, the interaction between universities and the for-profit sector, such as the presence of links to bookstores, and the financial and technical concerns…"

A study at the University of Calgary Library, Canada, using the "think aloud" method with 10 test questions, asked for users' comments on the usability of the website (Hayden et al., 2004). One of the results was that the participants wanted "the most important and most commonly used resources accessible with one click from the first page, ideally from a page that is tailored to their subject needs".

The difficulty of adequate terminology was one of the main results in a focus group study at Texas A&M University, US (Crowley et al., 2002). Participants complained not only about technical terms, but also about misleading everyday words. "When I see the link for information I get excited because I think that is what I am looking for: research articles. But I'm not looking for any of this kind of information (hours, telephone numbers, and directions)."

The indicator described here assesses the direct access to information and services **from** the library's homepage. Another important issue for the visibility and effective use of the library's website is the access **to** the library's website via its parent institution's website:

- How many clicks away is the library?
- Can the library be identified directly on the institution's website? As the library is always one of the most-used links, it should not be hidden in general terms like "central institutions", "services" or "organisation" (Bao, 2000, p.194; King, 1998, p.462).

Literature on library website design and usability tests is so extensive that only a few studies can be named that have addressed special topics related to this indicator or that can be seen as typical examples.

Bao, X. (2000), Academic library home pages: link location and database provision, *Journal of Academic Librarianship* 26,3, pp. 191-195

Brower, S. M. (2004), Academic health sciences library Website navigation: an analysis of forty-one Websites and their navigation tools, *Journal of the Medical Library Association* 92,4, pp. 412 – 420, available at: http://www.pubmedcentral.nih.gov/articlerender.fcgi?artid=521512

Crowley, G. et al. (2002), User perceptions of the library's web pages: a focus group study at Texas A&M University, *Journal of Academic Librarianship* 28,4, pp. 205-211

Hayden, A. et al. (2004), University library website usability study report, University of Calgary Library website usability study team, available at: http://hdl.handle.net/1880/43524

Holland, D. (2005), Practical experiences of using formal usability testing as a tool to support website redesign, *SCONUL Focus* 36 Winter, pp. 31-35

Hutcherson, N. B. (2004), Library jargon: student recognition of terms and concepts commonly used by librarians in the classroom, *College & Research Libraries* 65,4, pp. 349 - 354

ISO 9241 (1998), Ergonomic requirements for office work with visual display terminals (VDTs) -- Part 11: Guidance on usability, International Organization for Standardization, Geneva

Jasek, C. (2004), How to design library web sites to maximize usability, *Library Connect, pamphlet 5,* available at:
http://www.elsevier.com/framework_librarians/LibraryConnect/lcpamphlet5.pdf

Jeng, J. (2005), Usability assessment of academic digital libraries: effectiveness, satisfaction, and learnability, *Libri* 55, pp. 96 – 121

King, D. L. (1998), Library home page design: a comparison of page layout for front ends to ARL library web sites, *College & Research Libraries* 59,5, pp. 457-464, available at:
http://www.ala.org/ala/acrl/acrlpubs/crljournal/backissues1998b/september98/king.pdf

Kupersmith, J. (2007), Library terms that users understand, available at:
http://www.jkup.net/terms.html

Kupersmith, J. (2006), Library terms evaluated in usability tests and other studies, available at: http://www.jkup.net/terms-studies.html

Letnikova, G. (2003), Usability testing on academic library websites: a selective bibliography, *Internet Reference Services Quarterly* 8,4, pp. 53 - 68

Library usability bibliography, NCSU Libraries, North Carolina State University, available at:
http://www.lib.ncsu.edu/usability/library-usability.html

Nielsen, J. (1994), 10 usability heuristics, available at:
http://www.useit.com/papers/heuristic/heuristic_list.html

Nielsen, J. (2002), Top 10 guidelines for homepage usability, *Alertbox*, May 12 2002, available at: http://www.useit.com/alertbox/20020512.html

Nielsen, J. (2006), Outliers and luck in user performance, *Alertbox*, March 6 2006, available at: http://www.useit.com/alertbox/outlier_performance.html

Nielsen, J. and Loranger, H. (2006), Prioritizing web usability, Berkeley, Cal., New Riders

Norris, A. and M. Freeman (2005), Improving library website usability: a user focus, Paper presented at ALIA National Library & Information Technicians Conference, available at:
http://e-prints.alia.org.au/archive/00000062/

Raward, R. (2001), Academic library website design principles: development of a checklist, *Australian Academic & Research Libraries* 32,2, pp. 123-136, available at:
http://alia.org.au/publishing/aarl/32.2/full.text/raward.html

Report on the 2004 usability study of the e-library at Iowa State University (2005), available at: http://www.lib.iastate.edu/cfora/pdf/3000000.pdf

Robins, D, and Kelsey, S. (2002), Analysis of web-based information architecture in a university library: navigating for known items, *Information Technology and Libraries* 21,4, pp. 159-170, available at: http://www.ala.org/ala/lita/litapublications/ital/2104robins.htm

Schulz, U. (2006), Web usability, available at: http://www.bui.fh-hamburg.de/pers/ursula.schulz/webusability/webusability.html

Spivey, M. E. (2000), The vocabulary of library home pages: an influence on diverse and remote end-users, *Information Technology and Libraries* 19,3, pp. 151-156

Still, J. M. (2001), A content analysis of university library Web sites in English speaking countries, *Online Information Review* 25,3, pp. 160-165

Useit.com: Jacob Nielsen's website, available at: http://www.useit.com/

VandeCreek, L. M. (2005), Usability analysis of Northern Illinois University Libraries' website: a case study, *OCLC Systems & Services* 21,3, pp. 181 - 192

B. Use

B.1 Market penetration

Background

Libraries are usually founded and funded with the intent that they shall serve a defined population, e.g. the members of a university or the inhabitants of a community. Therefore the question to what extent a library reaches its population to be served with its services is an important issue for assessing whether the library fulfils its mission by offering services that meet the interests and needs of its population.

When measuring the market penetration or percentage of the population reached, libraries have generally concentrated on borrowing: They count the number of persons in the population that have borrowed an item from the library during a specified time. But library use can include many other activities besides borrowing:

- Working in the library with user-owned materials
- In-house use of the library collection, including copying
- Use of interlibrary lending and document delivery services
- Use of help services (reference service)
- Attending user training lessons
- Attending library events
- Using the library's electronic services and resources, inside or outside the library

Assessing the library's market penetration should therefore, if possible, include all user activities concerned with library services and resources.

Definition of the indicator

The percentage of the population to be served that are active users of the library.

The population to be served is the number of persons to whom the library is commissioned to provide its services. For public libraries, this will normally be the population of the community (or part of the community); for academic libraries, this will normally be the total of students and academic staff in the institution..

An active user is defined as a registered user who has visited the library or made use of library facilities or services during a specified period. This may include the use of electronic library services within or outside the library.

Aims of the indicator

The indicator assesses the library's success in reaching its population.

The indicator is relevant for all libraries with a defined population to be served.

Comparison of results between libraries with similar mission, structure and clientele is possible.

Methods

1. A representative sample of the population to be served is questioned by survey whether they have visited the library or made use of library services in any form during the last year. Surveys can be sent by mail or e-mail, or an online survey can be made available on the library's website. Questions in the survey could be:
   - Have you visited the library during the last year?
   - Have you visited the library's website during the last year?
   - Have you used the library's electronic services from outside the library during the last year?

   The market penetration of the library is calculated by the percentage of respondents answering "yes" at least once of the total number of respondents.

2. As an estimate for market penetration, the number of active borrowers can be used.

   Active borrowers are registered users who have borrowed at least one item during the last year. The data should be available via the records of the library's loan system.

   The market penetration of the library is calculated by the percentage of active borrowers of the total population to be served.

   As members of the population may have visited the library or used electronic library services without borrowing, the market penetration calculated by this method can be lower than in reality, especially if borrowing is not a main user activity. This can be the case in libraries of medicine or sciences, where electronic collections are more heavily used than the loan collection. In such cases, methods 1 or 3 should be preferred.

3. If the library's authentication procedures for the use of its electronic services make it possible to identify which users out of its population have used the electronic services, these data can be compared with those of active borrowers.

   The market penetration of the library is then calculated as the percentage of persons in the population to be served that have either borrowed at least one item and/or have used electronic library services during the last year.

When measuring market penetration, some libraries have also used the number of "registered users" (persons having registered for using library services). But this number may be too high, if users are registered automatically when enrolling in the institution, or if the library does not "weed" its user data regularly.

In order to get a more detailed view of market penetration, in all three methods the population to be served could be split into groups. For a university library this could be:

- Undergraduate students
- Graduate students
- Academic staff
- Students and academic staff of a faculty (e.g. medicine)

For a public library, this could be:

- Children (up to and including age 14)
- Adults
- Adults over 65 years

Market penetration could also be measured for special target groups differentiated as to gender or ethnic origin.

Interpretation and use of results

High market penetration will be considered as good. "A library that appeals to only a small proportion of prospective clients could not be seen as being effective in comparison with one which attracted 100% of prospective users" (Revill, 1990, p.303). But the degree of market penetration that can be achieved will depend on the library's mission and clientele. While libraries in institutions of higher education may reach nearly the whole population, especially if there is no other library nearby that could deliver similar services, public libraries will probably reach only part of the total population in the community.

The indicator can be influenced by several issues:

- Other libraries nearby supplying services to the library's clientele

- The distance of potential users to the library
- The level of education in the population

If the market penetration seems too low compared with other libraries of similar mission and population, the library could

- try to improve its services,
- introduce new attractive services (e.g. group working areas, wireless access, e-books),
- promote its services via its website or public media,
- tailor services to special target groups in the population.

Examples and further reading

When assessing market penetration, libraries as yet have used either active borrowers or registered users for the calculation. No example was found of a library including all types of usage as described in this indicator.

The German benchmarking project BIX (BIX. Der Bibliotheksindex) used the indicator "market penetration" in 2004 for academic libraries, calculated by the number of active borrowers in the population (BIX, 2004). The results were:

Percentage of active borrowers in the population	mean	maximum	minimum
Universities of applied sciences	87.9%	99.6%	68.4%
Universities: One-tier systems	85.8%	98.1%	67.2%
Universities: Two-tier systems (only the central library considered)	69.3%	98.5%	49.5%

Market penetration seemed to be lower in the traditional two-tier systems, but in their first terms many students use mainly the departmental or institute libraries, that may not yet participate in the central computerized loan system.

A study in Polish academic libraries used the indicator "registered users as % of potential users" (Derfert-Wolf, Górski and Marcinek, 2005). The results for 2003 were:

Registered users as percentage of potential users	average	median
University libraries	70,56%	75,76%
Technical university libraries	65,88%	70,17%
All academic libraries	69,93%	74,52%

Market penetration is of course lower in public libraries. The Finnish public library statistics show a percentage of 44.77% active borrowers of the population for 2005 and 43.33% for 2006 (Finnish public library statistics).

The statistics of public libraries in British Columbia compare the number of "resident borrowers" to the population to be served (British Columbia public library statistics, 2004). Resident borrowers are persons residing in the library's service area with borrower cards that have been used during the last three years. In 2004, 55.48% of the population to be served were resident borrowers.

The Council of Australian State Libraries published a report with accumulated data for the states or territories, using among others the indicator "percent of population who are library members" (Australian public libraries comparative report, 2005). This indicator calculates market penetration with the number of registered users. The percentage will therefore be higher than when active borrowers are compared to the population. The results for 2003/04 showed a maximum of 60% for South Australia and a minimum of 38% for the Northern Territory.

Australian public libraries comparative report 1998 – 2004 (2005), presented to CASL meeting Sydney, NSW, July 2005, available at: http://www.nsla.org.au/publications/statistics/2004/pdf/NSLA.Statistics-20040701-Australian.Public.Library.Comparative.Report.1998.2004.pdf

BIX. Der Bibliotheksindex, available at: http://www.bix-bibliotheksindex.de/

BIX. Der Bibliotheksindex (2004), Bertelsmann Stiftung, Gütersloh

British Columbia public library statistics (2004), Ministry of Education, Victoria, British Columbia, available at: http://www.bced.gov.bc.ca/pls/bcplstats_2004.pdf

Derfert-Wolf, L., Górski, M. and Marcinek, M. (2005), Quality of academic libraries – funding bodies, librarians and users, *World Library and Information Congress, 71th IFLA General Conference and Council,* available at: http://www.ifla.org/IV/ifla71/papers/080e-Derfert-Wolf.pdf#search=%22Derfert-Wolf%22

Finnish public library statistics, Culture and Media Division of the Ministry of Education, available at: http://tilastot.kirjastot.fi/Default.aspx?&langId=en

Revill, D. (1990), Performance measures for academic libraries, in Kent, E. (Ed.), Encyclopedia of Library and Information Science, Vol.45, Suppl.10, Dekker, New York, Basel, pp. 294 - 333

B.2 User satisfaction

Background

"In a service environment, how users perceive and value what is available is central to effective service design and delivery." (Creaser, 2006, p.1)

Most libraries are trying to assess their users' opinion on the services they supply. This is usually done by surveys handed out or mailed to a random sample of users or by a web-based survey on the library's website. Other methods used are focus groups or personal interviews with users.

User surveys can ask for different levels of experience with library services:

- The particular experience and satisfaction with the last library visit or the last use of a library service
- The long-time experience and satisfaction with all or individual library services
- The experience and satisfaction compared with the expected quality level

Surveying users is today very common in libraries. A questionnaire by the Association of Research Libraries to its members in 2004 showed, that only one library did not survey its users (Diamond, 2004, p.9). For a long time most libraries designed their own surveys according to their tasks and clientele. The advantage of such individual surveys is that each library can address its special problems and specified user groups. More recently, libraries tend to make use of standard surveys, designed for a group or type of libraries. The advantage is that benchmarking of the results will become possible, especially if the survey is applied regularly over years. A standardized survey will also give the individual library more confidence in its surveying process and will add reliability to the data when reporting to funding institutions. If libraries join in a user survey project, it will be possible to evaluate the data centrally and to save workload in the individual library.

User surveys will assist in tailoring library services to the needs and interests of the population. They show areas of dissatisfaction and thus help to detect problems and shortcomings in the service delivery.

Definition of the indicator

The average rating given by users on a numeric scale ranging from very unsatisfactory to very satisfactory expressing their perception of the library services as a whole and of individual services offered by the library.

The numeric scale can have different numbers of points; scales with four, five, seven, nine or ten points have been used. For the description of this indicator, a five-point- scale is used with 1 as the lowest value.

Aims of the indicator

To assess the degree to which users are satisfied with the library services as a whole and with individual services offered by the library.

The indicator is relevant for all libraries.

Comparison with other libraries, as well of the overall satisfaction with the library as of the satisfaction with individual services, will be possible, if the same kind of survey is used and if differences in the libraries' tasks and clientele are taken into consideration.

The indicator can be used separately for different target groups in the library's population, e.g. for undergraduates, the faculty of medicine, external users, or elderly people.

Methods

The library designs a questionnaire that lists the specific services and/or aspects of services which it wants to evaluate. A numeric scale, usually a five-point scale, is provided for answering the questions. Space should be given for additional comments.

The questionnaire should be tested by a small sample of users to see whether the questions are clear and understandable.

If the library decides to use a standard survey, if possible in a joint project together with other libraries, it should ensure that relevant local questions can be added to that survey.

Questions about user status should be included in the questionnaire in order to allow differentiating between the needs of the different user groups.

The contents of the questionnaire could be as follows

- **Questions as to user status:**
  Questions in an academic library could ask for age group, status (undergraduate, postgraduate, academic staff, others), faculty.

Questions in a public library could ask for age group, gender, ethnic origin, employment status.

- **Questions as to the frequency of library use**
  e.g. frequency of library visits, preferred branch or departmental library, frequency of using specified services (lending, reference, online catalogue, etc.)

- **Questions as to the last time use of library services and the satisfaction**
  What did you do when you last visited the library and how satisfied were you? (Options for activities and for a satisfaction rating on a five-point scale)
  What did you do when you last accessed library services from a computer and how satisfied were you? (Options for activities and for a satisfaction rating on a five-point scale)

- **Questions as to satisfaction with an individual library service and its importance for the respondent** (Satisfaction and importance are each rated on a numeric scale.)
  The services named could be:
  - collection (differentiated as to books, e-books, print and electronic journals, databases, audiovisual materials, children's books, etc.)
  - studying and reading facilities (differentiated as to seats, computer workstations, copying, etc.)
  - opening hours
  - library environment (differentiated as to noise, climate, security, etc.)
  - lending service
  - interlibrary lending
  - online catalogue
  - library website
  - reference service
  - user training
  - Internet access
  - staff (helpfulness, competence)

The survey could also ask for the overall satisfaction with the library's services, again on a five-point scale.

Method 1:
A random sample of users is asked to fill out the questionnaire. The questionnaires could be handed out directly to users visiting the library or sent by post or

e-mail to active users. If the questionnaire is handed out in the library, "normal" weeks should be chosen and an equal spread over times of the day and week in order to include different types of users.

Non-users should generally not be included, as they would have no experience with library services.

Method 2:

An online survey is put on the library's website at certain times, with an equal spread over times of the day and week. With this method, non-users might be included if they choose to answer the questions. The advantage is that the evaluation of the data will be much easier.

In both methods, user satisfaction is then calculated for the overall satisfaction with the library and for each service separately. The satisfaction scores given by respondents for each service are summed up and divided by the number of re-spondents.

Example:

In a sample of 371 users rating their satisfaction with the electronic journal collection on a five- point scale, 8 consider the collection as very unsatisfactory, 24 as unsatisfactory, 120 as moderately satisfactory, 164 as satisfactory, and 55 as very satisfactory.

8	x	1	=	8
24	x	2	=	48
120	x	3	=	360
164	x	4	=	656
55	x	5	=	275

$$1.347 \; : \; 371 \; = \; 3.63$$

The satisfaction rate with the electronic journal collection would be 3.63, between moderately satisfactory and satisfactory. The statements of the respondents about the frequency of use and the importance of individual services could then be compared to the results in order to decide whether more resources should be spent on this service.

Interpretation and use of results

High satisfaction rates will of course be seen as good and can be used as an efficient marketing tool of the library. The results, even if worse than expected, should in any case be publicised as well to library staff as to the user community and the parent institution.

Low satisfaction with a service points to shortcomings in the service deliv-ery. The open comments of users in the questionnaire can give more information about the reasons for dissatisfaction. The library could follow up the problem by conducting focus groups or interviews for the specified service. The comments might also have addressed issues that were not considered in the questionnaire.

For the interpretation of the scores it will be of vital importance to bear in mind that the results are based on the subjective opinion of a random sample of users. The problems are:

- Individual circumstances at the time of the survey can influence the answers. For example, a user who had to queue at the reference desk may rate the whole reference service as unsatisfactory.
- The previous experience of users will influence their expectations and therewith the satisfaction with a library service. If users have no experience of high quality services they may be satisfied with lower quality.
- Loyalty may influence the answers. Library staff often gets good scores for friendliness and helpfulness, because users know staff members personally.

The indicator "user satisfaction" should always be used together with other indicators for service quality and with usage statistics for the services that are evaluated.

Examples and further reading

Over years, many libraries have developed and used individual satisfaction surveys. But the trend is going to standard surveys and to joint projects for reasons of benchmarking and practicality of data evaluation.

There are a number of options available for standard surveys. For public libraries, surveys are sometimes mandatory, if a quality assessment program is prescribed for them by a central institution. This is for instance the case in UK public libraries (Creaser, 2006, p.1).

In academic libraries, the LibQUAL+ survey developed by the Association of Research Libraries has found wide acceptance. The survey asks library users to rate the library services on a nine-point scale as to

- the minimum acceptable service level,
- the desired level,
- the perceived service performance.

An overview of studies about LibQUAL+ and it's applications is given in the LibQual+[TM] bibliography and the LibQUAL+[(R)] study bibliography.

In the UK, a standard survey has been developed by SCONUL, Society of College, National and University Libraries. The survey asks not only for the "last time experience", but also for the satisfaction with individual services along with how important each individual service is to the user. This supports management decisions, where important services with low satisfaction rates would be tackled first.

In Australia, the Rodski survey, now Insync survey is used in many libraries. As in the SCONUL survey, it measures satisfaction with performance against importance of the service to the user (Saw and Clark, 2004).

A survey similar to SCONUL and Rodski, again asking for satisfaction and importance, was used in the joint user survey of 15 German university libraries in 2001 (Follmer, Guschker and Mundt, 2002; Mundt, 2003).

A joint project of 10 Austrian university libraries in 2003 concentrated on user satisfaction with electronic library services, with an online questionnaire on the library websites (Bauer, 2004).

Bauer, B. (2004), Die elektronische Bibliothek auf dem Prüfstand ihrer Kunden: Konzeption und Methodik der gemeinsamen Online-Befragung 2003 an zehn österreichischen Universitäts- und Zentralbibliotheken, *Bibliotheksdienst* 38,5, pp. 595-610

Creaser, C. (2006), User surveys in academic libraries, *New Review of Academic Librarianship* 12,1, pp. 1-15

Diamond, T. (2004), Library user surveys, SPEC Kit 280, Association of Research Libraries, Washington D.C.

Follmer, R., Guschker, S. and Mundt, S. (2002), Gemeinsame Nutzerbefragung der nordrhein-westfälischen Universitätsbibliotheken – methodisches Vorgehen und Erfahrungen, *Bibliotheksdienst* 36,1, pp. 20-33, available at: http://bibliotheksdienst.zlb.de/2002/02_01_02.pdf

LibQUAL+TM , available at: http://www.libqual.org/

LibQUAL+TM bibliography (2004), available at: http://www.libqual.org/documents/admin/LibQUALBibliography3.1.pdf

LibQUAL+(R) study bibliography, available at: http://www.coe.tamu.edu/~bthompson/servqbib

Mundt, S. (2003), Benchmarking user satisfaction in academic libraries – a case study, *Library and Information Research* 27 (87), pp. 29-37, available at: http://www.lirg.org.uk/lir/pdf/article87_mundt.pdf

Saw, G. and Clark, N. (2004), Reading Rodski: user surveys revisited, *IATUL Proceedings* 14, available at:
http://www.iatul.org/doclibrary/public/Conf_Proceedings/2004/Grace20Saw20and20Nicole20Clark.pdf

SCONUL service templates, available at:
http://www.sconul.ac.uk/groups/performance_improvement/surveys/templates.html

B.3 Library visits per capita

Background

Traditionally, libraries offer the use of their collections and services via a user's visit to the library as physical place. As users' visits can be seen as a measure for the library's attractiveness, national library statistics have in most cases included the number of library visits in their counts.

With the development of electronic collections and services libraries have started to offer a new virtual "entrance" to their services: the library website. Users can "visit" the library and use many of its services from remote places, e.g. from their workplace or from home. Such visits, in analogy to the traditional physical visits, are called "virtual visits".

Both forms of "visits" are used side by side, often by the same users. In some libraries physical library visits have decreased, due to a high number of the library's services and resources being available for remote use. In other cases, physical visits have remained stable or have even increased. This may be due to a growing tendency for group work in libraries, to the trend of users working with their own material in libraries, and to the advantage of using both print and electronic resources together with help and training services.

The library has remained attractive as a place to meet and study. Therefore, physical library visits are still a relevant measure of a library's attractiveness. But in order to additionally assess the attractiveness of the library's web services, the indicator proposed here tries to combine physical and website visits in order to show the growing use of library services via the library's website.

Definition of the indicator

The total number of visits to the library per year, either physical or virtual, by members of the population to be served, divided by the number of persons in the population.

A physical visit is defined as the act of a person's entering the library premises. Visits are counted independently of the purpose of the visit (borrowing, working in the library, or taking part in events and guided tours).

A virtual visit is defined as a user's request on the library's website from outside the library premises in order to use one of the services provided by the library.

The population to be served is the number of persons to whom the library is commissioned to provide its services. For public libraries, this will normally be the population of the community (or part of the community); for academic libraries, this will normally be the total of students and academic staff in the institution.

Aims of the indicator

The indicator assesses the library's success in attracting users either to the library as place or to its web services and the adequacy of the library's traditional and new web-based services to its population.

The indicator is relevant for all libraries with a defined population to be served and with both traditional and web-based services.

Comparison between libraries of similar mission, structure and clientele is possible, if special conditions (e.g. a new building) are considered.

The indicator does not consider users' activities during physical or virtual visits.

Methods

a) **Physical visits**: Count the number of visits made by persons (individuals) to the library premises annually. This is usually done by using a turnstile or similar device to automatically count the number of people leaving or entering the library. Count either entries or exits, not both.

If manual counts have to be used, samples of "normal" times could be taken and grossed up to give an annual estimate. Times with normal activity could be identified by using circulation data.

The method used (turnstile or manual count) should be reported.

Entrances and exits of library staff should be estimated and deducted.

Visits by external users (users not belonging to the population to be served) will be included in the counts. If external users' activities constitute a high proportion of library use, the library could try to estimate the number of external users' visits by calculating the percentage of loans to external users (see Indicator B.9 "Percentage of loans to external users").

b) **Virtual visits**: Counting virtual visits is not as straightforward as counting physical visits. Following the international standard ISO 2789, the following rules apply for this indicator:

- A virtual visit is a series of requests for data files from one and the same website visitor.
- A website visitor is either a unique and identified web browser program or an identified IP address that has accessed pages from the library's website.
- Only requests coming from outside the library premises are defined as virtual visits. Website visits from inside the library premises and page views by changing over from another page of the website are excluded. This can be difficult if the server cannot extract such visits.
- The interval between two consecutive requests must not be longer than a time-out period of 30 minutes if they are to be counted as part of the same virtual visit. A longer interval initiates a new visit.
- Website visits from robot or spider crawls and from page reloads may increase the numbers and should be excluded from the counts.
- If a request results in opening a HTML page that consists of several frames, the HTML document should be counted that comprises the most essential contents of the frameset.
- If a website exists in several languages, counting has to be done separately for every language and the partial results have to be added.

Ideally, the indicator should only consider virtual visits made by members of the population. Visits from outside the population should be excluded. IP-addresses inside an institution might be used for this purpose, but this would exclude the virtual visits from home addresses by members of the population.

Separating the virtual visits made by members of the population from other virtual visits would be possible if each website visitor were asked to register. But as most libraries want to offer information about their services to every interested person, registration is only used for services restricted to the population like licensed databases. Visitors from outside the population will therefore in most cases be included in the count of virtual visits. But as that will probably also be the case for physical visits, and as certainly the highest number of both physical and virtual visitors are members of the population, data of physical and virtual visits will still be comparable and can be summed up for this indicator "Library visits per capita".

Another problem for counting virtual visits is caching. Caching means that the user's browser has stored the page the user visited and at the next visit will pull the page from the cache, so that the visit will not be recorded in the server's log files. "The number of requests does not translate into number of unique visitors, and the numbers may not reflect all usage because of caching" (Bauer, 2000).

Libraries measuring website visits have used different counts:

- All page views, but excluding page accesses via another page of the website
- Only accesses to the homepage and the most-used pages
- Only accesses to the homepage

The home page is the page which serves as the visual unit that is displayed when accessing the library's website. The home page may appear after the redirection through an entry page.

A method for joint use by a group of libraries was developed by the German benchmarking project BIX (BIX. Der Bibliotheksindex) and will be used from 2007 following. The counts include only the library's homepage and the start page for the online catalogue. A "pixel" with a short text is inserted on each of the pages for counting purposes. The number of deliveries of the pixel is identical to the number of page deliveries. The advantage of this method is that it is easy to use; the disadvantage is that access to other pages is not counted.

The method chosen and the pages included in the count of virtual visits should be specified in the statistics, especially if the data are aggregated on a national basis and if the results are used for comparison and benchmarking.

For calculating "Library visits per capita", the total number of physical + virtual visits is divided by the number of persons in the population.

Interpretation and use of results

A high number of visits per member of the population show the library's attractiveness and the adequacy of its services to the population to be served.

The results for the number of physical visits per member of the population may be too high if visits by external users cannot be excluded from the counts. The number may also be influenced by users frequently leaving and re-entering the library, e.g. if the cafeteria is located outside the library premises.

If physical visits seem too low or are decreasing, the library could

- introduce new attractive services (e.g. group working areas, wireless access, a cafeteria and recreation areas),
- address problems of in-house library use by a user satisfaction survey,
- offer longer opening hours (see Indicator A.3 "Opening hours compared to demand")
- try to enlarge the space offered to users for reading and working (see Indicator A.1 "User area per capita").

If virtual visits per member of the population seem too low compared with other libraries, the library could

- align the homepage and other relevant pages to the main needs of its population (see Indicator A.10 "Direct access from the homepage"),
- change to a more user-friendly and consistent terminology,
- offer various instruments for orientation like a search function, a sitemap, or an "A – Z" register.

Another issue might be to offer special homepage entrances for special target groups. For academic libraries this could be:

- first-time visitors
- first-year students
- postgraduates
- faculty
- senior students
- disabled persons
- external visitors

For public libraries this could be:

- first-time visitors
- children, juveniles
- seniors
- disabled persons

Examples and further reading

The only example found where both physical and virtual visits are counted and compared to the population is that of the Finnish public libraries (Finnish public library statistics). The data of the last 4 years show a slight decrease in physical visits, a considerable increase in virtual visits, and an increase in total library visits.

	physical visits per inhabitant	virtual visits per inhabitant	total visits per inhabitant
2003	12,72	6,76	19,48
2004	12,84	7,90	20,74
2005	11,98	9,04	21,02
2006	11,38	10,15	21,53

As yet, most libraries count only the **physical visits** to the library.

The German benchmarking project BIX (BIX. Der Bibliotheksindex) uses for academic libraries the indicator „visits per capita", that aims at counting the total number of visits, including both physical and virtual visits, per member of the population. The count of virtual visits will start in 2007. The results for only physical visits in 2005 were (BIX, 2006):

Visits per capita	mean	maximum	minimum
Universities of applied sciences	32,0	51,4	7,0
Universities: One-tier systems	63,8	166,1	5,7
Universities: Two-tier systems (only the central library considered)	36,4	70,9	13,8

Visits seem to be lower in the traditional two-tier systems, but in their first terms many students use mainly the institute libraries.

The statistics of the Australian university libraries (CAUL online statistics) show for 2005 a mean score of 22,18 visits per member of the total population (students and staff). Visits increased during the last years.

In UK academic libraries the statistics of 2004/05 show an average of 57 visits per full time equivalent member of the population, including academic staff and students (Creaser, 2006, p.15). Visits decreased from 1994/95 to 2001/02, but remain stable since 2002/03.

The Finnish research libraries had in 2005 a score of 39,2 visits per member of the population, including students and staff (Finnish research libraries statistics database).

There are of course fewer visits per member of the population in public libraries. The German project BIX uses for public libraries the indicator "visits per capita", which is defined as the number of all physical visits to the library, including attendances at events, compared to the population to be served. The results in 2005 were (BIX, 2006):

Visits per capita	mean	maximum	minimum
Libraries in communities under 15.000 inhabitants	4,3	7,0	1,7
Libraries in communities from 15.000 to 30.000 inhabitants	3,5	6,3	0,6
Libraries in communities from 30.000 to 50.000 inhabitants	3,1	6,2	1,1
Libraries in communities from 50.000 to 100.000 inhabitants	2,7	5,0	0,9
Libraries in communities over 100.000 inhabitants	3,0	5,3	0,7

The mean score of visits per capita seems to be somewhat higher in smaller communities.

Public library statistics in British Columbia show 30.531.306 visits per 4.071.176 members of the population = 7,5 visits per member in 2003 (British Columbia public library statistics, 2004).

In UK public libraries, the 10-years statistics show a slight decrease in visits, but an increase again from 2002/03 to 2003/04 (Creaser, Maynard and White, 2005):
- 1993/94 = 8,0 visits per capita
- 2002/03 = 6,9 visits per capita
- 2003/04 = 7,1 visits per capita

The US public library statistics for 2004 count 4,67 visits per capita (Public libraries in the United States, 2006).

Virtual visits are a new issue in library statistics. Only a few national or regional statistics have started counting virtual visits in addition to physical visits.

In the German library statistics of 2005, data from 28 university libraries for both kinds of visits show the following results (DBS, 2005):
- total physical visits: 21.151.999
- total virtual visits: 43.323.411
- total visits: 64.475.410 (physical visits = 32,81 %)

Virtual visits were about double the physical visits, but in 9 libraries the number of virtual visits was lower than that of physical visits. The statistics count only accesses to a page from outside the library website, not changing to another page inside the website.

The Finnish university libraries counted in 2005 a total of 38.143.761 "downloads" from the library website and in 2006 a total of 49.629.268 "downloads" (Finnish research library statistics database).

The Association of Research Libraries has started counting virtual visits in its supplementary statistics, but the data are not yet published, as there is no standard method used in the libraries.

Measuring not only physical, but also virtual library visits will certainly be an important issue for library statistics in the next years in order to show on the one side the gradual shift from traditional to virtual library use, on the other side the continuing appreciation of the library as physical place.

Bauer, K. (2000), Who goes where? Measuring library web site usage, *ONLINE* January 2000, available at: http://www.infotoday.com/Online/OL2000/bauer1.html

BIX. Der Bibliotheksindex, available at: http://www.bix-bibliotheksindex.de/

BIX. Der Bibliotheksindex (2006), *B.I.T. online* Sonderheft 2006

British Columbia public library statistics (2004), Ministry of Education, Victoria, British Columbia, available at: http://www.bced.gov.bc.ca/pls/bcplstats_2004.pdf

CAUL online statistics, Council of Australian University Libraries, available at: http://www.anu.edu.au/caul/stats/

Creaser, C. (2006), SCONUL library statistics: trends 1994-95 to 2004-05, LISU, Loughborough University

Creaser, C., Maynard, S. and White, S. (2005), LISU annual library statistics 2005, featuring trend analysis of UK public and academic libraries 1994 – 2004, LISU, Loughborough University, available at: http://www.lboro.ac.uk/departments/dils/lisu/downloads/als05.pdf

DBS. Deutsche Bibliotheksstatistik (2005), available at: http://www.hbz-nrw.de/angebote/dbs/auswertung/

Finnish public library statistics, Culture and Media Division of the Ministry of Education, available at: http://tilastot.kirjastot.fi/Default.aspx?&langId=en

Finnish research library statistics database, Helsinki University Library, available at: https://yhteistilasto.lib.helsinki.fi/language.do?action=change&choose_language=3

Public libraries in the United States: fiscal year 2004 (2006), National Center for Education Statistics, available at: http://nces.ed.gov/pubs2006/2006349.pdf

B.4 Seat occupancy rate

Background

Libraries are highly-valued places for reading, learning and working. In some libraries physical library visits are decreasing, due to a high number of the library's services and resources being available for remote use. In others physical visits remain stagnant or are even increasing. Users appreciate the possibility of using both print and electronic resources together with help and training services inside the library. Other aspects add to a new attractiveness of the library: There is a growing tendency for group work in libraries and for users working with their own material in libraries. Therefore a sufficient number of working places with adequate equipment will be one of the most important issues for user satisfaction

Especially in institutions of higher education, the library is the physical place where students meet for studying singly or in groups. In public libraries, where users primarily need seats for a shorter time of reading and browsing, the number of seats for the population to be served will be significantly lower than in academic libraries, where users might need a seat for the whole day.

If a library wants to know whether the number of seats provided is adequate to the library's visitors, measuring the occupancy rate of the seats will give valuable information.

Definition of the indicator

The mean occupancy rate of user seats in the library over the year.

The definition includes seats with or without equipment, seats in carrels, in seminar and study rooms and in the audiovisual and children's departments of the library.

Seats in halls, lecture and auditory theatres intended for audiences of special events are excluded. The definition also excludes informal seating, e.g. floor space on which users may sit.

Aims of the indicator

The indicator assesses the adequacy of seats provided in the library to users' needs and therewith the priority given to the library's role as physical place for reading, learning and working.

The indicator is relevant for all libraries that offer reading and working facilities. It will be most relevant for libraries in institutions of higher education.

Comparison between libraries of similar mission, structure and clientele is possible.

The indicator does not measure the ratio of seats provided to the population to be served (see Indicator A.2).

Method

Count the number of seats available to users and the number of those occupied at random intervals over the year, including peak times and times of lower use, e.g. inside and outside term. By cumulating the results, the mean occupancy rate over the year can be calculated. Seats where users have placed their working material, notebooks etc. are defined as occupied, even if the user is absent at the time of counting.

It might also be useful to measure the seat occupancy rate in peak times separately, as the results show whether the library can also provide for high demand.

If there are different forms of reading and working areas, e.g. group working areas or laptop areas, the seat occupancy could be measured separately for such areas in order to find out what kind of reading and working facilities users prefer.

Interpretation and use of results

A low mean occupancy rate shows that there is sufficient seating available. This would be user-friendly, but it might also point to a decrease in user visits and an under-use of the facilities offered.

A high occupancy rate shows that the library is efficiently used, but over a certain level of occupancy users may feel uncomfortable. There is no standard to say what occupancy rate is appropriate for comfortable space and quiet working. This may depend on the space allowed for one user working place. In the German Technical Report for academic library buildings, the following space is defined as adequate for a workplace (Bau- und Nutzungsplanung, 1998).

- normal workplace = 3 m^2
- computer workplace = 3,50 m^2
- multimedia workplace or carrel = 4 m^2

All three types of workplaces would need an additional space of 0,90 m^2 for access to the place.

To assess whether the number and equipment of seats correspond to users' wishes, the issue could be addressed in a user satisfaction survey.

Examples and further reading

In a survey in Glasgow Caledonian University Library, UK, the highest occupancy rate was 43%, at a point of time just prior to examinations (Crawford and MacNicol, 2001).

La Trobe University Library, Australia, used an interesting categorization of workplaces in its 2-weeks seating usage survey in three campuses (King, Sheridan and Beranek, 2004). The survey also differentiated between times of the day/week. The highest occupancy rates occurred from Monday to Wednesday, chiefly between 11.30 am and 2.30 pm. Computer workstations had the highest occupancy, sometimes more than 100% (waiting queues). Group study places were often used in preference to single study places that generally had a low use. The average occupancy rates on one campus (Bendigo) were:

- Single study places or carrels   25%
- Group study seating   24%
- Casual seating   12%
- Computer workstations (seated)   74%
- Computer workstations (standing)   46%

The statistics of SCONUL, Society of College, National and University Libraries, UK count the average percentage of seats occupied. For 2004/05 the mean value was 36% (SCONUL, 2006).

As occupancy rates may not give a definite view of whether users feel comfortable with the number of seats, many libraries have assessed user opinion on this topic by satisfaction surveys.

In a joint user satisfaction survey of the university libraries in North Rhine-Westphalia, Germany, only 56% of respondents were satisfied with the number of user workplaces in the libraries, 65% with the working atmosphere, and 60% with quietness in the reading rooms (Follmer, Guschker and Mundt, 2002).

In the satisfaction survey of Glasgow Caledonian University Library mentioned above, only two respondents mentioned a need for additional study places, and general satisfaction with the study environment got the note 3.5 on a 5-point scale, with 5 the best note. This corresponds with the low occupancy rate in that library.

Bau- und Nutzungsplanung von wissenschaftlichen Bibliotheken (1998), *DIN-Fachbericht* 13, DIN – Deutsches Institut für Normung e.V., Berlin

Crawford, J. C. and MacNicol, C. (2001), Report on the general satisfaction survey conducted at Glasgow Caledonian University Library, February/March 2001, available at: http://www.learningservices.gcal.ac.uk/library/research/gss01.pdf#search=%22Glasgow% 20Caledonian%20University%20Library%202001%22

Follmer, R., Guschker, S. and Mundt, S. (2002), Alles was man zum Lernen braucht..., Übergreifende Ergebnisse der Benutzerbefragung in den nordrhein-westfälischen Universitätsbibliotheken 2001, *ProLibris* 2002,1, pp. 20-25

King, H., Sheridan, L. and Beranek, L. (2004), Seating usage survey 2004, La Trobe University Library, available at: www.lib.latrobe.edu.au/about/surveys/seatingsurvey2004.pdf

SCONUL annual library statistics 2004-2005 (2006), SCONUL, Society of College, National & University Libraries, London

B.5 Number of content units downloaded per capita

Background

In both public and academic libraries the number of electronic resources increases continually. Consequently, the question arises in how far this collection is adjusted to the needs of the population to be served.

In the international standard ISO 2789, the electronic library collection is subdivided as to databases, electronic serials, and digital documents. What makes it difficult to apply performance measures is the heterogeneous nature of these electronic resources. Databases for instance may contain only descriptive records such as bibliographic descriptions of books and articles, or they may be pure full-content databases with large quantities of digital documents or non-textual material, where the user is actually provided with the complete content and not only with meta-information that has to be followed up. Another type of electronic resources is a mixture of both descriptive records and full-content units.

Measures for the use of the electronic collection have been defined in ISO 2789 as follows:

- Search: specific intellectual query
- Session: successful request of a database
- Rejected session (turnaway): unsuccessful request of a database by exceeding the simultaneous user limit
- Session time: the period of time between a log-in to and an implicit or explicit log-off from a database
- Contents downloaded: a content unit being successfully requested from a database, electronic serial or digital document
- Records downloaded: a descriptive record being successfully requested from a database

Downloads of content units indicate that users have found items that seem to be relevant for their interests. The measure could be seen in analogy to loans of print materials, while sessions could be seen in analogy to browsing the shelves. Therefore, downloads can be regarded as the most expressive measure for the relevance of the electronic collection to users.

Definition of the indicator

The number of content units downloaded from electronic resources - databases, electronic serials or digital documents - in the library's collection per member of the population to be served during a specified time, usually a year.

A content unit is defined as a computer-processed uniquely identifiable textual or audiovisual piece of published work that may be original or a digest of other published work.

A content download is defined as a content unit being successfully requested from a database, electronic serial or digital document

The population to be served is the number of persons to whom the library is commissioned to provide its services. For public libraries, this will normally be the population of the community (or part of the community); for academic libraries, this will normally be the total of students and academic staff in the institution.

Downloads from free Internet resources (Internet resources with unrestricted access) are excluded, even if they have been catalogued by the library in its online catalogue or a database.

Aims of the indicator

The indicator assesses the use of the library's electronic collection by the population to be served and therewith the adequacy of the collection for the population. The number of requests for content units indicates the relevance attributed to the electronic collection by the users.

The indicator is especially useful for comparison over time.

Comparison between libraries, even of similar structure and clientele, will be difficult. It might be possible between libraries with the same subject collections (e.g. medicine), if a similar number and type of electronic resources is offered.

The indicator is relevant for all libraries with an electronic collection and a defined population to be served.

Method

Count the number of content units downloaded from all electronic resources during a year.

In case there are various manifestations of the same unit (HTML, PDF for text files and JPEG or WAV for non-textual material) all requests are counted.

Usually, the vendors of online resources provide detailed statistics separating the number of retrieved database entries or hits from the number of documents viewed or downloaded. Such a distinction should also be made for electronic resources hosted by the library itself.

For each electronic resource the total number of views or downloads over a certain time period – usually correlating to the subscription period of one year – is recorded. The numbers are summed up for all electronic resources and divided by the number of members of the population to be served, counted as persons (not full-time equivalent).

Downloads by library staff and for user training are included in the calculation.

With the population to be served as a data element all electronic resources freely available on the Internet should be left out of consideration. They can be accessed by anyone and give an incomplete picture of how relevant the electronic collection is for the primary users.

It is necessary to bear in mind that the data recorded by library suppliers are not always comparable, since not all vendors adhere closely to the recommended standards such as COUNTER (2005) or ICOLC (2006).

Interpretation and use of results

A high score will be seen as good as it shows high acceptance of the library's electronic collection by the members of the population to be served.

A low score points to inadequacy of the electronic collection to the needs of the population or to users' not being familiar with the collection. The library could try to promote its electronic resources by drawing attention to them in user training lessons.

As downloads are counted for each electronic resource separately, the library will know what resources have a low degree of acceptance. For such resources subscriptions might be cancelled and other resources might be licensed instead. But in such decisions the library should consider the special interests of small user groups.

The indicator may be affected by factors outside the control of the library, for example the level of network access and fees charged for access or downloading.

The number of content units downloaded could also be affected by the quality and efficiency of users' search strategies.

Examples and further reading

The project EQUINOX (2000) used the indicator "Number of documents and entries (records) viewed per session for each electronic library service". EQUINOX as well as the international standard 11620 for library performance indicators do not compare total downloads to the population.

Not many library statistics have already dared to count downloads on a national scale. The German national library statistics try to count downloads from databases and electronic journals, but in 2006 only 9 percent of the reporting libraries were able to deliver data for databases and 13 percent for electronic journals (DBS, 2006).

It will be easier to count only the downloads from licensed resources on external servers. The Danish research libraries count in their statistics downloads from electronic resources on external servers. In 2005, there were 7.014.143 such downloads. Compared to active borrowers of the same year (the total population is not counted) this would be 64,48 downloads per borrower.

Counter (2005), Release 2 of the COUNTER code of practice for journals and databases (Published April 2005), available at:
http://www.projectcounter.org/r2/Appendix_A_Glossary.pdf

DBS – Deutsche Bibliotheksstatistik (2006), Hochschulbibliothekszentrum, Köln, available at: http://www.hbz-nrw.de/angebote/dbs/

Equinox. Library performance measurement and quality management system (2000), available at: http://equinox.dcu.ie/index.html

Folke- og Forskningsbiblioteksstatistik (2005), Biblioteksstyrelsen, København, available at:
http://www.bs.dk/content.aspx?itemguid={D9A1DF3D-6DE9-42F1-B13E-D04CEF1941E0}

ICOLC, International Coalition of Library Consortia (2006), Revised guidelines for statistical measures of usage of web-based information resources, available at:
http://www.library.yale.edu/consortia/webstats06.htm

B.6 Collection use (turnover)

Background

If storing books on shelves is not an end in itself – as may be the case in libraries with an archival function - the degree to which the library collection is used is an essential measure to determine in how far the library meets the needs and interests of its users. Public libraries in particular have made this measure an integral part of the evaluation process for their collection development policy. Each item that was never issued within a certain period of time is seen as failure in providing what users want (see indicator B.7 "Percentage of stock not used"). The aim is to reach as high a collection turnover as possible.

The indicator is restricted to the loan collection and to loans, not including in-house use. It also leaves out of consideration the growing number of electronic resources, especially e-books, even though some providers follow the example of the printed book and restrict the use of an e-book to certain loan periods.

Definition of the indicator

The total number of loans in a certain period of time (usually one year) is divided by the total number of documents in the loan collection.

Loans in the sense of this indicator are lending transactions of physical items to one user. This includes user-initiated renewals, on-site loans (loans within the library) and copies supplied in place of original documents.

Automatic renewals by the system without user initiation and interlibrary loans are excluded.

Aims of the indicator

The indicator assesses the use rate of the loan collection and therewith quantifies the library's effort to match the loan collection and the information needs of its users. It is relevant for all libraries with a loan collection.

The indicator can be used separately for specified collections, subject areas, or branch and departmental libraries. For academic libraries that have to store and preserve collections for a longer time it might be useful to measure collection turnover only for materials acquired in the last 2 or 3 years.

Comparison between libraries of similar mission, structure and clientele will be possible, if differences in the collection subjects are considered.

Method

Define the number of documents in the loan collection and the number of loans during a specified period, usually a year. Most automated library systems contain data of a document's location as well as lending status. This makes it easy to determine the exact size of the loan collection, respectively parts of it, at any given moment. The library system also provides the number of loans that can be attributed to the loan collection as a whole or a particular part of it within a certain period of time.

Sometimes it may be useful to apply the indicator not to the loan collection as a whole but to special parts of it such as the junior library or the short-loan collection. New insights can be gained from distinguishing between various subject collections, since the lifespan of a book in the humanities differs considerably from that of a book in the natural sciences.

Since users are mostly interested in that part of the loan collection that has been acquired recently, it could also be useful to restrict the indicator to those documents added to the loan collection within the last two years, based on the date of acquisition as recorded by the automated library system.

The collection turnover is calculated by dividing the number of loans during a year by the number of documents in the loan collection.

Interpretation and use of results

A higher score will be seen as good. There are a number of factors influencing the indicator:

- The adequacy of the collection to current research topics or interests
- The weeding policies of the library
- The accessibility of the collection in regard to opening hours or physical arrangements
- The number of multiple copies for titles in high demand
- The lending regulations (loan periods, number of documents that may be borrowed simultaneously by a user, number of renewals that are possible)
- The proportion of in-library use to loans

If collection turnover seems too low, the library should above all try to assess the needs and wishes of its population and to adapt its collection policies accordingly. User satisfaction surveys can help to identify what users are missing in the collection. The library could also evaluate interlibrary lending or document supply requests in order to tailor its acquisitions policy to user needs.

Adapting the collection policy to user demand can only succeed as long-term strategy. It asks for a regular repetition of the indicator and a constant effort to keep pace with new trends and topics as well as with the sometimes quick changes in the users' research topics and interests.

Examples and further reading

Many public libraries use the indicator regularly. Texas public libraries have even developed a standard, distinguishing between three levels of performance (essential, enhanced, excellent) for various categories of public libraries based on the size of the population to be served (Texas public library standards, 2005). For libraries serving a population of more than 200,000 a collection turnover rate of 1.0 is considered essential, 2.5 is rated as enhanced, and 3.5 as excellent.

In 2006 Finnish public library statistics reached an overall collection turnover of 2.51 (Finnish public library statistics). In addition, they recorded the turnover for document types such as books and printed music (2.02 in 2006), other than books and printed music (7.54), music recordings (4.50) and video cassettes (7.60).

British Columbia public libraries use a slightly altered version of the indicator (British Columbia public library statistics, 2006). They divide the number of loans by the total number of volumes held. For 2005 they recorded the average score of 4.29.

The German project BIX (BIX. Der Bibliotheksindex) uses the indicator for public libraries. Loans include renewals; stock in closed access is excluded. The results for 2005 were (BIX, 2006):

Collection turnover	mean	maximum	minimum
Communities under 15.000 inhabitants	4,3	7,4	2,1
Communities from 15.000 to 30.000 inhabitants	4,8	7,8	1,2
Communities from 30.000 to 50.000 inhabitants	4,8	9,2	1,8
Communities from 50.000 to 100.000 inhabitants	4,5	6,5	2,2
Communities over 100.000 inhabitants	5,0	7,1	2,6

Academic libraries using this indicator restrict it to loans of recently acquired documents. The benchmarking project of the Netherlands university libraries measures "loans in the past year to acquisitions over the past five years" (Laeven and Smit, 2003, p.297). The results for 2004 for 13 libraries ranged between 1,02 and 4,89, with an average of 1,92 (UKB, 2004).

BIX. Der Bibliotheksindex, available at: http://www.bix-bibliotheksindex.de/

BIX. Der Bibliotheksindex (2006), *B.I.T. online* Sonderheft 2006

British Columbia public library statistics (2006), British Columbia Ministry of Education, Victoria, British Columbia, available at: http://www.bced.gov.bc.ca/pls/bcplstats_2005.pdf

Finnish public library statistics database, Culture and Media Division of the Ministry of Education, available at: http://tilastot.kirjastot.fi/?langId=en

Laeven, H. and Smit, A. (2003), A project to benchmark university libraries in the Netherlands, *Library Management* 24, 6/7, pp. 291-304

Texas Public Library Standards [draft document] (2005), Joint TSLAC/TLA Task Force on Public Library Standards and Accreditation, available at: http://www.tsl.state.tx.us/cgi-bin/ld/plstandards/plstandards.php

UKB (2004), Benchmarking, Samenwerkingsverband van de Nederlandse universiteitsbibliotheken en de Koninklijke Bibliotheek, results only available to participants

B.7 Percentage of stock not used

Background

In the context of collection development and collection use the question of non-use and its reasons has always been discussed, in the case of the Pittsburgh Study (Kent, 1979) in much detail. The study found that 48,37% of the collection had never circulated during the seven years of the study period and followed the results up by differentiations as to the acquisition year, the language and subject of a non-used document and the frequency of circulation of each document.

Ten years earlier Fussler and Simon (1969) had already tried to determine the probability of a book in the collection being used by analysing circulation statistics.

Many studies found results that correspond to the famous 80/20 rule, namely that 80% of the circulations in a library come from a relatively small proportion of the collection, often from about 20%. This small proportion usually coincides with the more recently acquired titles in the collection. "…it is important to recognize that the longer a book goes without being used the less probable it becomes that it will ever be used" (Lancaster, 1993, p.56).

Circulation analysis is usually the main method for libraries evaluating their collection. Non-use is seen as violation of the first of Ranganathan's five laws of library science, namely that "books are for use" (Ranganathan, 1931). Each library has to decide on its own to what extent it is willing to accept that documents in its collection are not used. For libraries with an archival function (e.g. legal deposit) non-use during a certain time period will be tolerable. But especially for public libraries use will be the main issue for collection quality, and non-use will be the criterion for weeding decisions. "Non-use is the kiss of death" was an answer in a survey on weeding practices in public libraries (Dilevko and Gottlieb, 2003).

Definition of the indicator

The percentage of documents in the loan collection that have not been used during a certain period of time, usually a year.

A longer time period, e.g. 2 or 3 years, would be used if the library has a collection with highly specified materials that would probably not be used every year, but will yet remain important for research. "Use" in the sense of this indicator means borrowing. Registered loans within the library (on-site loans) are included.

Browsing and other forms of in-house use are not considered. Interlibrary lending is excluded.

Documents in the collection that are not available for loan are excluded.

Aims of the indicator

The indicator identifies parts of the collection that are not used and is thus a valuable instrument for fine-tuning the collection profile to users' needs. It will support weeding decisions as well as changes in selection policies and resource allocation to subjects.

The indicator has often been used together with the indicator B.6 "Collection use". "Collection use" compares the number of documents in the collection to the number of loans, irrespective of the fact that some documents have been used frequently while others have not been used at all. This indicator deals with the single document and its use, as there may be "dead areas" in the collection though the collection as a whole is heavily used.

The indicator is relevant for all libraries with a loan collection. It will be especially interesting for public libraries. For academic libraries that have to store and preserve collections for a longer time it might be useful to measure non-use only for materials acquired in the last 2 or 3 years.

Comparison between libraries of similar mission, structure and clientele will be possible, if differences in the collection subjects are considered.

Methods

1. For a random sample of books in the collection all loans over a certain period of time (usually one year) are recorded. Documents not available for loan should be excluded from the sample. If the indicator is used to monitor the collection development policy the sample chosen should relate to a particular subject collection, since the interpretation of the results depends on the subject. The time-point of obsolescence (the time when documents "age" and will be less used) varies considerably between subjects.
   Sampling should be used with caution, as there may be clusters of unused documents in different parts of the collection.

2. With the help of an automated library system it will be possible to identify the overall number of items in the collection that are available for loan

and the number of those items which were on loan at least once during the period in question. The rest consists of unused material, so-called "zero loans".

In the context of this indicator it is irrelevant whether an item was used once or several times. What matters is that it has been used at all. But a library may want to raise its standards and decide to count those cases when an item has been used only once or twice as "zero loans". This will of course result in a much higher score for "stock not used".

The "stock not used" is calculated as the percentage of documents not used of all documents in the loan collection.

Interpretation and use of results

A low percentage of stock not used will be seen as good. What percentage would be tolerated will depend on the library's goals.

The indicator will be influenced by high in-house use that may reduce circulation. It will also be affected by storage conditions: Documents in closed stacks will probably be used less than documents in open access areas. Documents placed in small collections that are easy to survey might have a higher chance of being used than documents "lost" in large collections. Use may also be influenced by a complicated shelf classification, and even by the shelf level the document is placed on. A study in the Southeast Missouri State University found that "books sitting on the bottom shelf circulate the least, followed by those sitting on the top shelf" (Banks, 2002. p.115).

There are basically two ways of dealing with a large percentage of books not used:

- If loans are the essential criterion for collection development, any document that has not been used could be removed from the collection in order to improve the turnover rate. The period for "not used" may vary in libraries according to their goals.
- The collection development policies should be revised and adapted to user needs. When applied to different subjects the indicator may influence resource allocation so that subjects with a low percentage of non-use will receive more funds than others.

The non-used documents should be further examined as to language, publication date, type and subject of the document in order to identify the reasons for non-use.

134

Some libraries deliver so-called "flop-lists" to staff in charge of collection development in order to give them a feel of what did not meet the demands of the users.

Examples and further reading

The results of circulation analysis have often been disappointing for librarians who have taken great care with the collection building. Only a few examples are given her:

Institution	Year	Collection	Titles examined	% not used
4 libraries participating in the project EQLIPSE (EQLIPSE, 1995-97)	1995/6	Monographs of one acquisition year		3, 29, 30, 39
Southeast Missouri State University (Banks, 2002)	2002	Political science	531	43
Duke University Libraries (Littman and Connaway, 2004)	2002	Titles available both as print and e-book	7.880	print: 64 e-books: 60
Rowan University's Campbell Library (Brush, 2006)	2004/05	Engineering	227	77

Results in public libraries will show a much lower percentage of stock not used, due to the continuous weeding of the collection. A project in the Huntington Beach Public Library in 1984/85 showed that only 4,4% of 290.000 volumes did not circulate at least once in three years (Hayden, 1987).

The weakness of this indicator is that it does not consider in-house use of a document. In-house use can come up to a considerable amount and may be even higher than circulation. The University Library Münster, Germany, found a relation of 0,6 to 1 between in-house use and circulation (te Boekhorst, 1997, p.209).

At the moment most libraries have a routine to monitor the use and non-use of their material. Electronic resources, especially e-books, will make the monitoring process both easier and more complicated. For an electronic document every single form of usage can be recorded, on the other hand usage statistics have to be collected from different sources.

An interesting project in the Duke University Libraries, Durham, NC compared the usage of 7.880 titles that were available both in print and e-book format (Littman and Connaway, 2004). For e-books, the measure of usage was "access", including both a short browsing and a "checkout", where an e-book is in circulation to a user for a specified period. E-books received 11% more usage than comparable print books, but in either format 3.597 titles remained unused. Non-use for e-books was 60%, for print books 64%.

Banks, J. (2003), Weeding book collections in the age of the Internet, *Collection Building* 21,3, pp. 113-119

Dilevko, J. and Gottlieb, L (2003), Weed to achieve: a fundamental part of the public library mission? *Library Collections, Acquisitions & Technical Services* 27,1, pp. 73-96, available at: http://www.ugr.es/~alozano/Translations/Weeding.pdf

EQLIPSE. Evaluation and Quality in Library Performance: System for Europe (1995-1997), available at: http://www.cerlim.ac.uk/projects/eqlipse/ (The low score of 3% was reached in a special library.)

Fussler, H. and Simon, J. (1969), Patterns in the use of books in large research libraries, Chicago University Press, Chicago

Hayden, R. (1987), If it circulates, keep it, *Library Journal* 112,10, pp. 80-82

Kent, A. (1979), Use of library materials: the University of Pittsburgh study, *Books in library and information science* 26, New York, Dekker

Lancaster, F. W. (1993), If you want to evaluate your library…, 2nd ed., University of Illinois, Graduate School for Library and Information Science, Champaign, Ill.

Littman, J. and Connaway, L. S. (2004), A circulation analysis of print books and e-books in an academic library, *Library Resources & Technical Services* 48,4, pp. 256-262

Ranganathan, Shiyali Ramamrita (1931), The five laws of library science, Madras Library Association, Madras, *Madras Library Association Publication Series* 2, available at: http://dlist.sir.arizona.edu/1220/

te Boekhorst, P. (1997), Zum Verhältnis von Präsenznutzung und Ausleihe, eine Stichprobe der ULB Münster, *Bibliotheksdiens*t 31,2, pp. 208-210, available at: http://bibliotheksdienst.zlb.de/1997/1997_02_Benutzung01.pdf

B.8 Loans per capita

Background

In spite of growing electronic library collections, the loan collection is still one of the most-used library services. Borrowing books for reading and studying at home or inside the library ranks high in users' priorities. In a joint user satisfaction survey of the university libraries in North Rhine-Westphalia, Germany, nine from 10 respondents said that they visited the library for borrowing books (Follmer, Guschker and Mundt, 2002). Though in some libraries the number of loans is decreasing, due to resources, especially journals, being offered in electronic form, this is not generally the case even in academic libraries. "Overall, the number of loans per FTE student has increased by 11.5 % over the ten year period covered" (Creaser, 2006).

Therefore, the number of loans per member of the library's population to be served is still an important indicator for the acceptance of the library's services.

Definition of the indicator

The total number of loans per year by members of the population to be served divided by the number of persons in the population.

The population to be served is the number of persons to whom the library is commissioned to provide its services. For public libraries, this will normally be the population of the community (or part of the community); for academic libraries, this will normally be the total of students and academic staff in the institution.

Loans in the sense of this indicator are lending transactions of physical items to one user. This includes user-initiated renewals, on-site loans (loans within the library) and copies supplied in place of original documents.

Automatic renewals by the system without user initiation and interlibrary loans are excluded.

Aims of the indicator

The indicator assesses the use of the library's non-electronic collection by the population to be served and therewith the adequacy of the collection to the population.

The indicator is relevant for all libraries with a defined population to be served and with a loan collection.

Comparison of results between libraries with similar mission, structure and clientele is possible.

Method

The number of loans by members of the population to be served during a year is set in relation to the number of persons in the population to be served. The loan data should be available via the automated lending system.

The members of the population to be served are counted as persons, not as FTE (full time equivalent). Thus, part-time students or staff in academic institutions will be counted each as one person.

Interpretation and use of results

A high score will be seen as good.

The indicator can be affected by the library's loan periods and the number of books that users can borrow simultaneously. Cutting down loan periods will probably result in a higher number of loans and user-initiated renewals.

Other libraries nearby supplying services to the library's clientele can also influence the score.

A low score points to inadequacy of the collection for the population's interests. In order to find more details about collection use, the library could try the indicators B.6 "Collection use" or B. 7 "Percentage of stock not used". User satisfaction surveys can help to identify what users are missing in the collection. The library could also evaluate interlibrary lending or document supply requests in order to tailor its acquisitions policy to user needs.

The indicator will be less relevant in libraries where borrowing is not a main user activity. This can be the case in libraries of medicine or sciences, where electronic collections are more heavily used than the loan collection. In such cases, the indicator should be used together with indicator B.5 "Number of content units downloaded per capita".

Examples and further reading

The German benchmarking project BIX (BIX. Der Bibliotheksindex) uses for public libraries the indicator „loans per capita", which is defined as the number of all materials borrowed, including renewals, compared to the population to be served. The results in 2005 were (BIX, 2006):

Loans per capita	mean	maximum	minimum
Libraries in communities under 15.000 inhabitants	9,8	14,9	4,8
Libraries in communities from 15.000 to 30.000 inhabitants	8,7	20,0	0,9
Libraries in communities from 30.000 to 50.000 inhabitants	7,6	16,0	1,6
Libraries in communities from 50.000 to 100.000 inhabitants	6,9	12,5	2,5
Libraries in communities over 100.000 inhabitants	6,8	13,4	1,4

The number of loans per capita seems to be higher in small communities, comparable to the number of visits per capita (see the table in Indicator B.3 "Library visits per capita").

In public libraries in British Columbia, Canada, "circulation per capita" had in 2003 an average value of 12,33 (British Columbia public library statistics, 2004).

The Council of Australian State Libraries published a report with accumulated data for the states or territories, using among others the indicator "circulation per capita" (Australian public libraries comparative report, 2005). The results of 2003/04 showed a maximum of 11,2 for South Australia and a minimum of 4,8 for the Northern Territory.

The US public libraries had in 2004 a score of 7,1 loans per capita, including renewals (Public libraries in the United States, 2006).

In academic libraries, the results of the indicator will be much higher, as students and researchers rely for their work on the library collection. The statistics of UK academic libraries in 2004/05 show an average of 56 loans per full time equivalent student (Creaser, 2006, p.17).

The statistics of the Australian university libraries (CAUL online statistics) show for 2004 a mean score of 19,64 loans per student and 24,11 loans per member of the total population (students and staff).

The libraries in the Association of Research Libraries had in 2005 a mean value of 16.82 initial loans per FTE (full-time equivalent) student and 29,01 loans including renewals (ARL statistics interactive edition).

The Finnish university libraries had in 2005 a score of 63,6 loans per member of the target population (Finnish research library statistics database).

When comparing the results of this indicator, it will be important to state the individual definition of "circulation" or "loans" (possibly including renewals or interlibrary loans) and the definition of "population" or "capita".

ARL statistics interactive edition, available at: http://fisher.lib.virginia.edu/arl/index.html

Australian public libraries comparative report 1998 – 2004 (2005), presented to CASL meeting Sydney, NSW, July 2005, available at: http://www.nsla.org.au/publications/statistics/2004/pdf/NSLA.Statistics-20040701-Australian.Public.Library.Comparative.Report.1998.2004.pdf

BIX. Der Bibliotheksindex, available at: http://www.bix-bibliotheksindex.de/

BIX. Der Bibliotheksindex (2006), *B.I.T. online* Sonderheft 2006

British Columbia public library statistics (2004), Ministry of Education, Victoria, British Columbia, available at: http://www.bced.gov.bc.ca/pls/bcplstats_2004.pdf

CAUL online statistics, Council of Australian University Libraries, available at: http://www.anu.edu.au/caul/stats/

Creaser, C. (2006), SCONUL library statistics: trends 1994-95 to 2004-05, LISU, Loughborough University

Finnish research library statistics database, Helsinki University Library, available at: https://yhteistilasto.lib.helsinki.fi/language.do?action=change&choose_language=3

Follmer, R., Guschker, S. and Mundt, S. (2002), "Alles was man zum Lernen braucht...", Übergreifende Ergebnisse der Benutzerbefragung in den nordrhein-westfälischen Universitätsbibliotheken 2001", *ProLibris* 2002,1, pp. 20-25

Public libraries in the United States: fiscal year 2004 (2006), National Center for Education Statistics, available at: http://nces.ed.gov/pubs2006/2006349.pdf

B.9 Percentage of loans to external users

Background

Many libraries extend the use of their collections and services to users outside their primary clientele, called "external" or "unaffiliated" users. For a university library, this could be for instance the inhabitants of the community or students of other universities. For public libraries, this would be persons from outside their legal community.

Services to external users are offered free or with specified fees; policies differ considerably between countries and types of libraries. In many cases, the libraries offer only a certain range of services to external users. Onsite use of materials and borrowing rights are in most cases included, but may be restricted to the general collection, excluding e.g. undergraduate libraries, or to a limited number of simultaneous loans. Access to licensed electronic collections will generally be allowed only as in-house use because of licensing agreements. Temporary login may be provided for external users.

External users can come up to a high percentage of a library's users and can create considerable workload for library staff and therewith costs. Serving the needs of the general public is not often accounted for in the budgets. Therefore, external users will not always be welcome, as the services delivered to them may interfere with the main tasks of the library. One of the most-cited articles on external users is entitled "Barbarians at the gate" (Courtney, 2001).

Though external users are an important factor in many libraries, there is not much literature about this topic, and few national statistics count external users. Probably the libraries did not consider it advisable to point to this issue, as the funding institutions might deem this a possible source for income generation. "The point of view of the unaffiliated user is not often represented in the library literature; the arguments for and against opening academic libraries to the use of the public are generally made by librarians who find themselves caught between a professional instinct to provide access to all and the realities of budgets, space, and the needs of their own clientele" (Courtney, 2001, p.473).

But on the other side, a high number of external users can prove the attractiveness of the library's services and the importance of the library in the regional environment. Academic libraries often see services to external users "as means to maintain good public relations in their communities" (Courtney, 2003, p.3).

Whether the indicator described here should be used as quality measure for a library will depend on that library's mission and on the priority given to its educational and cultural role outside its institution or community.

Definition of the indicator

The percentage of loans to external users of the total loans during one year.

An external user of a library is a person who does not belong to that library's population to be served.

The population to be served is the number of persons to whom the library is commissioned to provide its services. For public libraries, this will normally be the population of the community (or part of the community); for academic libraries, this will normally be the total of students and academic staff in the institution.

Loans in the sense of this indicator are lending transactions of physical items to one user. This includes user-initiated renewals, on-site loans (loans within the library) and copies supplied in place of original documents.

Automatic renewals by the system without user initiation and interlibrary loans are excluded.

Aims of the indicator

The indicator assesses the extent to which the library's loan services are used by users outside the library's population to be served and therewith the attractiveness of the library to external users. Loans are taken exemplarily for the services delivered to external users as in most libraries borrowing represents the main activity of external users.

The indicator can also be used to determine the workload connected with services to users outside the population.

The indicator is relevant for all libraries with a defined population to be served that offer borrowing rights to external users. It will be especially interesting for libraries with cooperation policies in a region.

Comparison of results between libraries is possible, if the mission and policies of the library in regard to external users are taken into consideration.

Method

Count the number of total loans and the number of loans to external users during one year. The data should be accessible via the library's circulation system. Then calculate the percentage of all loans that are delivered to external users.

Interpretation and use of results

Whether a higher score would be considered as good will depend on the library's mission and goals and its institution's or community's conception of the library's role outside the institution and in the region.

A higher score could be reached by promoting library services outside the institution or community and by offering usage privileges to external users.

The results of the indicator can be used for promoting the library's importance and role. They could also be used for requesting support for services to external users from the institutions or communities the external users belong to.

Examples and further reading

The indicator is used in the Norwegian set of performance indicators (Forslag til indikatorer, 2007, p.17). It includes loans + interlibrary loans to external users.

The German national library statistics count the number of external users that are active users (persons who have borrowed at least one item during the reporting year). The statistics of 2006 for academic libraries show a total of 2.633.128 active users, of those 782.386 external users = 29,7 % (DBS, 2006).

The percentage of loans to external users of all loans must not necessarily be the same as the percentage of external users of all users. External users' utilization of a library service may be disproportionately higher or lower than the absolute number of external users would suggest. For example, surveys showed that the reference service in university libraries was used more frequently by an external user than by a user out of the library's population (Verhoeven, Cooksey and Hand, 1996). In Münster University and Regional Library, Germany, data over years showed that external users borrowed fewer items than the members of the university.

A survey of academic libraries in the US asked for the privileges accorded to external users and for different privileges accorded to certain groups (Courtney, 2003). 88,9 % of the responding libraries allowed unrestricted access to the building to all external users, but borrowing privileges varied considerably between user groups. Groups with higher borrowing privileges were alumni, fac-

143

ulty and students of consortia institutions, and persons in the local or regional area. Libraries of publicly funded institutions were more liable to grant unrestricted borrowing to all external users than libraries of private institutions.

Courtney, N. (2001), Barbarians at the gates: a half-century of unaffiliated users in academic libraries, *The Journal of Academic Librarianship* 27,6, pp. 473-480

Courtney, N. (2003), Unaffiliated users' access to academic libraries: a survey, *The Journal of Academic Librarianship* 29,1, pp. 3-7

DBS – Deutsche Bibliotheksstatistik (2006), Hochschulbibliothekszentrum, Köln, available at: http://www.hbz-nrw.de/angebote/dbs/

Forslag til indikatorer for fag- og folkebibliotek (2007), ABM-utvikling, Oslo, available at: http://www.abm-utvikling.no/bibliotek/statistikk-for-bibliotek/indikatorer-for-fag-og-folkebibliotek

Verhoeven, S., Cooksey, E. and Hand, C. (1996), The disproportionate use of reference desk service by external users at an urban university library, *RQ* 35,3, pp. 392-397

B.10 Attendances at training lessons per capita

Background

Most libraries have always offered training in the use of their services, either as guided library tours or as general introductory lessons about the library services or a specified service.

Today, information resources and ways of information seeking have changed dramatically. "Information overload" has become a main problem in research, and academic teachers are complaining about the "Google mentality" of students who do not proceed beyond a quick search on the web. The difficulty today is how to find and select relevant information.

Libraries have taken up the new task of teaching information literacy, as well in public as in academic libraries. In universities, libraries often join with faculties in offering training courses within the curriculum, whether as face-to-face training or as online training modules. There is abundant literature about libraries and information literacy teaching. An international overview is given by Lau (2007).

Developing and offering training courses will involve considerable effort and input of resources. Therefore, libraries should be able to show at least basic data about input and output of their training activities. But judging from national library statistics it seems that libraries are only recently starting to collect data about the number, duration, and costs of training lessons and the number of attendants. If possible, libraries should also try to assess the effect and impact of user training activities by satisfaction surveys or interviews and by tests of the attendants' skills and competences before and after training.

The indicator described here concentrates on the acceptance of library training by the population. It was chosen because of its practicality and its suitability for benchmarking purposes.

Definition of the indicator

The number of attendances at formal user training lessons per 1.000 members of the population to be served during one year.

User training is defined as a programme with a specified lesson plan, which aims at specific learning outcomes for the use of library and other information services. This definition includes guided tours of the library. Online tutorials offered as web-based services and personal one to one instructions (point-of-use training) are excluded. The duration of lessons is irrelevant.

The population to be served is the number of persons to whom the library is commissioned to provide its services. For public libraries, this will normally be the population of the community (or part of the community); for academic libraries, this will normally be the total of students and academic staff in the institution.

Aims of the indicator

The indicator assesses the library's success in reaching its population by user training services.

The indicator is relevant for all libraries with a defined population to be served and with user training services. It will probably be more interesting for academic than for public libraries.

Comparison of results between libraries with similar mission, structure and clientele is possible.

The indicator does not measure the quality or the impact of the training.

Method

Count the number of attendants at each training lesson, including guided tours. If training lessons are not aiming at the library's population, but at external user groups, the attendants of these lessons should be excluded. The numbers are accumulated at the end of the year.

The number of attendances is set in relation to the number of persons in the population to be served, divided by 1.000.

As a subset, the number of attendances at training lessons on electronic services and information technology could be counted.

In order to get a more detailed view of training lessons attendance, the population to be served could be split into groups. For a university library this could be:

- Undergraduate students
- Graduate students
- Academic staff
- Students and academic staff of a faculty (e.g. medicine)

For a public library, this could be:

- Children (up to and including age 14)
- Adults

- Adults over 65 years

Interpretation and use of results

A high score will be generally seen as good.

The indicator will be affected by the number of training lessons offered and by the quality of the training. Libraries should therefore also count the number of lessons. The quality of the lessons should be monitored by satisfaction questionnaires and/or by tests that assess the learning outcome.

The indicator will also depend on the library's mission and clientele. In academic libraries, teaching information literacy is now more or less acknowledged by the parent institutions as a library task, and students are more apt to recognize the need of training in this sector than users of public libraries.

In case of low attendance at training lessons, the library could

- promote its user training services via its website or other media,
- tailor the services to special target groups in the population,
- try to improve the quality of training,
- offer information literacy training within the curriculum in collaboration with faculties.

Examples and further reading

The statistics of the Australian university libraries (CAUL online statistics) show for 2005 a mean score of 0,34 training attendances per member of the total institutional population (students, academic and non-academic staff) and 0,49 attendances per student. The number of training lessons show a mean value of 0,0244 per member of the population and 0,0349 per student.

The Swedish research libraries statistics show in 2005 a total number of 115.546 attendants at training lessons and 325.800 members of the population (students and academic staff), which would be 0,35 attendances per member of the population (Forskningsbiblioteken, 2005). The results are similar to CAUL.

The Netherlands university libraries counted 47.443 attendances at training lessons per 226.669 members of the population, which would come out 0,21 attendances per member (UKB, 2004).

The Finnish university libraries had in 2005 a total of 177.756 students and 47.371 participants in user training = 0,27 attendances per student (Finnish research libraries statistics database).

The Canadian Association of Research Libraries compared attendances in group presentations with the number of students, counted as FTE (full-time equivalent). In 2003/04, participation in group presentations in university libraries ranged from the equivalent of 14 % to 99 % of the students, with a median of 50 % equivalent participation (Hoffmann, 2005).

The German benchmarking project (BIX. Der Bibliotheksindex) uses the indicator "User training hours per 1.000 members of the population" for academic libraries. The hours of duration are counted for each training session and added up. The results in 2005 were (BIX, 2006):

User training hours per 1.000 members of the population	mean	maximum	minimum
Universities of applied sciences	23,5	84,1	2,9
Universities: One-tier systems	32,0	159,8	5,1
Universities: Two-tier systems (only the central library considered)	17,6	64,0	4,5

No examples were found for public libraries, probably because many public libraries include the count of training sessions in the count of "library events" (see Indicator B.12 "Attendances at events per capita").

BIX. Der Bibliotheksindex, available at: http://www.bix-bibliotheksindex.de/

BIX. Der Bibliotheksindex (2006), *B.I.T. online* Sonderheft 2006

CAUL online statistics, Council of Australian University Libraries, available at: http://www.anu.edu.au/caul/stats/

Finnish research library statistics database, Helsinki University Library, available at: https://yhteistilasto.lib.helsinki.fi/language.do?action=change&choose_language=3

Forskningsbiblioteken 2005 (2005), KB/Bibsam och SCB, Sveriges officiella statistik, available at: http://www.scb.se/statistik/_publikationer/KU0102_2005A01_BR_KUFT0601.pdf

Hoffmann, E. (2005), CARL statistics 2003 – 2004, trends and observations, Canadian Association of Research Libraries, available at: http://www.carl-abrc.ca/projects/statistics/statistics-e.html

Lau, J. et al. (2007), Information literacy, an international state-of-the-art report, second draft, available at: http://www.infolitglobal.info/

UKB (2004), Benchmarking, Samenwerkingsverband van de Nederlandse universiteitsbibliotheken en de Koninklijke Bibliotheek, results only available to participants

B.11 Reference questions per capita

Background

Offering help in information seeking and library use by answering reference questions has always been an important library service as well in public as in academic libraries. This is still more the case in times of electronic information sources and the Internet.

Reference service has traditionally been offered as face-to-face reference, users coming to the help-desk with point-of-use questions. Today it is complemented by e-mail or online (chat) reference and cooperative online reference.

In some countries, reference questions per year seem to decrease. The statistics of the Association of Research Libraries show a decrease by 48% in reference questions from 1991 to 2005 (Kyrillidou, and Young, 2006, p.9). This may be due to users relying most on the Internet, especially for factual or subject questions. But the number of reference transactions is still high overall, and the workload may even be higher than before, as users confronted with multiple information resources may need more differentiated assistance than before.

Statistics of reference questions are not yet common in national library statistics, but the number of such statistics is growing, and probably there are more data available in individual libraries. "Reference statistics constitute a poorly developed area of library statistics. ... The only recognized indicator that has been established so far is he number of reference questions per inhabitant per year" (Høivik, 2003, p.30/31).

Definition of the indicator

The total number of reference questions per year by members of the population to be served divided by the number of persons in the population.

Reference questions can regard facts, documents, or advice on sources for the user's subject.

The definition excludes directional and administrative inquiries, e.g. for locating staff or facilities, regarding opening times, about handling equipment such as reader printers or computer terminals, using self-service functions, or locating items of stock that have already been identified bibliographically.

The population to be served is the number of persons to whom the library is commissioned to provide its services. For public libraries, this will normally be the population of the community (or part of the community); for academic libraries, this will normally be the total of students and academic staff in the institution.

Aims of the indicator

The indicator assesses the use of the library's reference service by the population to be served and therewith the importance of the service to the population. It can also be used to assess the workload for the reference service per member of the population. The indicator does not measure the quality of the reference service.

The indicator is relevant for all libraries with a defined population to be served and with a reference service.

Comparison of results between libraries with similar mission, structure and clientele is possible.

Method

For a sample period, count all incoming reference questions, whether face-to-face at the reference desk, by mail, e-mail or online (chat) reference, that come from the population to be served.

The members of the population to be served are counted as persons, not as FTE (full time equivalent). Thus, part-time students or staff in academic institutions will be counted each as one person.

The number of reference questions is set in relation to the number of persons in the population to be served.

As single counts can be misleading, sample counts should be conducted at random intervals over the year, including peak times and times of lower use, e.g. inside and outside term. By cumulating the results, the mean reference questions per capita over the year can be calculated.

In order to get a more detailed view of the use of reference service, the population to be served could be split into groups. For a university library this could be:

- Undergraduate students
- Graduate students
- Academic staff
- Students and academic staff of a faculty (e.g. medicine)

For a public library, this could be:

- Children (up to and including age 14)

- Adults
- Adults over 65 years

If reference questions submitted in electronic form are counted separately, the results can also be used for calculating the percentage of reference questions in electronic format in order to show to what extent users are switching to electronic media for asking questions.

Interpretation and use of results

A high score will be generally seen as good.

The indicator will be affected by the quality of the reference service. Quick and correct answers, friendly and helpful staff will induce users to repeatedly using the service. Waiting times, unsatisfying answers, or an unfriendly atmosphere will reduce the number of questions.

The indicator will also be influenced by the structure and contents of the library's website. If the website offers effective guidance and explanations for the library's services, there may be less need for questions pertaining to how to use the services.

The indicator will also be affected by socio-economic factors, e.g. the level of information literacy in the population.

If the score seems too low, the library should assess user satisfaction with the reference service. Waiting times should be considered, and staffing might be increased in peak times.

The quality of reference answers could be evaluated by using the indicator C.12 "Reference fill rate".

Examples and further reading

In UK public libraries, the 10-years statistics show a slight decrease in "enquiries per capita" (Creaser, Maynard and White, 2005):
- 1993/94 = 1,05 enquiries per capita
- 2003/04 = 0,98 enquiries per capita

In public libraries in British Columbia, Canada, "reference transactions per capita" had an average of 1,04 in 2003 (British Columbia public library statistics, 2004). This corresponds to the British data.

The Australian public library statistics report for 2003/04 a number of 525 "information enquiries per 1.000 persons" = 0,52 enquiries per capita, but add that the data have not been uniformly reported across all States and Territories, and that the reported annual figure can vary markedly according to the States and Territories that supply the data.

In Norwegian public libraries there was a rate of 0,8 enquiries per capita in 2000 (Høivik, 2003, p.31).

In academic libraries, the results of the indicator will be much higher, as students and researchers working in the library will have many point-of-use questions.

For UK academic libraries the statistics of 2004/05 show an average of 7,1 "enquiries per FTE student" (Creaser, 2006, p.20). Directional questions are included. Statistics of the last years show a slight decrease in questions.

The statistics of the Australian university libraries (CAUL online statistics) show for 2005 a mean score of 3,52 reference transactions per person in the population to be served and 5,09 per student. Simple directional questions are excluded.

When comparing results of this indicator, it will be important to state what kind of reference questions have been included in the count.

Australian public libraries statistical report 2003 – 2004 (2006), Public Library Services, State Library of Queensland, available at:
http://www.nsla.org.au/publications/statistics/2004/pdf/NSLA.Statistics-20040701-Australian.Public.Library.Comparative.Report.1998.2004.pdf

British Columbia public library statistics (2004), Ministry of Education, Victoria, British Columbia, available at: http://www.bced.gov.bc.ca/pls/bcplstats_2004.pdf

CAUL online statistics, Council of Australian University Libraries, available at:
http://www.anu.edu.au/caul/stats/

Creaser, C. (2006), SCONUL library statistics: trends 1994-95 to 2004-05, LISU, Loughborough University

Creaser, C., Maynard, S. and White, S. (2005), LISU annual library statistics 2005, featuring trend analysis of UK public and academic libraries 1994 – 2004, LISU, Loughborough University, available at:
http://www.lboro.ac.uk/departments/dils/lisu/downloads/als05.pdf

Høivik, T. (2003), Why do you ask? Reference statistics for library planning, *Performance Measurement and Metrics* 4,1, pp. 28-37

Kyrillidou, M. and Young, M. (2006), ARL statistics 2004-05, Association of Research Libraries, available at: http://www.arl.org/bm~doc/arlstat05.pdf

B.12 Attendances at events per capita

Background

Libraries, beside their regular services, offer various kinds of "events" to their population and the general public. Such events can have a cultural or literary intent, e.g. promoting the cultural heritage by exhibitions, author visits and literary discussions, or an educational intent, e.g. organizing reading groups or storytelling sessions. In most cases, such events are offered free of charge to all interested persons.

Events are more popular and various in public libraries. In academic libraries, events are often restricted to exhibitions, lectures and workshops.

Organizing library events will involve considerable effort and input of resources, especially staff resources. The funding institutions might not always be convinced of the importance of library events. Therefore, libraries should be able to show at least basic data about input and output of such activities. But judging from national library statistics it seems that libraries are only recently starting to collect data about the number of events offered and the number of attendants.

It would of course be most interesting to the funding institutions if the libraries could show the impact of events on the attendants, e.g. a better understanding of the local cultural heritage, or a higher knowledge of literature. Libraries could try to assess the effect and impact of their events by satisfaction surveys or interviews of attendants.

But such methods would be time-consuming, and the results would only yield an "anecdotal evidence" of an event's impact. Therefore the indicator described here uses the number of attendances at library events as a measure for assessing the attractiveness of the events to the population. It was chosen because of its practicality and its suitability for benchmarking purposes.

Definition of the indicator

The number of attendances at library events per 1.000 members of the population to be served during one year.

Library events in the sense of this indicator include events organized by the library with literary, cultural or educational intent, e.g. author visits, reading groups, literary discussions, workshops, etc.

Events inside the library premises organized by institutions outside the library and user training sessions are excluded. The definition also excludes exhibitions, as they are often accessible inside the library premises and entrance counts are not possible.

The population to be served is the number of persons to whom the library is commissioned to provide its services. For public libraries, this will normally be the population of the community (or part of the community); for academic libraries, this will normally be the total of students and academic staff in the institution.

Aims of the indicator

The indicator assesses the library's success in attracting its population by library events. It may also be used for demonstrating the library's cultural role in the community or institution.

The indicator is relevant for all libraries with a defined population to be served that organize events. It will be of special interest for public libraries.

Comparison of results between libraries with similar mission, structure and clientele is possible.

Method

Count the number of attendants at each event. The numbers are accumulated at the end of the year.

The total number of attendances is set in relation to the population to be served, divided by 1.000.

If events aim at a specified target group inside the population, e.g. children, only attendances by that target group should be counted (if possible) and set in relation to the number of members in that target group, divided by 1.000.

Attendants not belonging to the population to be served will probably be included in the counts, as it will not be possible to count them separately.

Interpretation and use of results

A high score will be generally seen as good. It shows that the events the library organized were suited to the interests of its population.

The indicator will be affected by the number of events offered and by the attractiveness of the events to a broad population. Specialized events, though possibly with high impact on attendants, may attract fewer visits than popular topics. The indicator will also be influenced by socio-demographic variables in the population, e.g. the level of education, by the distance of the library to parts of the population, and by the timing and opening times of events.

In addition to the results of this indicator, the quality of the events could also be monitored by satisfaction questionnaires.

In case of low attendance at events, the library could try to

- intensify the promotion of events via the media,
- assess the attendants' satisfaction with events by exit questionnaires or interviews,
- tailor events to special target groups in the population.

Libraries might also ask their population for preferences of events, e.g. by an online survey. They could ask for the kind of events and activities in libraries that people would like to attend, e.g. author talks, history themed events, workshops for writers, or events for children.

In order to get more insight into the attractiveness of special events, the attendances to each event could be calculated separately.

Examples and further reading

The statistics of public libraries in British Columbia, Canada, count the number of program attendances and the members of the population in the service area (Ministry of education, British Columbia). The average data are:

- 2003 = 0,19 attendances per member of the population

For public libraries in Ontario, Canada, the average data for the same statistics are (Ministry of culture, Ontario):

- 2003 = 0,21 attendances per member of the population
- 2004 = 0,22 attendances per member of the population

No example was found for this indicator in the statistics of academic libraries. But several national statistics count the number of exhibitions and/or other events for academic libraries. The German and Finnish statistics count exhibitions and other events (DBS. Deutsche Bibliotheksstatistik; Finnish research library statistics database).

DBS. Deutsche Bibliotheksstatistik,, available at: http://www.hbz-nrw.de/angebote/dbs/

Finnish research library statistics database, Helsinki University Library, available at: https://yhteistilasto.lib.helsinki.fi/language.do?action=change&choose_language=3

Ministry of culture, Ontario (2004), Ontario public library statistics, available at: http://www.culture.gov.on.ca/english/culdiv/library/statistics2004/2004stats.htm

British Columbia public library statistics (2004), Ministry of education, British Columbia,, available at: http://www.bced.gov.bc.ca/pls/bcplstats_2004.pdf

C. Efficiency

C.1 Cost per user

Background

Libraries today are confronted with a general demand for transparency as to costs and quality. Funding institutions as well as the general public want to see how resources are spent and what values are achieved. In addition, libraries are experiencing growing problems when organising their work and offering their services within their given budget and resources. Therefore, measures of cost-effectiveness are becoming important in library evaluation.

For measuring cost-effectiveness, a library's expenditure can be set in relation to its output, e.g. loans or library visits. It can also be compared with the number of registered or active users in order to assess the totals costs per user.

When calculating the cost per user, the total operating expenditure is set in relation to the number of active users in the library's population, users that have made use of library services during the reporting year. Active users are preferred to the number of registered users. The statistics of "registered users" may be misleading, if users are registered automatically when enrolling in the institution, or if the library does not "weed" its user data regularly. Another advantage for comparing with active users is that the library can actively influence the number of active users by attractive and effective services.

Definition of the indicator

The total operating or recurrent expenditure of the library during the reporting year divided by the number of active users in the population to be served.

The total operating expenditure includes expenditure for

- acquisitions (including binding, licenses, and pay-per-view costs),
- staff (including project staff, student assistants, etc.),
- operations and maintenance of computers and network, software licenses and telecommunication,
- repair or replacement of existing equipment,
- other items like cataloguing records, copying, postage, promotion of services, insurance, transport, consulting, etc.

Utility costs (heating, electricity, water, sewage, cleaning, security) and calculatory depreciations of assets (buildings, IT- and other equipment) are excluded.

Capital expenditure (expenditure on building sites, new buildings and extensions, furnishings and equipment for new and expanded buildings, new computer systems) is also excluded.

The population to be served is the number of persons to whom the library is commissioned to provide its services. For public libraries, this will normally be the population of the community (or part of the community); for academic libraries, this will normally be the total of students and academic staff in the institution.

An active user is defined as a registered user who has visited or made use of library facilities or services during the year. This may include the use of electronic library services within or outside the library. For libraries in which loans are the principal activity, the number of active borrowers (users who have borrowed at least one item during the year) could be used as an estimate of the number of active users.

Aims of the indicator

The indicator assesses the library costs per active user in the population and therewith the cost-efficiency of library services.

The indicator is relevant for all libraries with a defined population to be served.

Comparison of results between libraries with similar mission, structure and clientele is possible, if the operating expenditure is calculated in the same way.

Methods

1. A random sample of the population to be served is asked by survey whether they have visited the library, borrowed a book, or made use of library services in any form during the last year. Surveys can be sent by mail or e-mail, or an online survey can be made available on the library's website.

   Questions could be:

   - Have you visited the library during the last year?

   - Have you borrowed a book or other material during the last year?

   - Have you visited the library's website during the last year?

   - Have you used the library's electronic services from outside the library during the last year?

Calculate the percentage of respondents answering "yes" at least once of total respondents in the sample. Then calculate the number of total active library users by applying the same percentage to the population to be served.

Assess the total operating expenditure of the library during the reporting year.

The "cost per user" is then calculated by dividing the total operating expenditure by the number of active users in the population.

2. As an estimate for the cost per user, the number of active borrowers in the population could be used.

   Active borrowers are registered users who have borrowed at least one item during the last year. The data should be available via the records of the library's loan system.

   The "cost per user" is calculated by dividing the total operating expenditure by the number of active borrowers of the population to be served. As members of the population may have visited the library or used electronic library services without borrowing, the "cost per user" calculated by this method can be higher than in reality.

3. If the library's authentication procedures for the use of its electronic services make it possible to identify what users out of its population have used the library's services, these data can be compared with those of active borrowers.

   The "cost per user" is then calculated by dividing the total operating expenditure by the number of persons in the population to be served that have either borrowed at least one item and/or have accessed electronic library services during the last year.

Most libraries will probably prefer method 2 as the easiest method. But using the number of "active borrowers" may result in higher cost per user than in reality, if borrowing is not a main user activity. This can be the case in libraries of medicine or sciences, where electronic collections are more heavily used than the loan collection. In such cases, methods 1 or 3 should be preferred.

Interpretation and use of results

Low cost per user would generally be considered as showing high cost-effectiveness of the library. But a higher score may be justified by special tasks of the library and special needs of the clientele. For libraries in institutions of higher education that have to offer specialized and labour-intensive services to their users the cost per user will be higher than in public libraries. Therefore, this indicator should not be used by itself, but together with indicators of service quality.

The indicator will be useful for evaluating the cost-effectiveness of a library in different periods or compared with other libraries of a similar type. It can be used for justifying the library's expenditure and for budget appliances.

The indicator can be influenced by several issues:

- Other libraries nearby supplying services to the library's clientele
- Special library services like rare or specialized collections, electronic publishing, or special teaching modules
- Specialized needs of the population to be served
- A high percentage of external active users (not belonging to the population) that may increase the costs
- Fees for library use

If the cost per user seems too high compared with other libraries of similar mission and population, the library might try to reduce costs, e.g. by streamlining processes, cutting down less-used services, or replacing professional staff in certain services by non-professionals.

As this will not often be possible without lower service quality, it may be more effective to attract a higher number of active users in order to reduce the cost per user. This might be done by

- introducing new attractive services,
- promoting services via the library website or public media,
- tailoring the services to special target groups in the population.

Examples and further reading

Not many library statistics compare the library's expenditure to active users. The indicator as described here was introduced in a German project using the Balanced Scorecard for academic libraries (Ceynowa and Coners, 2002, pp.73-76).

The German benchmarking project BIX (BIX. Der Bibliotheksindex) uses the indicator "library expenditure per user" for academic libraries, calculated by the operating expenditure as described above and the number of active borrowers in the population (BIX, 2006). The results in 2005 were:

Library expenditure per user	mean	maximum	minimum
Universities of applied sciences	179,38 €	279,64 €	95,27 €

Universities: One-tier systems	526,01 €	1224,34 €	217,98 €
Universities: Two-tier systems (only the central library considered)	426,78 €	798,13 €	206,55 €

The cost per user was lower in the universities of applied sciences, probably because they offer fewer specialized services.

The Finnish research library statistics allow comparing the total operating expenditure to active borrowers (Finnish research library statistics database). In 2005, the expenditure of all research libraries was 135.039.700 €. Divided by 397.811 active borrowers this is 339,46 € per active borrower. For university libraries only, total operating expenditure = 96.671.900 € divided by 207.440 active borrowers came up to 466,02 € per active borrower.

Other statistics compare the library expenditure to the number of persons in the population to be served.

The statistics of the UK academic libraries compare expenditure to students. The statistics of 2004/05 show an average of 307 £ per full time equivalent student (Creaser, 2006, p.23). Since 1994/95, expenditure per student increased by 24,3 %.

The statistics of SCONUL, Society of College, National and University Libraries, UK count the total expenditure per full-time equivalent user, meaning potential users (students and academic staff). For 2004/05 the mean value was 243 £ (SCONUL, 2006).

The statistics of the Australian university libraries (CAUL online statistics) show for 2005 a mean expenditure of 399 AUD per member of the population which would be about 233 €. Expenditure excludes capital expenditure

The cost per member of the population will be lower in public libraries. In UK public libraries, the 10-years statistics show a continuous increase of expenditure per capita, expenditure including capital expenditure (Creaser, Maynard and White, 2005):
- 1993/94 = 12,85 £
- 2003/04 = 17,64 £

The US public library statistics for 2004 count 32,21 $ of operating expenditure per capita = population of the legal service area (Public libraries in the United States, 2006).

The Finnish public library statistics show an operating expenditure of 47,69 € per inhabitant in 2005 and 48,71 € in 2006 (Finnish public library statistics).

The examples show that for comparing results it is extremely important to know whether active users, registered users, or members of the population are compared to expenditure, and what is included in the calculation of expenditure.

BIX. Der Bibliotheksindex Available at: http://www.bix-bibliotheksindex.de/

BIX. Der Bibliotheksindex (2006), *B.I.T. online* Sonderheft 2006

CAUL online statistics, Council of Australian University Libraries, available at: http://www.anu.edu.au/caul/stats/

Ceynowa, K. and Coners, A. (2002), Balanced Scorecard für wissenschaftliche Bibliotheken, *Zeitschrift für Bibliohekswesen und Bibliographie, Sonderheft 82,* Klostermann, Frankfurt a.M.

Creaser, C. (2006), SCONUL library statistics: trends 1994-95 to 2004-05, LISU, Loughborough University

Creaser, C., Maynard, S. and White, S. (2005), LISU annual library statistics 2005, featuring trend analysis of UK public and academic libraries 1994 – 2004, LISU, Loughborough University, available at: http://www.lboro.ac.uk/departments/dils/lisu/downloads/als05.pdf

Finnish public library statistics, Culture and Media Division of the Ministry of Education, available at: http://tilastot.kirjastot.fi/Default.aspx?&langId=en

Finnish research library statistics database, Helsinki University Library, available at: https://yhteistilasto.lib.helsinki.fi/language.do?action=change&choose_language=3

Public libraries in the United States: fiscal year 2004 (2006), National Center for Education Statistics, available at: http://nces.ed.gov/pubs2006/2006349.pdf

SCONUL annual library statistics 2004-2005 (2006), SCONUL, Society of College, National & University Libraries, London

C.2 Cost per visit

Background

Libraries today are confronted with a general demand for transparency as to costs and quality. Funding institutions as well as the general public want to see how resources are spent and what values are achieved. In addition, libraries are experiencing growing problems when organising their work and offering their services within their given budget and resources. Therefore, measures of cost-effectiveness are becoming important in library evaluation.

For measuring cost-effectiveness, a library's expenditure can be set in relation to its output.

While indicator C.1 compares expenditure to users, this indicator sets the library's expenditure in relation to library visits.

Traditionally, libraries offer the use of their collections and services via a user's visit to the library as physical place. With the development of electronic collections and services libraries have started to offer a new virtual "entrance" to their services: the library website. Users can "visit" the library and use many of its services from remote places, e.g. from their workplace or from home. Such visits, in analogy to the traditional physical visits, are called "virtual visits".

Both forms of "visits" together can be seen as a measure for the use of library services and therewith as a cost driver for the library's expenditure. During a physical visit, visitors make use of the library's building, equipment, collection, or loan and help services. During a virtual visit, they use the electronic collections and services of the library. Therefore, this indicator calculates the total number of physical + virtual visits in order to assess the cost of a user's "entering the library".

Definition of the indicator

The total operating or recurrent expenditure of the library during the reporting year divided by the number of physical + virtual library visits.

The total operating expenditure in the sense of this indicator includes expenditure for

- acquisitions (including binding, licenses, and pay-per-view costs),
- staff (including project staff, student assistants, etc.),

164

- operations and maintenance of computers and network, software licenses and telecommunication,
- repair or replacement of existing equipment,
- other items like cataloguing records, copying, postage, promotion of services, insurance, transport, consulting, etc.

Utility costs (heating, electricity, water, sewage, cleaning, security) and calculatory depreciations of assets (buildings, IT- and other equipment) are excluded.

Capital expenditure (expenditure on building sites, new buildings and extensions, furnishings and equipment for new and expanded buildings, new computer systems) is also excluded.

A physical visit is defined as the act of a person's entering the library premises. Visits are counted independently of the purpose of the visit (borrowing, working in the library, or taking part in events and guided tours).

A virtual visit is defined as a user's request on the library's website from outside the library premises in order to use one of the services provided by the library.

For this indicator, both physical and virtual visits include visits made by external users (users not belonging to the population to be served), as it would be difficult to identify such visits.

Aims of the indicator

The indicator assesses the library costs per library visit and therewith the cost-efficiency of library services.

The indicator is relevant for all libraries with both traditional and web-based services.

Comparison between libraries of similar mission, structure and clientele is possible, if special conditions (e.g. a new building) are considered and if the operating expenditure is calculated in the same way.

The indicator does not consider users' activities during physical or virtual visits.

Method

Calculate the total operating expenditure of the library during the reporting year.

Count the number of physical and virtual visits during the same time. For the methods of counting, compare Indicator B.3 "Library visits per capita".

For calculating the cost per visit the total operating expenditure is divided by the number of physical + virtual visits.

Interpretation and use of results

Low cost per visit would generally be considered as showing high cost-effectiveness of the library. But a higher score may be justified by the special tasks of the library and special needs of its clientele. For libraries in institutions of higher education that have to offer specialized and labour-intensive services to their users the cost per visit will be higher than in public libraries. Therefore, this indicator should not be used by itself, but together with indicators of service quality.

The indicator will be useful for evaluating the cost-effectiveness of a library in different periods or compared with other libraries of a similar type. It can be used for justifying the library's expenditure and for budget appliances.

The indicator can be influenced by several issues:

- Other libraries nearby supplying services to the library's clientele
- Special library services like rare or specialized collections, electronic publishing, or special teaching modules
- Specialized needs of the population to be served
- A high percentage of external users (not belonging to the population) that may increase the costs

If the cost per visit seems too high compared with other libraries of similar mission and population, the library might try to reduce costs, e.g. by streamlining processes, cutting down less-used services, or replacing professional staff in certain services by non-professionals.

As this will not often be possible without lower service quality, it may be more effective to attract a higher number of visits, e.g. by

- introducing new attractive services,
- offering more space or seats for user (see Indicators A.1 "User area per capita" and A.2 "Seats per capita"),
- offering longer opening hours,
- promoting services via the library website or public media,
- tailoring the services to special target groups in the population,
- improving the usability of the library website.

Satisfaction surveys including non-users can help to identify issues that detain members of the population from visiting the library.

Examples and further reading

As yet, there is no example of practical appliance of the indicator as described here. Libraries using cost measures have compared their expenditure only to the number of physical visits.

The German benchmarking project BIX (BIX. Der Bibliotheksindex) uses the indicator "library expenditure per visit" for public libraries, calculated by the operating expenditure + capital expenditure and the number of physical visits (BIX, 2006). The results in 2005 were:

Total expenditure per visit	mean	maxi- mum	mini- mum
Libraries in communities under 15.000 inhabitants	3,87 €	8,30 €	1,58 €
Libraries in communities from 15.000 to 30.000 inhabitants	4,90 €	35,34 €	2,45 €
Libraries in communities from 30.000 to 50.000 inhabitants	4,08 €	6,19 €	2,41 €
Libraries in communities from 50.000 to 100.000 inhabitants	5,06 €	7,86 €	3,07 €
Libraries in communities over 100.000 inhabitants	5,38 €	11,82 €	2,36 €

The cost per visit seems to be higher in libraries of large communities, possibly due to more specialized services.

The Finnish public library statistics show an operating expenditure of 3,89 € per library visit in 2005 and 4,28 € in 2006 (Finnish Public Library Statistics).

The Swiss public libraries had in 2005 a total expenditure of 110.746.930 CHF and 5.762.836 visits, that is 19,22 CHF or 13,09 € per visit (Schweizerische Bibliothekenstatistik, 2005). The higher score is explained by expenditure including calculatory costs.

The cost per visit is generally somewhat higher in academic libraries because of the specialized services offered and the special activities of users in the library.

The Finnish research library statistics allow comparing the total operating expenditure to physical visits (Finnish research library statistics database). In 2005, the expenditure of all research libraries was 135.039.700 €. Divided by 16.284.641 visits, this is 8,29 € per visit. For university libraries only, the total operating expenditure = 96.671.900 € divided by 9.675.617 visits came up to 9,99 € per visit.

The statistics of the Australian university libraries (CAUL online statistics) show for 2005 a mean expenditure per visit of 10,82 AUD which would be about 6,30 €. Expenditure excludes capital expenditure; visits are measured by turnstile count.

The Swiss university libraries had in 2005 a total expenditure of 180.095.610 CHF and 5.088.574 visits, that is 35,39 CHF or 24,10 € per visit (Schweizerische Bibliothekenstatistik, 2005). Expenditure here includes calculatory costs.

The examples show that for comparing results it is extremely important to know how the expenditure was calculated and what is included in the calculation.

BIX. Der Bibliotheksindex, available at: http://www.bix-bibliotheksindex.de/

BIX. Der Bibliotheksindex (2006), *B.I.T. online* Sonderheft 2006

CAUL online statistics, Council of Australian University Libraries, available at: http://www.anu.edu.au/caul/stats/

Finnish public library statistics, Culture and Media Division of the Ministry of Education, available at: http://tilastot.kirjastot.fi/Default.aspx?&langId=en

Finnish research library statistics database, Helsinki University Library, available at: https://yhteistilasto.lib.helsinki.fi/language.do?action=change&choose_language=3

Schweizerische Bibliothekenstatistik (2005), Bundesamt für Statistik, available at: http://www.bfs.admin.ch/bfs/portal/de/index/themen/kultur__medien__zeitverwendung/kultur/blank/analysen__berichte/bibliotheken.html

C.3 Cost per use

Background

Libraries today are confronted with a general demand for transparency as to costs and quality. Funding institutions as well as the general public want to see how resources are spent and what values are achieved. In addition, libraries are experiencing growing problems when organizing their work and offering their services within their given budget and resources. Therefore, measures of cost-effectiveness are becoming important in library evaluation.

For measuring cost-effectiveness, a library's expenditure can be set in relation to its output.

While indicators C.1 and C.2 compare expenditure to users and library visits, this indicator sets the library's expenditure in relation to all forms of collection use.

The traditional measure for collection use is the number of loans. But this measure ignores the extent of non-lending (in-house) use of library materials and thus underrates the usage of the physical collection. The amount of in-house usage should therefore be counted additionally.

Since libraries offer electronic resources beside their physical collection, the use of the electronic collection should also be considered when comparing collection use to the library costs. Electronic usage could be counted as

- sessions (requests of electronic material),
- or downloads (successful requests of a content unit or descriptive record out of the electronic collection).

A session on a database shows the user's interest in a topic, while the download of a content unit or descriptive record out of the database would show that users have found items they deem relevant. The relation of downloads to sessions is somewhat similar to that of loans to browsing. Downloads are therefore preferred as measures for the electronic use of the collection.

The indicator described here tries to count all forms of collection use and sets them in relation to the library's expenditure.

Definition of the indicator

The total operating or recurrent expenditure of the library during the reporting year divided by the number of loans + in-house uses + downloads from the electronic collection.

The total operating expenditure in the sense of this indicator includes expenditure for

- acquisitions (including binding, licenses, and pay-per-view costs),
- staff (including project staff, student assistants, etc.),
- operations and maintenance of computers and network, software licenses and telecommunication,
- repair or replacement of existing equipment,
- other items like cataloguing records, copying, postage, promotion of services, insurance, transport, consulting, etc.

Utility costs (heating, electricity, water, sewage, cleaning, security) and calculatory depreciations of assets (buildings, IT- and other equipment) are excluded.

Capital expenditure (expenditure on building sites, new buildings and extensions, furnishings and equipment for new and expanded buildings, new computer systems) is also excluded.

Loans in the sense of this indicator are lending transactions of physical items to one user. This includes user-initiated renewals, on-site loans (loans within the library) and copies supplied in place of original documents. Automatic renewals by the system without user initiation and interlibrary loans are excluded.

In-house use in the sense of this indicator means that a user takes a document from the open access collections for using it inside the library. This includes browsing the contents of a document while standing at the shelves.

A **download** is the successful request of a content unit or descriptive record from a database, electronic serial or digital document. In the sense of this indicator, a content unit means a published document or a part of a document, either textual or audiovisual. A descriptive record is a bibliographic or other record that describes a document or a content unit with elements such as title, author, subject, date of origin etc.

Aims of the indicator

The indicator assesses the library costs per case of collection use and therewith the cost-efficiency of library services.

The indicator is relevant for all libraries with both a physical and an electronic collection.

Comparison between libraries of similar mission, structure and clientele is possible, if differences in the collections are considered and if the operating expenditure is calculated in the same way.

Method

Calculate the total operating expenditure of the library during the reporting year.

Count the numbers of the different forms of collection use during the same time.

The **loan** data should be available via the automated lending system.

In-house use is measured by sampling. The samples should be taken in one or more normal weeks and grossed up for the year. During the sampling period the users are asked not to reshelve documents used in the library. The documents are counted before reshelving. On-site loans (items lent for use inside the library) should, if possible, be excluded or deducted, as they are counted as loans.

The number of **downloads** must be collected from different sources. For electronic documents on a supplier's server, the statistics should be delivered by the supplier. For electronic documents on the library's own server, the server statistics should be used.

Only downloads from the library's electronic collection are counted. This comprises all documents acquired or licensed by the library, but excludes free Internet resources, even if the library has included them in its online catalogue.

For calculating the cost per use, the total operating expenditure is divided by the number of loans + in-house uses + downloads.

If a library does not see its way to gather the data for in-house use and for downloads, and if lending is one of the main services, the cost per loan only might be used as an estimate for the cost per use. For public libraries that do not yet offer a large electronic collection this might afford an insight into cost-effectiveness. In academic libraries, in-house use will probably represent a high percentage of usage of the physical collection and should be counted in addition to loans. For all libraries offering a growing electronic collection, ignoring electronic use in an indicator of cost-effectiveness would be misleading, as the use of the physical collection might decrease and be replaced by electronic usage.

Interpretation and use of results

Low cost per use would generally be considered as showing high cost-effectiveness of the library. But a higher score may be justified by the special tasks of the library and special needs of its clientele. Therefore, this indicator should not be used by itself, but together with indicators of service quality.

The indicator will be useful for evaluating the cost-effectiveness of a library in different periods or compared with other libraries of a similar type. It can be used for justifying the library's expenditure and for budget appliances.

The indicator can be influenced by several issues:

- Ease of access to the physical and the electronic collection
- Studying and reading facilities in the library
- Other libraries nearby supplying services to the library's clientele
- The level of user skills
- Fees for library use

The number of downloads could also be influenced by users' search strategies.

If the cost per use seems too high compared with other libraries of similar mission and population, the library might try to reduce costs, e.g. by streamlining processes, cutting down less-used services, or replacing professional staff in certain services by non-professionals.

As this will not often be possible without lower service quality, it may be more effective to try attracting higher collection use, e.g. by

- promoting the collection via the library website or public media,
- adapting the collection policy to the needs of the population,
- opening closed magazines for open access.

In order to find more details about collection use, the library could use the Indicators B.6 "Collection use", B.7 "Percentage of stock not used" or B.5 "Number of content units downloaded per capita".

User surveys can help to identify issues of dissatisfaction with the collection or with the options for collection use.

Examples and further reading

As yet, there is no example of practical appliance of this indicator. Libraries using cost measures have compared their expenditure only to the number of loans.

The German public libraries had in 2006 an expenditure of 795.333.000 € and 348.982.000 loans which is about 2,28 € per loan (DBS - Deutsche Bibliotheksstatistik).

The Finnish public libraries counted in 2006 2,48 € per loan, similar to the German score (Finnish public library statistics).

The Swiss public library statistics had in 2005 a total expenditure of 110.746.930 CHF and 17.426.571 loans, that is 6,35 CHF or 4,32 € per loan (Schweizerische Bibliothekenstatistik, 2005). Expenditure here includes calculatory costs.

The cost per loan is generally higher in academic libraries because of the specialized services and collections offered.

The Swedish university libraries had in 2005 an expenditure of 1.265.863 (in 1.000 SEK) and 10.694.594 loans which is 118.36 SEK or 13,02 € per loan (Forskningsbiblioteken, 2005).

The Finnish research library statistics allow comparing the total operating expenditure to loans (Finnish research library statistics database). In 2005, the expenditure of all research libraries was 135.039.700 €. Divided by 4.508.633 loans, this is 29,95 € per loan. For university libraries only, total operating expenditure = 96.671.900 € divided by 2.619.610 loans came up to 36,90 € per loan. The score is higher because renewals are excluded.

The statistics of the Australian university libraries (CAUL online statistics) show for 2005 a mean expenditure per loan of 23,94 AUD which would be about 13,95 €. Expenditure excludes capital expenditure; loans include all renewals which would make the cost lower.

The Swiss university libraries had in 2005 a total expenditure of 180.095.610 CHF and 3.439.162 loans, that is 52,37 CHF or 35,66 € per loan (Schweizerische Bibliothekenstatistik, 2005). Expenditure here includes calculatory costs.

The examples show that for comparing results it is extremely important to know how the loans and the expenditure are calculated and what is included in the calculation.

CAUL online statistics, Council of Australian University Libraries, available at: http://www.anu.edu.au/caul/stats/

DBS. Deutsche Bibliotheksstatistik, Hochschulbibliothekszentrum des Landes Nordrhein-Westfalen, available at: http://www.hbz-nrw.de/angebote/dbs/

Finnish public library statistics, Culture and Media Division of the Ministry of Education, available at: http://tilastot.kirjastot.fi/Default.aspx?&langId=en

Finnish research library statistics database, Helsinki University Library, available at: https://yhteistilasto.lib.helsinki.fi/language.do?action=change&choose_language=3

Forskningsbiblioteken 2005 (2005), KB/Bibsam och SCB, Sveriges officiella statistik, available at:
http://www.scb.se/statistik/_publikationer/KU0102_2005A01_BR_KUFT0601.pdf

Schweizerische Bibliothekenstatistik (2005), Bundesamt für Statistik, available at:
http://www.bfs.admin.ch/bfs/portal/de/index/themen/kultur__medien__zeitverwendung/kultur/blank/analysen__berichte/bibliotheken.html

C.4 Ratio of acquisitions costs to staff costs

Background

Staff costs are in most libraries the highest factor in the budget. Libraries offer services that in many cases need experienced professional staff. During the last decades libraries have tried to cut down staff costs by resource sharing, e.g. in cataloguing or portal building, and by streamlining processes, e.g. in book processing. But new tasks like online services and teaching activities have raised staff costs on the other side.

As one of the main tasks of a library is to offer print and electronic collections that are adequate to its population, the problem arises whether staff costs are becoming so high that they narrow the library's funds for collection building. This can be the case in libraries that have flexible or global budgets and that can shift resources between staff and collection expenditure.

Therefore, the relation between acquisitions and staff costs can be seen as an indicator for the library's cost-effectiveness and its ability to keep a good balance between the collection and other library services. This issue will be interesting as well to the funding institution as to users and to the general public.

Definition of the indicator

The acquisitions expenditure divided by the expenditure on regular staff.

Acquisitions expenditure in the sense of this indicator includes binding, licenses and pay-per-view costs. If the library joins in consortia or other over-all contracts, only the library's own share in the contractual expenses should be counted.

Staff expenditure in the sense of this indicator includes the expenditure for regular staff (staff in the position chart). Staff members paid by special grants and student helps are excluded. If the actual expenditure cannot be calculated, average rates can be used. Lists of average rates for each level of the position chart, published by governmental departments, are available in many countries.

Aims of the indicator

The indicator assesses whether the library has organized its processes so efficiently that staff costs do not prevent the library from investing a relevant part of its income in the collection.

The indicator is relevant for all libraries. The indicator is most informative for libraries that have flexible or global budgets and that can shift resources between staff and acquisitions expenditure.

Comparison of results between libraries with similar mission, structure and clientele is possible, if differences in collection policies are taken into account and if the acquisitions and staff expenditure is calculated in the same way.

Method

Calculate the total acquisitions expenditure and the total staff expenditure of the library during the reporting year. Staff expenditure includes only the expenditure for regular staff.

For calculating the ratio of acquisitions costs to staff costs, the total acquisitions expenditure is divided by the total staff expenditure.

Interpretation and use of results

A higher score is usually considered as good. It shows that by efficient organisation staff costs are kept within reasonable bounds that allow the library to invest a relevant part of its income in the collection. But a lower score may be justified by labour-intensive special tasks of the library. Therefore, this indicator should not be used by itself, but together with indicators of service quality.

The indicator can be influenced by
- the library's collection policies,
- labour-intensive services,
- specialized needs of the population to be served,
- external means (e.g. special grants) for consortia,
- cuts in collection building funds,
- raises in staff salaries.

If staff costs seem too high, the library should try to reduce staff costs, especially in background services like media processing and administration. This might be done by
- streamlining processes,
- using as much automation of procedures as possible,

- intensifying cooperative services between libraries,
- replacing professional staff in certain services by non-professionals.

It should be kept in mind that such actions must not result in lower service quality.

Examples and further reading

The German benchmarking project BIX (BIX. Der Bibliotheksindex) uses the indicator "ratio of acquisitions expenditure to staff expenditure" for academic libraries as described above. The results in 2005 were (BIX, 2006):

Ratio of acquisitions expenditure to staff expenditure	mean	maximum	minimum
Universities of applied sciences	0.52	1.24	0.28
Universities: One-tier systems	0.77	2.13	0.39
Universities: Two-tier systems (only the central library considered)	0.55	0.83	0.31

The statistics of the UK academic libraries allow comparing total expenditure on information provision to total staff expenditure. The statistics of 2004/05 count 11.800.000 £ expenditure on information provision and 21.200.000 £ expenditure on staff, which is a score of 0.56 for the indicator and comparable to the BIX results (Creaser, 2006, p.123).

The Finnish research library statistics for 2005 show for all research libraries "library materials costs" of 28.877.200 € and "staff salaries and social costs" of 63.236.500 €, which is a ratio of 0.46 (Finnish research library statistics database). For university libraries only, "library materials costs" are 20.908.800 € and "staff salaries and social costs" are 41.901.800 €, which is a ratio of 0.50. The ratio is somewhat lower in the Finnish libraries, because social costs are included in staff costs.

The statistics of the Association of Research Libraries show in 2004 8.286.431 $ expenditure for library materials and 9.088.732 $ total salary expenditure, which is a ratio of 0.91 (Kyrillidou and Young, 2005). 10 years earlier, in 1994, the ratio was 0.75. From 1986 to 2004, materials expenditure had risen by 206 %, salary expenditure only by 122 %.

In public libraries staff expenditure comes up to a higher percentage and acquisition costs are lower.

The US public library statistics for 2004 count a total operating expenditure of 8.643.028.000 $, of which 65.8 % are staff costs and 13.2 % collection costs (Public libraries in the United States, 2006). This results in a ratio of 0.20.

The Finnish public library statistics show for 2005 an "expenditure on library materials" of 35.944.205 € and "expenditure on staff" of 142.604.435 €, which is a ratio of 0.25, comparable to the US libraries (Finnish public library statistics).

The cost structure of public libraries differs from that of academic libraries.

In Finnish public libraries 2005, distribution of expenditure was as follows (Finnish public library statistics):

- staff   = 57.39 %
- library materials   = 14.47 %
- other   = 28.14 %

The university libraries in the Association of Research Libraries had in 2003/04 the following distribution of expenditure (Kyrillidou and Young, 2005):

- staff   = 46 %
- library materials   = 40 %
- other   = 13.88 %

CARL, the Canadian Association of Research Libraries, had in 2004/05 the following distribution of expenses (Holmes, 2006):

- staff   = 51.6 %
- library materials   = 39.7 %
- other   = 8.7 %

A survey of library spending in 29 countries found the following resource allocation pattern over all types of libraries (OCLC, 2001):

- staff   = 53 %
- collection   = 30 %
- other   = 17 %

When comparing results of this indicator, it will be extremely important to compare only with libraries of similar type and clientele and to define clearly what has been included in the calculation.

BIX. Der Bibliotheksindex, available at: http://www.bix-bibliotheksindex.de/

BIX. Der Bibliotheksindex (2006), *B.I.T. online* Sonderheft 2006

Creaser, C., Maynard, S. and White, S. (2005), LISU annual library statistics 2005, featuring trend analysis of UK public and academic libraries 1994 – 2004, LISU, Loughborough University, available at:
http://www.lboro.ac.uk/departments/dils/lisu/downloads/als05.pdf

Finnish public library statistics, Culture and Media Division of the Ministry of Education, available at: http://tilastot.kirjastot.fi/Default.aspx?&langId=en

Finnish research library statistics database, Helsinki University Library, available at: https://yhteistilasto.lib.helsinki.fi/language.do?action=change&choose_language=3

Holmes, D. (2006), CARL statistics 2004-05, trends and observations, Canadian Association of Research Libraries, available at: http://www.carl-abrc.ca/projects/statistics/statistics-e.html

Kyrillidou, M. and Young, M. (2005), ARL statistics 2003-04, Association of Research Libraries, available at: http://www.arl.org/bm~doc/arlstat04.pdf

OCLC (2003), Worldwide education and library spending, in 2003 environmental scan: a report to the OCLC membership, available at:
http://www.oclc.org/reports/escan/economic/educationlibraryspending.htm

Public libraries in the United States: fiscal year 2004 (2006), National Center for Education Statistics, available at: http://nces.ed.gov/pubs2006/2006349.pdf

C.5 Cost per document processed

Background

Libraries need data about the costs of their individual products and services, on the one side for resource management, on the other side for reporting, for budget appliances and for justifying the library's expenditure. Especially financing authorities often ask for the cost of one loan, document delivery, or catalogue entry.

If the costs per unit of individual products and services are known, benchmarking with other libraries will be possible. Additionally, staff will gain a better understanding of the cost implications of practices and policies. The data will also be extremely helpful for decisions on outsourcing processes.

Media processing is taken as example for unit costs, as the processing activities are necessary in all libraries, and the results can therefore be compared between libraries.

The first edition of the International Standard ISO 11620 included the indicator "Cost per title catalogued". But in many libraries acquisition and cataloguing processes are now combined in a media processing department and will be carried out in one. Therefore "cost of document processed", including both acquisition and cataloguing, will be more adequate to the present situation in libraries.

Definition of the indicator

The staff costs of processing acquired media (print and electronic documents) divided by the number of documents processed.

Media processing includes acquisition and descriptive cataloguing.

For the purpose of this indicator, acquisition is defined as all processes after documents have arrived at the library and it has been decided to add them to the collections (e.g. accession list, accounting procedures).

Classification and/or subject cataloguing are excluded, as the rules and procedures in libraries are too different to render comparison possible.

Media acquired by gift, exchange or legal deposit are included.

Aims of the indicator

The indicator assesses the staff costs of a library's procedures for processing acquired documents and therewith the efficiency of processes.

The indicator is relevant for all libraries.

Comparison between libraries is possible, if the type and language of acquired media, the percentage of copy and/or minimal cataloguing and differences in salaries are taken into account.

The indicator is not applicable if the processing or some part of the processing has been outsourced.

Method

The library chooses a sampling period with normal workload.

To obtain the number of hours spent on processing acquired media, time cost analysis is necessary. Because staff members are often involved in several tasks, the time they spend on processing should be logged during the sampling period. If time logging is not possible, the proportion of time spent on processing can, instead, be estimated.

The time spent on processing by all staff during the sampling period is summed up to hours. The hours are then multiplied with the cost per hour of labour (wages divided by the regular working time of the relevant staff) to obtain the staff costs of processing.

The number of documents processed during the sampling period is recorded.

The cost per document processed is calculated by dividing the staff costs of processing during the sampling period by the number of documents processed during the same period.

It should be stated clearly what part of the processing is included in the calculation

Interpretation and use of results

A low score for "cost per document processed" will be seen as good.

The indicator will be greatly influenced by the type and language of the processed documents. Processing of non-commercial publications will probably take longer, as copy cataloguing data might not be available. Cataloguing of publications in foreign languages may offer more problems than cataloguing of publications in the national language.

The indicator will also be influenced by the procedures of media processing, the level of bibliographic description, the degree of automation, and the qualification and expertise of staff.

If the cost per document processed seems too high compared to other libraries, the library might

- revise workflows,
- use more automated procedures,
- try to increase the percentage of copy cataloguing,
- replace highly paid professional staff by support staff.

Examples and further reading

The indicator is adapted from a method described by Deriez and Giappiconi (1994) that calculated "cost per title catalogued".

One of the most comprehensive time and cost studies was conducted by the Technical Services of the Iowa State University Library between 1987 and 2001 (Morris, 1992; Morris and Osmus, 1992; Morris et al., 2000). The study focussed on aspects of staff time and costs for cataloguing. The average cost of cataloguing per title decreased from $20.83 to $ 16.25 between 1990-91 and 1997-98, and at the end of 1999 the cost was about $6.13 per title. The decrease of costs was due to shared cataloguing, process automation and more cataloguing done by support staff.

The National Library of Australia calculates the cost per collection item acquired and/or processed or digitised. Over the last three years the costs increased from AUD 38.43 to AUD 42.10.

A study of the Library at Curtin University of Technology and the three other publicly funded universities in Western Australia (known collectively as WA-GUL) compared cost savings to be achieved by re-engineering cataloguing and related operations with savings to be expected from outsourcing (Wade and Williamson, 2007). In Curtin, the cost of one title catalogued before re-engineering was 21,13 AUD. The expectation was to reach a cataloguing cost per title of 10,11 AUD by organisational measures.

When comparing results of this indicator it will be especially important to state which activities have been included in "cataloguing" or "processing".

Deriez, R. and Giappiconi, T. (1994), Analyser et comparer les coûts de catalogage, *Bulletin des Bibliothèques de France* 39,6, pp. 28-33

Morris, D. E. (1992), Staff time and costs for cataloguing, *Library Resources & Technical services* 36,1, pp. 79-92

Morris, D. E. and Osmus, L. (1992). Serials cataloguing time and costs: results of an ongoing study at Iowa State University, *The Serials Librarian* 22, 1/ 2, pp. 235-248

Morris, D. E. et al. (2000), Cataloguing staff costs revisited, *Library Resources & Technical Services*, 44,2, pp. 70-83, available at:
http://www.ala.org/ala/alcts/alctspubs/librestechsvc/LRTSarchive/44n2.pdf

National Library of Australia (2006), 46th Annual Report 2005/06, available at:
http://www.nla.gov.au/policy/annrep06/index.html

Wade, R. and Williamson, V. (2007), Cataloguing costed and restructured at Curtin University of Technology, available at:
http://www.unilinc.edu.au/services/consult_curtin.html

C.6 Cost per download

Background

Over the last two decades the electronic collections of libraries have been growing steadily. Bibliographic databases were the first to replace their printed version, followed by journals that nowadays often appear in two formats – both in print and electronically. Compared to the printed books the proportion of e-books is still rather small but growing continuously.

Since an ever increasing part of the library budget is spent on electronic resources, the library will have to justify the expenditure for each resource by showing that the cost per use does not exceed limits the library itself is willing to accept as reasonable in the context of its information provision.

Downloads indicate that users have found items that seem to be relevant to their interests. The measure could be seen in analogy to loans of print materials, while sessions could be seen in analogy to browsing the shelves. Therefore, downloads can be regarded as the most expressive measure for the relevance of the electronic collection to users.

If the number of downloads from an electronic resource is compared with the costs of that resource, the cost per use will show whether the expenditure is justified.

Definition of the indicator

The costs of each electronic resource – a database, an electronic serial or an e-book – are divided by the number of downloads from that resource during a specified period, usually a year.

The costs of an electronic resource consist of its subscription or licensing costs. One-time purchases of electronic resources are excluded, since usage period and cost period do not correspond. Regular payments for server maintenance fees if the resource is not hosted on the library's server are included. Maintenance of computers and network and software licences for the provision of electronic resources on the library's own servers as well as other operational costs are excluded.

Pay-per-view arrangements are excluded since costs per download for such a service are determined in advance.

If the costs of an individual electronic resource cannot be clearly established, because it has been acquired by bulk purchase or in a package with a print version, this indicator will not be applicable for that resource.

A download is the successful request of a content unit or descriptive record from a database, electronic serial or digital document. In the sense of this indicator, a content unit means a published document or a part of a document, either textual or audiovisual. A descriptive record is a bibliographic or other record that describes a document or a content unit with elements such as title, author, subject, date of origin etc.

Downloads by library staff and in user training are included in the number of downloads.

Aims of the indicator

The indicator assesses the cost-efficiency of the library's electronic collection on a titles basis so that the library can decide at regular intervals if it is still willing to accept the cost per use or if it decides to cancel a resource.

The number of downloads is also an indication of the relevance attributed to the electronic resource by the users.

The indicator is relevant for all libraries with an electronic collection. It will be especially useful for comparison over time.

Comparison of the same or similar resources between libraries may be possible, if differences in the libraries' clientele are considered.

Method

To begin with the electronic collection has to be checked through for those resources for which access fees are paid at regular intervals.

For each electronic resource for which payments are made on a regular basis the costs per year are calculated and divided by the number of downloads recorded for that resource during the same period. In case there are various manifestations of the same unit (HTML, PDF for text files and JPEG or WAV for non-textual material) all requests are counted.

In an automated library system it will be easy to identify the costs of an individual resource. Bibliographic as well as full text databases are usually paid annually. The cost structure of electronic journals is simple in the case of e-only subscriptions. It becomes complicated when there is an extra fee for electronic access that has to be added to the price of the print subscription. When a consortium agreement or other contractual arrangements with a journal publisher exist it is often difficult to determine the access fee for the individual journal. In that case the total access fee (including cross access) has to be divided by the number of journals in the package (including the journals to be accessed because of cross access within the consortium). As long as e-books are mainly sold in packages it seems reasonable to apply the indicator on the basis of the package as a whole.

If the costs of an individual electronic resource cannot be clearly established, because it has been acquired by bulk purchase or in a package with a print version, this indicator will not be applicable for that resource.

The collection of usage statistics may be time-consuming because publishers and database suppliers provide separate statistics of downloads for each product. For the usability of the data COUNTER compliancy is a necessity.

With more and more libraries making use of Electronic Resource Management Systems, where both cost and usage data are integrated, the data collection process will become easier in the future.

Interpretation and use of results

In general low cost per download is considered a good cost-benefit relation for an electronic resource. It is for the library to decide what it regards as a good cost-benefit relation – there are no generally applicable standards. For a full text database of medieval manuscripts a price of 2,45 € per download may be acceptable while 1,95 € per download may be deemed high for downloads from a widely used bibliographic database in the STM sector.

The indicator will be affected by the users' browser cache configurations and use of proxy servers. The real number of downloads could be higher than the numbers shown by server statistics.

If the cost per session seems too high, the library could either promote the use of the electronic resource, e.g. in user training, or cancel it. Especially in the case of electronic journals, a subscription could be replaced by document delivery, with the library covering the delivery costs.

Before cancelling a database or journal with high cost per session, the library should assess whether the resource is of crucial importance for a comparatively small user group. User surveys or interviews could help to determine the importance of an electronic resource beyond the confines of pure usage statistics.

The indicator will be useful for improving the library's cost-efficiency in regard to its electronic collection. It can be used for justifying the library's expenditure and for budget appliances.

Examples and further reading

The indicator was introduced in the project EQUINOX in the form "Cost per document or entry (record) viewed for each electronic library service" (EQUINOX, 2000).

Being confined to single resources it is not surprising that the indicator is not used in the framework of national library statistics. Many libraries use it, however, to prove the cost-efficiency of their electronic resources. In the context of the transition from print to electronic journal collections cost per use data have been analysed and found to "hold tremendous potential for libraries and library consortia to increasingly employ reliable cost and use data to support collection development and management decisions." (Franklin, 2004)

At Drexel University Library in Philadelphia detailed usage statistics of both print and electronic journal use were collected (Montgomery and King, 2002). For electronic journals subscriptions the average cost per download amounted to 1,40 $ with considerable differences between individual subscriptions (3,20 $), publisher's packages (2,25 $), aggregator journals (1,35 $) and full text database journals (0,40 $). A similar result of 1,64 $ per download was given for the University of Virginia (Franklin, 2004).

The medical branch library of the University Library in Münster conducted a similar study (Obst, 2003). The cost per download for electronic journals turned out to be 3,47 €, producing evidence for great difference between various publishers between 15,10 € (Academic Press) and 0,31 € (HighWire).

At the University of Connecticut as at many libraries of other universities the indicator is used – on an annul basis - as decision-making tool in collection development (Franklin, 2004). Expensive databases are compared in regard to their cost-efficiency. In 2003 the cost per download ranged from 0,37 $ for WorldCat to 2,17 $ for Web of Science with FirstSearch (0,47 $) and JStor (0,62 $) in between.

Equinox. Library performance measurement and quality management system (2000), available at: http://equinox.dcu.ie/index.html

Franklin, B. (2004), Managing the electronic collection with cost per use data, *World Library and Information Congress: 70th IFLA General Conference and Council, 22-27 August 2004, Buenos Aires*, available at: http://www.ifla.org/IV/ifla70/papers/098e-Franklin.pdf

Montgomery, C. H. and King, D.W. (2002) Comparing library and user related costs of print and electronic journal collections: a first step towards a comprehensive analysis, *D-Lib Magazine* 8,10, available at:
http://www.dlib.org/dlib/october02/montgomery/10montgomery.html

Obst, O., (2003), Patterns and cost of printed and online journal usage, *Health information and libraries journal*, 20, pp. 22 - 32

C.7 Acquisition speed

Background

New publications – in whatever format – are of high interest for users, especially for researchers who want to be up-to-date in their subject. It will therefore be important for them that newly published documents are acquired by the library as quickly as possible.

The speed of acquisition has two aspects:
- The library's promptness to react on the publication of a document
- The vendor's quickness in delivering the item

The library can influence the speed of ordering a document by quick reaction on publication announcements, but is at the mercy of the vendors in respect to the timely delivery of a document as soon as it is published. This indicator is restricted to the second aspect, the delivery speed of vendors. Besides pricing conditions and the correct fulfilment of orders, delivery speed is one of the most important criteria in the dealings between libraries and their suppliers. In a questionnaire to community colleges in 1990 that asked for top criteria for choosing vendors, speed of delivery ranked fourth, after accuracy of order fulfilment, discounts and customer service (Alessi, 1992).

Definition of the indicator

The median number of days between the date the library orders a document and the date the document is received in the library.

Documents ordered before publication are excluded, as the time elapsed between ordering and actual publication of the document cannot be seen as shortcoming of the vendor.

Days are counted in working days, not calendar days.

Aims of the indicator

The indicator assesses whether the library has chosen vendors with efficient workflows and whether users can expect speedy availability of new titles.

The indicator is relevant for all libraries. It will be especially useful for measuring the acquisition speed of monographs, but can be applied to different types of documents. Useful results can be expected from a comparison of vendors among different libraries.

Methods

1. The library chooses a sample period. For each document that is received by the library within this period the day of ordering, the day of receipt and the supplier's name are recorded, either from the computerized acquisition system or from the order forms and similar records. It should be made certain that there is no delay between documents arriving in the library's mail room and in the acquisitions or processing department.

   Documents acquired by gift, exchange or legal deposit are excluded. Documents ordered before publication should also be excluded, but this may prove difficult. If the source for the ordered title was a pre-announcement or a CIP (cataloguing in publication) bibliography, such titles can be excluded from the sample. Another way would be to mark documents not yet published with a code when ordering. This would also be useful for differentiating within overdue orders when claiming. In many cases it will be necessary to identify titles not yet published individually by consulting online vendors or national catalogue databases.

   For each vendor the titles are ranked according to the number of working days that elapsed between ordering and delivery. The median acquisition speed is the number of days that is in the middle of the ranking list. In order to facilitate comparisons between different vendors or an individual vendor's speed over time it is useful to separate domestic from foreign orders. It is also necessary to keep normal acquisition procedures apart from special procedures such as rush orders for documents already requested by users or orders for antiquarian titles that might take a longer delivery time.

2. A simpler method uses the claiming procedures of the automated library system. When the library orders a title, it will usually fix the time period until a claim is sent out. Such periods are for instance: 20 days for rush orders, 60 days for domestic orders, 90 days for foreign orders.

   For a sample time, the library fixes for all orders a shorter claiming period, e.g. 15 days. The claims produced by the system after that period will show what percentage of orders was not delivered within that period.

Interpretation and use of results

According to the type of acquired material (domestic/foreign/antiquarian) and the acquisition procedure (express/normal delivery) the performance of each vendor is quantified. The lower the number of days between order and receipt the better.

If the acquisition speed seems inadequate, the library could make up time by using online ordering. The time between order and receipt of an already published book can also be reduced by an approval plan, since it saves the time for ordering procedures.

The library may also consider changing vendors. Orders that have taken an especially long completion time should be discussed with the vendor in search of reasons for the delay. This may help the vendor to become aware of inefficient handling or shipment procedures.

The library may have to revise its procedures for claiming overdue books. In the case of already published documents a change to shorter claiming intervals may reduce the days it takes to deliver a document.

Comparisons on the basis of the median acquisition speed facilitate the choice of vendors delivering similar material, although speed is but one criterion for vendor quality.

Examples and further reading

Acquisition speed has increased visibly during the last years because of faster ordering procedures and improved handling procedures between suppliers and publishers.

In the project EQLIPSE (EQLIPSE, 1995-1997) that tested data collection for a large set of performance indicators, acquisition speed in three participating libraries varied from 24 days to 97 days.

In an evaluation of the Copenhagen Business School Library "supply times for receipt of new materials" were measured (Report on the 1992 evaluation study, 1993, p.89). The median supply time for all books in 1992 was 56 days, for Danish books 21 days and for foreign books 65 days.

The Swedish benchmarking project 2001 – 2004 (Edgren et al., 2005, pp.34-35) used a combined indicator for acquisition and processing speed, but measuring each issue separately. The median acquisition speed in 2004 for academic libraries varied from 7 days to 23 days, with an average of 12,1 days. For public libraries the time varied from 6 to 53 days, with an average of 28,8 days.

In 2005 the Appalachian State University conducted a study comparing Amazon.com with other library suppliers (Orkiszewski, 2005). While the main criteria were availability and pricing, speed of delivery was also analysed, ranging from two weeks for Amazon to an average of three weeks for all vendors and four weeks for the library's primary book vendor.

An overview of the literature on vendor assessment is given by Vargas (2006).

Alessi, D. (1992), Vendor selection, vendor collection, or vendor defection, *Journal of Library Administration* 16,3, pp. 117-130

Edgren, J. et.al. (2005), Quality handbook, performance indicators for library activities, The Swedish Library Association's Special Interest Group for Quality Management and Statistics , available at:
http://www.biblioteksforeningen.org/sg/kvalitet/handbook_eng.html

EQLIPSE. Evaluation and quality in library performance: system for Europe, 1995-1997, available at: http://www.cerlim.ac.uk/projects/eqlipse/

Orkiszewski, P. (2005), A comparative study of Amazon.com as a library book and media vendor, *Library Resources & Technical Services* 49,3, pp. 204-209.

Report on the 1992 evaluation study of the Copenhagen Business School Library (1993), Copenhagen Business School Library

Vargas, S. C. (2006), Library vendor assessment literature review, *BiblioTech, the online magazine of the Library Student Organisation (LSO) of the University of Arizona, Tucson, USA* 4/1, available at:
http://www.sir.arizona.edu/lso/bibliotech/2006sep_vol4_no1/Vargas.html

C.8 Media processing speed

Background

The activities needed for processing (acquiring and cataloguing) new media for the collection constitute one of the main background services of the library.

Media processing involves several steps:

- Accession: all processes after the item has arrived at the library and it has been decided to add it to the collections (accession list, accounting procedures)
- Cataloguing (bibliographic description)
- Classification and/or subject indexing
- Jacketing or binding (if applicable)
- Physical processing (stamping, labelling, bar-coding, applying a magnetic strip)
- Shelving

In a French survey in university libraries in 1989-1991, cataloguing (including classification and/or subject cataloguing) amounted to 51 % of the total time for processing; acquisition and physical processing each amounted to about 25 % (Deriez and Le Barbanchon, 1993).

In many libraries acquisition and cataloguing processes are now combined in a media processing department and will be carried out in one.

As media processing is a regular process occurring in all libraries, it can be easily used as example for the efficiency of processes in the library.

Definition of the indicator

The median number of days between the date a document arrives at the library and the date it is available for use, usually on the shelves or on the server.

Days are counted in working days, not calendar days.

Processing procedures include acquisition, descriptive cataloguing, subject indexing, if applicable binding, physical processing, and shelving.

Aims of the indicator

The indicator assesses whether the processing procedures are efficiently organized, and what priority the library gives to the speed of services.

The indicator is relevant for all libraries. It will be especially useful for measuring the processing speed of monographs, but can be applied to different types of documents.

Comparisons between libraries are possible, if differences in the level of automation, in descriptive cataloguing and subject indexing, in the percentage of copy cataloguing, in binding policies etc. are taken into account.

Method

The library chooses a sampling time with normal activity. For all incoming items the date of the following processes - if applicable - is noted on a manual recording sheet that accompanies the item through the processing:

- Arrival
- End of accession
- End of cataloguing/adding metadata
- End of classification and/or subject indexing
- End of binding
- End of physical processing (stamping, labelling, bar-coding, applying a magnetic strip)
- Shelving or installation on the server

For items received as gift or in exchange, it must be decided that the item will be added to the collection before processing starts.

For electronic documents, the end of processing will either coincide with cataloguing, when the URL for a document on an external server has been added, or with the installation of the document on the library's server and the URL being added in the catalogue.

Each staff member processing the item is asked to write down the exact date after handling the document. If all data are available via the automated system, no manual recording sheet will be needed.

In libraries with online cataloguing procedures, the document will be earlier in the catalogue than on the shelf. But as shelving is necessary for the availability of the document, the date of shelving determines the end of processing.

For each item, calculate the number of working days between arrival and availability for use. Rank the items according to the number of days elapsed. The median processing speed is the number of days that is in the middle of the ranking list.

A more detailed view of the processing speed is possible, if processing times are shown in cumulative distribution, e.g.:

Media processing speed	%
< 1 day	5
1 – 2 days	10
2 – 5 days	30
5 - 10 days	30
10 – 20 days	20
> 20 days	5

If processing speed is evaluated in cumulative distribution, transactions with especially long completion time could be followed up in order to find reasons for the delay, e.g. backlogs or inefficient procedures.

Apart from the usual way a document is processed, there may be special procedures for special document types that should be analyzed separately:

- Rush processing for items already requested by users
- Electronic media
- Legal deposit
- Special collections

It might also be interesting to assess media processing speed for each subject collection.

Items sent to a bindery before the physical processing should also be evaluated separately, as outside binding may considerably lengthen the processing time.

Interpretation and use of results

Processing speed will be influenced by the type of materials processed. Processing of rare material will take longer as special procedures have to be followed.

If there is a division of labour for certain types of documents, documents in foreign languages or in a special format may have to wait for the staff person with good knowledge of that language or that format.

The speed will also be influenced by peak times for incoming documents, e.g. end of the year, or by absence times of staff.

When a manual recording sheet is used, this may influence the processing speed, as staff might try to keep processing time for these items low.

In most libraries, priorities will be given to certain groups of documents, e.g. patron requested items or items for which high use is expected. Gift or exchange documents are often given lower priority. Another issue for priorities is that "human nature may succumb to the temptation to do the easier items first" (Holley, 1984, p.346).

If the processing speed is too low, the following measures could be taken:
- Streamlining workflows
- Quick forwarding of items from one department involved in the processing to the next
- Using as much automation of procedures as possible
- Using more copy cataloguing
- Integrating acquisition and cataloguing activities
- Adding more staff in peak times

Staff motivation will be important for speedy procedures, and backlogs can be demotivating. It has proved efficient to eliminate backlogs by assigning additional staff for a short period and then trying to keep up short processing times.

Examples and further reading

Processing speed has increased visibly during the last years due to higher automation of processes and higher availability of bibliographical data for copy cataloguing.

In the project EQLIPSE (EQLIPSE, 1995-1997) that tested data collection for a large set of performance indicators, document processing in three participating libraries varied from 17 days to 28 days.

The public library in Münster, Germany, measured processing time before and after reorganizing its processes (Rosenberger, 2001). In 1999, before the reorganisation, the average processing time was 43 days; in 2000, after the reorganisation, it was 26 days.

A study in Polish academic libraries used the indicator "time of document acquisition and processing in days" (Derfert-Wolf, Górski and Marcinek, 2005). The median result for all academic libraries in 2002 and 2003 was 14 days.

The Netherlands university libraries' benchmarking project counted in 2003 (UKB, 2003):

Books available for use	days
50 % within ...	from 3 to 32
80 % within...	from 5 to 67
90 % within...	from 14 to 109

The Swedish benchmarking project (Edgren et al., 2005) used a combined indicator for acquisition and processing speed, but measuring each issue separately. The median processing speed for 2004 varied from 1 day to 28 days,

The service standards of Headingley & Civic Quarter Libraries at Leeds Metropolitan University promise that "85 % of material requiring cataloguing/processing will be sent for shelving within 8 weeks of being unpacked" and that "we will make all new electronic information sources available to users within 1 working week of the subscription being activated" (Headingley & Civic Quarter Libraries, 2006)

In an evaluation of the Copenhagen Business School Library, the goal was that the maximal processing time for new books should be 2 weeks, and that external binding of books and periodicals should not take more than one month (Report on the 1992 evaluation study, 1993, p.89). Processing time showed a mean of 6 days, while binding time came up to 6 weeks.

Columbus Metropolitan Library, Ohio, had an average processing time (from receipt to the distribution to branch libraries) of 17 days when they started establishing productivity standards and looking at their workflow in 2003 (Hatcher, 2006). In 2004, they reached a "turnaround time" of 1.5 days, and since 2005, of 48 hours. Weekends and closed days are ignored in the calculation.

A survey in Carnegie Mellon University Libraries in 2001 monitored "the amount of time required to catalog materials from receipt in the Acquisitions Department to shelf-ready status" (Hurlbert and Dujmic, 2004). 75 % of all materials and 72 % of monographs were catalogued within 7 weeks. As acquisitions and cataloguing departments were still separate, the critical time was the period between receipt and cataloguing, as cataloguing staff tended to leave items with difficult cataloguing issues in the backlog. Gifts proved to have less priority in cataloguing and thus had a longer processing time.

Apart from the processing speed, libraries may also look at the efficiency of the processing staff (see Indicator C.9 "Employee productivity in media processing").

Derfert-Wolf, L., Górski, M. and Marcinek, M. (2005), Quality of academic libraries – funding bodies, librarians and users, *World Library and Information Congress, 71th IFLA General Conference and Council,* available at: http://www.ifla.org/IV/ifla71/papers/080e-Derfert-Wolf.pdf#search=%22Derfert-Wolf%22

Deriez, R. and Le Barbanchon, E. (1993), Le circuit du livre dans les bibliothèques universitaires: évaluation des tâches, *Bulletin des Bibliothèques de France* 38,2, pp. 50 – 55

Edgren, J. et.al. (2005), Quality handbook, performance indicators for library activities, The Swedish Library Association's Special Interest Group for Quality Management and Statistics , available at: http://www.biblioteksforeningen.org/sg/kvalitet/handbook_eng.html

EQLIPSE. Evaluation and quality in library performance: system for Europe (1995-1997), available at: http://www.cerlim.ac.uk/projects/eqlipse/

Hatcher, M. (2006), On the shelf in 24 hours, *Library Journal* September 15, pp. 30 - 31

Headingley & Civic Quarter Libraries (2006), Service standards 2005-06, available at: http://www.lmu.ac.uk/lis/lss/commitment/service_stds_cq-hy_2006-07.pdf

Holley, R. P. (1984), Priority as a factor in technical processing, *Journal of Academic Librarianship* 9,6, pp. 345-348

Hurlbert, T. and Dujmic, L.L. (2004), Factors affecting cataloging time: an in-house survey, *Technical Services Quarterly* 22,2, pp. 1 - 14

Report on the 1992 evaluation study of the Copenhagen Business School Library (1993), Copenhagen Business School Library

Rosenberger, B. (2001), "Der Kunde kommt schneller an neue Medien!", Ermittlung der Mediendurchlaufzeiten an der Stadtbücherei Münster, *BuB, Forum Bibliothek und Information* 53,8, pp. 471 - 477

UKB (2003), Benchmarking, Samenwerkingsverband van de Nederlandse universiteitsbibliotheken en de Koninklijke Bibliotheek, results only available to participants

C.9 Employee productivity in media processing

Background

Assessing employee productivity is an important issue when evaluating the efficiency of a library's organisation. Media processing is taken as example for employee productivity, as the processing activities are necessary in all libraries, and the results can therefore be compared between libraries.

The quality criteria for media processing are the speed and accuracy of processing. The efficiency of media processing can be measured by comparing the output of one FTE (full-time equivalent) staff over time and with results in other libraries. The results will be especially interesting for the funding institution, as the question of how much staff is necessary for the library's tasks is one that is always debated between libraries and their authorities.

Libraries have always been reluctant to assess staff performance, and they are still more reluctant to communicate such data. But staff productivity is a crucial issue for cost-effectiveness of libraries, as staff costs will often represent the main part of all costs. When assessing staff productivity it will be advisable to include staff representatives and to ensure that the evaluation does not consider the individual person, but the overall productivity in specified services.

Definition of the indicator

The average number of acquired media (print and electronic documents) processed per employee in a certain period (usually one year).

Media acquired by gift, exchange or legal deposit are included.

Staff is calculated as FTE (full-time equivalent). Figures for part-time employees are converted to the equivalent number of full-time workers.

Example:
If out of three persons employed as librarians, one works quarter-time, one works half-time, and one works full-time, then the FTE of these three persons would be 0,25+0,5+1,0=1,75 librarians (FTE).

Processing in the sense of this indicator includes both acquisition and cataloguing. Classification and/or subject cataloguing are excluded, as the rules and procedures in libraries are too different to render comparison possible.

The number of acquired media is divided by the number of employees (FTE) involved in media processing (acquisition and descriptive cataloguing, no retrospective cataloguing).

Aims of the indicator

The indicator demonstrates overall employee productivity by the example of media processing.

The indicator is useful for comparisons over time. Comparison to other libraries is possible, if differences in the type and language of acquired media and in the procedures of media processing are taken into account.

The indicator is not applicable if the processing or some part of the processing has been outsourced.

Method

Count the number of processed media during a specified period, usually a year, including all formats. For electronic periodicals and newspapers, an annual subscription is counted as one document acquired.

Calculate the number of staff in FTE that are involved in the acquisition and descriptive cataloguing of acquired media. Retrospective cataloguing and classification/subject cataloguing are excluded. The count includes all staff, whether permanent or temporary. Because staff members are often involved in several tasks, the time they spend on acquisition and cataloguing should be logged during a representative period. If time logging is not possible, the proportion of time spent on acquisition and cataloguing can, instead, be estimated.

The number of processed media is divided by the number of FTE staff involved in acquisition and cataloguing.

Interpretation and use of results

A high number of processed media per FTE person will be considered as good.

The indicator will be greatly influenced by the type and language of the acquired media. Processing of non-commercial publications will probably take longer, as copy cataloguing data might not be available. Cataloguing of publications in foreign languages may offer more problems than cataloguing of publications in the national language.

The indicator will also be influenced by the procedures of media processing, the degree of automation, and the qualification and expertise of staff.

If the employee productivity seems too low compared to other libraries, the library might

- revise workflows,
- use more automated procedures,
- intensify staff training,
- try to increase the percentage of copy cataloguing.

Examples and further reading

The indicator was introduced in a German controlling project for academic libraries (Ceynowa and Coners, 2002) and adopted by the German benchmarking project BIX for academic libraries (BIX. Der Bibliotheksindex). In 2005, BIX showed the following results (BIX, 2006):

Employee productivity in media processing	mean	maximum	minimum
Universities of applied sciences	1.996	4.425	934
Universities: One-tier systems	2.497	4.913	1.219
Universities: Two-tier systems (only the central library considered)	2.972	5.759	797

The indicator is also used in the benchmarking project of the Netherlands university libraries, but restricted to books (Laeven and Smit, 2003). The results for 2004 showed an average of 1.017 titles of books processed per FTE staff (UKB, 2004).

BIX. Der Bibliotheksindex, available at: http://www.bix-bibliotheksindex.de/

BIX. Der Bibliotheksindex (2006), *B.I.T. online* Sonderheft 2006

Ceynowa, K. and Coners, A. (2002), Balanced Scorecard für wissenschaftliche Bibliotheken, *Zeitschrift für Bibliohekswesen und Bibliographie, Sonderheft 82,* Klostermann, Frankfurt a.M.

Laeven, H. and Smit, A. (2003), A project to benchmark university libraries in the Netherlands, *Library Management* 24, 6/7, pp. 291-304

UKB (2004), Benchmarking, Samenwerkingsverband van de Nederlandse universiteitsbibliotheken en de Koninklijke Bibliotheek, results only available to participants

C.10 Lending speed

Background

Libraries store their collections either in open access, where users can browse and collect items for reading or borrowing, or in closed stacks, where users have no access. For materials in closed stacks users must consult the catalogue to find items of interest and must fill out a lending request. The kind of storage is influenced by building conditions and by the materials in the collection. Rare and old materials will in most cases be stored in closed magazines. Generally, open access storage is preferable not only for users, but also for the library, as users can deliberately select items, and the library will save the workload of retrieving the items. Open access, even if the documents are not shelved in systematic order, but in accession order, will need more space for users' browsing activities.

But even if a library has the possibility of offering large parts of its collection – preferably the most-used parts – in open access, in most cases certain parts of the collection have to be stored in closed stacks, due to lack of space or to the kind of materials stored.

Therefore, quick access to items in closed stacks is still an important issue for many libraries. Delivery speed will be even more important, if collections are housed in off-site storage.

Definition of the indicator

The median time between the moment a user requests an item out of closed stacks and the moment the item is available at the issue desk. The time is counted in hours and minutes, considering only the working hours of the retrieval services and the lending department.

Aims of the indicator

The indicator assesses whether the library's retrieval and lending services are efficiently organized.

The indicator is relevant for all libraries with at least part of their collection in closed stacks.

Comparison between libraries is possible if local differences in regard to means of transportation, construction of the library building, and especially remote storage are taken into account.

Method

The library chooses a sampling time with normal activity. For a random sample of documents stored in closed stacks and requested by a user note the date and time of the request and the date and time of the item being available at the issue desk. Requests for items in off-site storage should be evaluated separately.

In most cases these data will be available via the library's circulation system. If the system does not deliver the information, the following data are noted on a manual recording sheet:
- Date and time a request is received (in any format)
- Date and time the requested item is available at the issue desk

Failed requests because of incorrect shelving or other reasons are left out of the calculation.

The time needed for each delivery is calculated by counting only the business hours of the retrieval services and the lending department on the sampling days.

The lending delivery time is then calculated by ranking the requests in ascending order by the retrieval time. The median time is the value of the request in the middle of the ranking list.

A more detailed view of the delivery speed is possible, if delivery times are shown in cumulative distribution, e.g.:

Delivery time	%
0 – 30 minutes	20
30 minutes – 1 hour	35
1 – 2 hours	30
> 2 hours	15

If delivery times are evaluated in cumulative distribution, transactions with especially long completion time could be followed up in order to find reasons for the delay. In some cases, this may be due to wrong citations, e.g. when a requested article cannot be found in the journal issue cited and the library has to verify the citation.

Interpretation and use of results

A short delivery time will be considered as good.

Delivery speed will be influenced by the number of orders at peak times and by the storage conditions. If the requested item has to be fetched from remote storage, transportation time will be added to the total delivery time.

The indicator is also influenced by incorrect shelving, by an insufficient number of stack attendants, especially in peak times, and by staff competences, e.g. stack attendants' knowledge about the shelving system, locations of special collections etc.

If the delivery speed is too slow, the following measures could be taken:
- Examining workflows
- Using as much automation of procedures as possible
- Training staff in issues of the shelving system, storage problems etc.
- A higher number of stack attendants during peak times
- A more transparent shelf-location system
- Regular shelf-reading procedures (see Indicator C.13 "Shelving accuracy")
- Quick reshelving of returned items

Examples and further reading

The indicator was described early (Dougherty, 1973; Orr and Schless, 1972). Though probably many libraries actually measure the speed of their retrieval services, results are rarely published.

In the project EQLIPSE (EQLIPSE, 1995-1997) that tested data collection for a large set of performance indicators, "median time of document retrieval from closed stacks" was assessed by two participating libraries. The results differed considerably: 64 minutes and 3 days.

Some libraries have defined goals for delivery speed in their strategy. The National Library of Australia promises "that 60% of items requested from onsite storage areas will be delivered within 25 minutes, material stored in more distant locations onsite may take up to 45 minutes to deliver" (National Library of Australia, 2004).

The National Library of New Zealand reports for the period 2003-2004 that 90% of author/title requests for collection items were "completed within 20 minutes of request or advertised batch times for onsite use and within 48 hour for off-site use" (National Library of New Zealand, 2004, p.50).

Many libraries name a time when the requested item should normally be available to users.

The public library in Vienna, Austria, states that requests within opening times will be available after 45 minutes, while requests outside opening times will be available from 9.00 in the morning on the following day (Wienbibliothek im Rathaus, FAQ).

There are several libraries that name a time limit for retrieving requested items from remote storage. The University of Birmingham Library uses a performance indicator "Recovery from store/another site: time to recover" with the goal "90 % within 1 working day" (Key performance indicators, 2006).

Dougherty, R.M. (1973), The evaluation of campus library document delivery service, *College and Research Libraries* 34, pp. 29 – 32

EQLIPSE. Evaluation and quality in library performance: system for Europe (1995-1997), available at: http://www.cerlim.ac.uk/projects/eqlipse/

Key performance indicators (2006), University of Birmingham Information Services, available at: http://www.isquality.bham.ac.uk/kpi.htm

National Library of Australia (2004), Reader services policy, available at: http://www.nla.gov.au/policy/readerservices.html

National Library of New Zealand (2004), Statement of intent 2003/04, available at: http://www.natlib.govt.nz/en/about/2pubsoi03.html

Orr, R.H. and Schless, A. P. (1972), Document delivery capabilities of major biomedical libraries in 1968: results of a national survey employing standardized tests, *Bulletin of the Medical Library Association* 60, pp. 382 – 422, available at: http://www.pubmedcentral.nih.gov/picrender.fcgi?artid=197715&blobtype=pdf

Wienbibliothek im Rathaus, FAQ, available at: www.wienbibliothek.at

C.11 Interlibrary loan speed

Background

Interlibrary loan (ILL) and document delivery by libraries have not become less important in times of growing electronic resources. Some surveys show that ILL and document delivery transactions have decreased during the last years (Goodier and Dean, 2004; Brine, 2006). This may be due to a higher number of electronic resources being available free on the web, but also to – temporarily - increasing numbers of electronic journal subscriptions in libraries. On the other side, decreasing or stagnating library budgets cause journal cancellations. Libraries evaluating their journal subscriptions on a cost per use basis have partly replaced subscriptions by covering the ILL and document delivery costs for their users. This may again result in a higher number of ILL and document delivery requests for materials not available via the local library.

Data about the quantity and quality of ILL and document delivery have always been collected widely. ILL data have frequently been used for managing the collection:

- Identifying gaps in the collection
- Cancelling or ordering journals
- Finding a balance between giving and taking in library cooperation

Evaluating the quality of ILL and document delivery services can focus on different issues. "There is a general agreement that fill rate, turnaround time, cost and user satisfaction are the four primary criteria for evaluating ILL and document supply" (Stein, 2001, p.11).

The difficulty for measuring the performance of ILL and document delivery services is that only part of the performance can be influenced by the individual library. If a requesting library measures either the fill rate of requests (the number of successfully completed requests) or the "turnaround time" (the time between the initiation and the completion of a request), it will for the most part be measuring the performance of other institutions, namely the supplying libraries and – if applicable – the transport system (postal service or library courier services).

When evaluating the speed of delivery, a number of projects have assessed the total supply time ("turnaround time") for an ILL or document delivery request, starting from the requesting library. This would include (Line, 1991):

1. Request processing by the borrowing library
2. Request transmission
3. Processing by the supplying library (retrieval from shelves, copying etc.)
4. Supply transmission
5. Handling of supplied item in the requesting library

, Today, self-initiated user requests may go directly to a supplying library. The location of the requested item has either been verified in the online catalogues, or link resolvers lead from a citation in a database to a catalogue search and to an ILL or document delivery request. Request transmission will not be a time factor in online ILL or document delivery. The most important issue for the delivery speed will be the time taken in the delivering library. Therefore, this indicator measures the speed and quality of processes in the delivering library.

Definition of the indicator

The average time needed for completing an interlibrary loan or document delivery transaction in the lending/delivering library. The time is counted in hours, considering only the working hours of the interlibrary loan department.

The transaction starts when the library receives a request and ends when either the item is despatched to the requesting library/user, or when the library/user is notified about delivery not being possible (item unavailable for loan, missing, at the bindery, etc.), if the system did not notify this. The end is **not** the time when the requesting party receives the item.

Transactions include returnable items as well as non-returnable items (copies) and all methods of transmission (e.g. postal delivery, fax, electronic delivery).

The indicator includes mediated and end-user initiated interlibrary loan and document delivery, delivery from libraries to other libraries and delivery directly to individual users.

Document delivery from commercial suppliers is excluded.

Aims of the indicator

The indicator assesses whether the delivering services are efficiently organized, and what priority the library gives to its role in interlibrary cooperation.

The indicator does not intend to measure the success or fill rate of requests.

The indicator is relevant for all libraries participating in interlibrary loan and document delivery services.

Comparison between delivering libraries is possible, if the different methods of transmission are taken into account.

Method

The library chooses a sampling time with normal activity. All incoming requests are noted on a manual recording sheet as to:
- Date and time a request is received (in any format)
- Date and time the requested item is forwarded to the requesting library/user
- Or: Date and time the library/user is notified of the non-availability

If the library's system is able to record all that information, no manual recording will be needed.

Requests for material that is not included in the library's collection should be deleted from the sample.

The hours needed for completing each transaction are calculated by counting only the business hours of the ILL department on the specific day/s.

The hours for completing all transactions in the sample are summed up and divided by the number of transactions in the sample.

A more detailed view of the delivery speed is possible, if delivery times are shown in cumulative distribution, e.g.:

Completion time	%
0 – 2 hours	10
2 – 4 hours	12
4 – 6 hours	30
6 – 10 hours	25
10 – 15 hours	12
> 15 hours	11

Transactions with especially long completion time should be followed up in order to find reasons for the delay. In many cases, this may be due to wrong citations, e.g. when a requested article cannot be found in the journal issue cited and the library has to verify the citation.

Special rush services for urgent requests should be evaluated separately.

Non-availability of a requested item can be due to the item being on loan, misshelved, in in-house use, at the bindery, or not available for external loan.

Interpretation and use of results

Delivery speed will be influenced by the type of material requested. Delivery of an article from an electronic journal will be quickest, if copyright laws and the library's treaty with the publisher permit electronic delivery. Copyright issues hindering electronic delivery from electronic resources in the library and demanding instead copy and fax delivery will considerably influence the delivery speed.

All activities like fetching materials from the shelves, copying and sending by fax or normal mail will naturally prolong the transaction. Requests for copies out of rare material will probably take longer, as special procedures have to be followed. The speed will also be influenced by storage conditions. If the requested item has to be fetched from remote storage, transportation time will be added to the total delivery time.

If the library wants to find more details about possible delays in the delivery, the transaction could be split up into several processes (Measuring the performance of document supply systems, 1987):

- Time between receipt of a request and the handling of it
- Time spent searching the catalogue (if no shelf mark was given in the request)
- Time involved in actual retrieval of the item
- Time spent copying, microfilming or digitizing in cases where the original is not sent
- Time spent packing the item
- Time between packing the item and its dispatch

Thus, possible backlogs or lengthy procedures in different departments can be identified.

The indicator is influenced by insufficient staffing for the lending activities, especially in peak times, and by staff competences, e.g. stack attendants' knowledge about the shelf-location system, locations of special collections etc.

Speed must not be the main criterion for user satisfaction with ILL and document delivery services, at least not for all researchers. While users in natural sciences and engineering generally want their material very quickly, users in human and social sciences might deem the reliability of delivery and the quality of the copies more important. Therefore, delivery speed could also be split up as to subjects.

For all users, costs will be a very important issue, and they may be content to wait for some days, if the fees they have to pay are low. Maurice Line proposes that "timeliness", a reasonable average speed of supply, might be the best quality issue (Line, 1991, p.7).

In order to decide whether the delivery speed coincides with users' wishes, user satisfaction with ILL and document delivery could be assessed by a survey in the requesting library.

If the delivery times are too long, the following measures could be taken:

- Updating records in the online catalogue (union catalogue) to make sure that for items that are missing or not available for loan this information appears in the catalogue
- Streamlining workflows
- Using as much automation of procedures as possible
- Training staff in issues of the shelf-location system, storage problems etc.

Examples and further reading

A survey of the literature on performance measurement for ILL and document delivery from 1986 to 1998 is given by Stein (2001).

Most libraries assessing the ILL and document delivery speed have measured the total turnaround time, from the time the user makes the request to the time the user is notified that either the requested item has arrived or is not available. Only a few projects show a breakdown of the delivery time into stages so that the supplying library's delivery time can be identified.

Turnaround time has been measured as well in working days as in calendar days.

An Australian benchmarking study in 2001 in 97 libraries of all types found an average turnaround time of 11.5 calendar days (National Resource Sharing Working Group, 2001), of which 6.3 days were the average time from the date the request was sent by the requesting library to the date the material or a negative response was received.

A study in the Nordic countries in 2001 found a turnaround time of 10.4 calendar days, of which 8.1 days were the average time from the date the request was sent by the requesting library to the date the material or a negative response was received (Vattulainen, 2001). Turnaround time was longer for returnables (books) = 13.0 days than for non-returnables (copies) = 9.8 days.

Several studies of the Association of Research Libraries show the difference made by the introduction of online procedures in ILL services (Jackson, 2003). Turnaround time for mediated borrowing dropped by about 50% since the 1996 study.

Borrowing turnaround time	1996	2002
Turnaround time mediated	16.9 days (loans) 14.9 days (copies)	9.29 days (loans) 6.23 days (copies)
Turnaround time user-initiated (loans)	--	2.30 – 8.23 days

In the ARL study of 2001/2002, "turnabout time for lending" was measured, the time between a library receiving and shipping a request (Assessing ILL/DD services, 2004). This corresponds to the indicator described above.

Lending turnaround time	Calendar days
User-initiated requests	0.1 – 1.5 days
Mediated requests	1.5 days

A study in publicly-funded Tennessee colleges and universities in 1995 with 25 libraries cooperating looked at the different steps in ILL. "Lending turnaround time" (from the lending library receiving the order to shipping the item) was about one day (Phillips et al., 1999).

Delivery times were also evaluated for "Impala", the Belgian electronic document ordering system for research libraries (van Borm, Corthouts and Philips, 2000). Turnaround time was split into several segments, of which the segment "busy to success" includes the time from the moment the delivering library first looks at the request to the time when the requested item has been set ready for supply. The results show a growing speed of delivery time.

Busy to success =< 2 days	%
1994	41
1995	45
1996	56
1997	57
1998	63

Most studies have not assessed the speed of ILL and document delivery separately, but together with other quality measures like fill rate, cost per transaction, or user satisfaction.

Assessing ILL/DD services: new cost-effective alternatives, *ARL Bimonthly Report* 236, available at: http://www.arl.org/bm~doc/illstudy.pdf

Brine, J. (2006), The history of interlending and document supply in the UK, in Bradford, J. and Brine, J. (eds.), Interlending and document supply in Britain today, Chandos Publishing, Oxford

Goodier, R. and Dean, E. (2004), Changing patterns in interlibrary loan and document supply, *Interlending & Document Supply* 32, 4, pp. 206-214

Jackson, M. E. (2003), Assessing ILL/DD services study: initial observations, *ARL Bimonthly Report* 230/231, available at: http://www.arl.org/bm~doc/illdd.pdf

Line, M. B. (1991), Performance measurement with interlending and document supply systems, in Gallico, A. (Ed.), Interlending and document supply, proceedings of the second international conference, held in London, November 1990, British Library, London, pp. 5-13

Measuring the performance of document supply systems (1987), Prepared by the IFLA International Office for UAP, Unesco, Paris

National Resource Sharing Working Group (2001), Interlibrary loan and document delivery benchmarking study, National Library of Australia, available at: http://www.nla.gov.au/initiatives/nrswg/illdd_rpt.pdf

Phillips, L.L. et al. (1999), Interlibrary loan turnaround time: measuring the component parts, *Journal of Interlibrary Loan, Document Delivery & Information Supply.* 9,2, pp. 97-121

Stein, J. (2001), Measuring the performance of ILL and document supply: 1986 to 1998, *Performance Measurement and Metrics* 2,1, pp. 11-72

Van Borm, J., Corthouts, J. and Philips, R. (2000), Performance measurement in the Belgian document ordering and delivery system Impala, *Scientometrics* 47,2, pp. 207-225

Vattulainen, P. (2001), Nordic study of performance measurement of interlibrary loan and document delivery services, Nordic University and Research Libraries, available at: http://www.nrl.fi/nvbf/nordicpm.htm

C.12 Reference fill rate

Background

"Reference work is not **the** most important library service, but it ranks near the top."(Høivik 2003, p.2). The importance and the responsibilities of reference services differ between countries and sometimes between types of libraries. Libraries in Anglo-American countries have been more liable to consider the reference desk as a focal point than those in Europe, and while public libraries generally see it as their duty to directly deliver the information the user asks for, academic libraries tend to content themselves with showing the way to find that information.

Though reference service is seen as important, statistics of reference activities are still scarce. Looking into ten national library statistics (Europe, Australia and the ARL statistics), only half of them try to count reference transactions; and if the national statistics prescribe counting reference transactions, only part of the libraries deliver the data, even if sampling is allowed.

Example:
In the German library statistics for academic libraries 2006, only 68 of 224 participating libraries delivered data for reference transactions in their library (DBS. Deutsche Bibliotheksstatistik).

While already the quantity of reference transactions is often unknown, this is even more the case for the quality of reference answers. Yet the issue of reference quality has been discussed for decades, and there is a multitude of publications about reference service in general (Saxton and Richardson, 2002b) or digital reference (Smith, 2002; Wasik, 2005).

Quality of reference services has different aspects:
- Accuracy (of the information given)
- Utility, usefulness or relevance of the information in the user's view
- Satisfaction of the user (as well with the answer as with the reference transaction)

Accuracy, rated by experts, will in most cases be lower than usefulness (rated by users) and user satisfaction. Users tend to be satisfied if they have learned or found something they think relevant, not knowing that they may have missed more important information, or that the information they got was incorrect. User satisfaction also depends very much on staff behaviour (empathy, friendliness, apparent competence).

Reference questions address different topics. They can be subdivided into the following:

- Factual questions: Users ask for facts or data, e.g.
  - the etymological origin of a name,
  - the longest river in a country,
  - the year of an event.
- Subject (topical) questions: Users ask for advice on sources or reading about a subject, e.g.
  - a sociological method,
  - a political question,
  - an author.
- Document questions: Users ask for specific documents or their use, e.g.
  - a specific article or book,
  - the contents of a specific database,
  - search options in the online catalogue.

A study of 500 digital questions in Oslo Public Library showed the following differentiation (Høivik, 2003, p.4):

- subject   = 71%
- document = 19%
- factual   = 11%

The percentage of factual questions seems to be higher in public libraries than in academic libraries. "Public libraries offer more direct, fact-based answers, unencumbered by the need to teach the methodology of searching as a primary motivation." (Meserve, 2006, p.32) A study in a German university library in 1999 showed only 5.8% of factual questions (Scholle, 2000). Users apparently did not expect to get direct facts, but help in their search procedures. In the future, factual questions might even decrease, as users search for facts directly in the Internet. Tests of reference accuracy should therefore not focus on factual questions.

Today, traditional face-to-face reference is complemented by e-mail or online (chat) reference and cooperative online reference. The different forms of digital reference show varying advantages and disadvantages (Roesch, 2006). Guidelines for digital reference have been edited by several library associations (ALA, 2004 and 2006; IFLA, 2005). Publications on performance indicators for digital reference focus on staff skills and user satisfaction (Booth, Dawes and Kigbo, 2004; UNISON, 2006).

For reference transactions in electronic form, it is much easier to check what has been done in the transaction and whether the user got the right answer or was directed to the relevant resource for finding information. Questions and answers can be stored, and a sample of reference transactions can be evaluated without disturbing the reference interview or conducting time-consuming surveys. But it might be more difficult than in face-to-face interviews to get a definite notion of the specific user's needs.

Definition of the indicator

The percentage of reference questions that is answered correctly

Reference questions can regard facts, documents, or advice on sources for the user's subject.

The definition excludes directional and administrative inquiries, e.g. for locating staff or facilities, regarding opening times, about handling equipment such as reader printers or computer terminals, using self-service functions, or locating items of stock that have already been identified bibliographically.

Aims of the indicator

The indicator assesses the quality of the reference service in terms of accuracy and completeness of the supplied information. It does not measure:

- The usefulness of the supplied information to the user
- The user's satisfaction with the reference interview
- The speed of the reference transaction
- The quality of staff behaviour

The indicator is relevant for all libraries offering reference and information services. Comparison of results between libraries with similar clientele is possible, if the same method of data collection has been used.

Methods

This handbook recommends two methods for assessing reference fill rate (accuracy). In both methods, directional and administrative questions are excluded. Typical such questions are:

- Where is the next copying machine?
- How can I get a user card?
- What time is the library open?
- Who can help me to use the scanner?

If a reference interview addresses several questions, each question should be evaluated separately.

Method 1: Set of questions with predefined answers

Library experts choose a set of questions that mirror typical questions in academic or public libraries. The set should contain factual, subject and document questions in the distribution that seems appropriate to the library. If libraries have collected specified statistics as to the kind of questions asked in their reference service, this will be easier. The number of questions depends on the differentiation of user groups the library has to serve and therewith the variety of questions usually asked at the library's reference desk.

The correct answers to the questions must be added to the set. It should be checked that the library owns or has access to resources that would enable staff to answer correctly.

The questions should be pre-tested in order to avoid ambiguities and to decide on the different options of categorizing answers as correct or incorrect.

The method used for testing the set is unobtrusive observation (Hernon and McClure, 1986a). Proxy users (surrogate users) put the questions to the reference staff, either in face-to-face interviews or by phone, e-mail, or in an online reference service. In most cases, students have been used as proxies. They should be trained in order to guarantee the unobtrusiveness and uniformity of the reference interview. The interaction between reference staff and proxy should be as normal as possible, therefore proxy users must be convincing. The questioning should be spread over the day/week to include peak times and times with low use.

After finishing the interview, proxies should record carefully the procedure and outcome of the reference transaction. For questions put in electronic form it will be easy to keep a record of the reference interview for evaluation.

To avoid moral objections of staff members, the test should be strictly anonymous. The proxies should not note the name of the staff member. The reference staff as a whole is tested, not the individual staff member. Collaboration with staff representatives will be useful. If the library management decides that the study should be pre-announced, this should be done somewhat earlier and without defining the point of time of the study, so that staff behaviour will not be influenced.

After the interviews, the answers are rated by library experts. Whether an answer is rated as correct depends on what the library's reference policy aims at. Basically, there are two ways of answering questions:

- Telling the users directly the facts, bibliographical records etc. they are seeking for
- Telling the users the best way to find the answers themselves

In academic libraries, naming and/or showing the source where the user can find the information will in most cases be seen as correct answer.

As the correct answers have been predefined, evaluation of answers could be simple:

- Correct answer = fully correct; all aspects covered; user referred to the right sources
- Incorrect answer = simply wrong; only partially correct; not all aspects covered; user referred to wrong sources

The answer "don't know" without referral to other persons/sources would be counted as incorrect. If the user gets no answer at all (librarian too busy, user asked to return later), this should not be counted in the sample; the question should be put again at a later time.

The reference fill rate is the percentage of correct answers of all answers.

If more complicated questions have been used in the set, or if the library wants to know more details about failures and success, a more differentiated scoring could be used (Elzy et al., 1991).

- Fully correct; all aspects covered; users referred to sources that provided the right answer
- Partly correct; not all aspects covered; users sent to resources that provided only part of the answer
- Partly incorrect; users sent to inappropriate sources
- Simply wrong; question not answered without referral to other sources/persons

In order to calculate the reference fill rate, answers scoring 1 or 2 should be rated as correct, 3 or 4 as incorrect.

Method 1 is easy to use and not too time-consuming, but it does not consider ambiguous or open-ended questions occurring in actual reference service nor the often lengthy procedures where user and librarian join in seeking relevant sources. But if the choice of questions is adequate to the library's population, the results will suffice to get an insight into reference accuracy.

Method 2: A sample of actual questions in electronic form

This method uses a random sample of actual questions. There are no predefined answers as in the first method; therefore questions in electronic form should be preferred, as the answer and/or the whole reference interview can be stored and evaluated.

A team of experts rates the procedures and answers. In many cases, additional searches in sources will be needed to find the "right" answer/s. The time needed for evaluation will be higher than in the first method. When rating answers as "correct" or "incorrect", it should be kept in mind that an answer need not always cover all information possible for the topic, but that answers should be adequate to the specific user's need. An undergraduate writing a paper on "evidence-based medicine" will need some general sources to start from, while for a doctoral dissertation a graduate student will be glad to find specialized articles about that subject. If the protocol of the reference transaction shows that the referral to one source was what the user needed, that should be counted as correct.

The advantage of the method is that the questions are representative of the real situation, and that a high number of reference interviews can be evaluated. Reference questions put to staff members outside reference staff (e.g. subject specialists) could be included. But it should be kept in mind that answering questions in written form will make staff take more pains. Experience shows that answers in written form tend to be more correct, probably because the answering person feels that the answer might be controlled.

The problem of the method is that questions in electronic form, issued from home or the workplace, might be of a more complicated nature than point-of-use questions occurring when users work in the library. Questions could be ambiguous; several answers might be possible. There will be "escalator questions" (Christenson et al., 1989), requiring several steps to clarify the user's questions, as users tend to start with broader topics than they really seek. Therefore a simple rating of answers as "correct" or "incorrect" will not be possible; scoring should be more differentiated as shown above in method 1.

Method 2 will give a better insight into the causes of failure and success in reference service, e.g. what procedures staff followed in order to clarify the question, whether the user was referred to another person or library, and what the attitude of the staff was.

Interpretation and use of results

A high accuracy rate will be considered as good. But when interpreting the results, it must be kept in mind that the decision whether an answer is counted as correct or incorrect may be subjective, especially if actual questions are used.

The outcome of the reference interview can be influenced by
- staff skills (including communication skills),
- the users' skills (familiarity with the library, experience in information seeking; especially the ability to explain what they want to know),
- the point of time of the interview (especially busy times, long queues waiting),
- the variety and accessibility of reference sources,
- and – of course – the difficulty of the questions.

A low reference fill rate points to
- an inadequate reference collection,
- insufficient equipment of the reference desk,
- lack of staff skills,
- insufficient staffing at the reference desk, especially at peak times,
- low priority of the reference service in the library's policy.

More detailed information about reasons for failure could be gained from following the procedure of the reference interview (e.g. which sources were checked, or whether the user was asked to explain the question).

Expertise in conducting reference interviews can lead to higher accuracy. A study in Maryland in 1983 found that closing the reference transaction with "Does this answer your question?" increased the accuracy of answers from 52 to 76 percent (Gers and Seward, 1985).

It should always be borne in mind that this indicator measures only one aspect of reference service quality, namely accuracy. It is advisable to compare the results with users' rating of reference quality by conducting user satisfaction surveys. But accuracy is certainly the most important aspect of reference quality, though a well-conducted reference interview and empathy of reference staff can help to reach accuracy. Incorrect answers given by reference staff can have negative outcome on users' work, as users tend to believe in the competence of this service. Even if a user has got an incorrect or incomplete answer, he "may believe that because the service is providing the answer, that this, in some way, ensures correctness, definitiveness, or comprehensiveness." (McClure et al., 2002, p.41)

Examples and further reading

An overview of studies on reference accuracy till 1995 is given by Lorene Roy (Roy, 1995).

Using the indicator "reference fill rate" with a set of **predefined questions and answers and unobtrusive observation** has a long tradition. In 1986, a paper of Hernon and McClure (1986b) announced the startling result that reference staff generally answered only 50 to 60% of questions correctly – the famous "55% rule". This of course caused a vehement debate, especially as user surveys showed high satisfaction with reference service, and the 55%-rule was contradicted by studies that, by using other methods, found much higher accuracy rates. Even Thomas Childers, one of the two graduate students conducting the first unobtrusive reference studies in 1967 (Crowley and Childers, 1971), twenty years later cautioned against "oversimplification" when judging reference service quality (Childers, 1987). Still, as the method proved simple and – for its purpose – reliable, it has been used regularly. A study in 104 public and academic libraries in Canada in 1997/98, using questions related to government documents, resulted in only 29.3% of correct (complete) answers, 42.4% if partly complete answers were included (Dilevko, 2000).

A pilot study for assessing the quality of chat reference with unobtrusive observation was conducted in the University of Maryland (White, Abels and Kaske, 2003). A set of predefined questions, including "escalator" questions, was tested both in a public and an academic library. Answers were rated as accurate, if the proxies (experienced searchers) were able to locate the right answer in the sources the reference staff named. With this definition, accuracy reached 75%.

Other projects have used **actual reference questions** for assessing accuracy. Saxton and Richardson asked: "How can half-right reference service be found to have high utility and give great satisfaction to users?" (Richardson, 2002; Saxton and Richardson, 2002b). They evaluated 3500 actual questions in 12 public libraries with an expert panel that rated 90% of answers as correct (accurate source or accurate strategy). Comparing accuracy with other variables of the reference transaction, the only variable that was found to predict accuracy was the difficulty of the query.

Asking reference staff to rate the accuracy of their own answers resulted in high accuracy rates, as staff would naturally be convinced of working effectively (Rothstein, 1964).

An evaluation program asking both staff and users to rate reference quality is the Wisconsin-Ohio Reference Evaluation Program (WOREP) that uses actual reference interviews and survey forms for staff and users for detailed assessment of the success. WOREP has even set up quality criteria for success (Stalker and Murfin, 1996):

- poor   0 – 50.99 % successful
- fair   51 – 54.99 % successful
- adequate   55 – 59.99 % successful
- good   60 – 64.99 % successful
- very good   65 – 69.99 % successful
- excellent   70% plus successful

When WOREP was used in 110 academic libraries (Havener and Murfin, 1998), "satisfaction with what was found" reached 70.95%, but "success in finding exactly what was wanted" only 57.99%, which is not higher than the accuracy rate found in unobtrusive observation studies.

A great part of reference quality studies have focussed not on accuracy of the answers, but on **user satisfaction and on the usefulness of answers** as seen by users. In some cases, proxy users have been employed for putting questions out of their own study subjects and rating friendliness and competence of staff, the usefulness of the answer, their own satisfaction with the reference interview and their "willingness to return" to the same staff member with another question. Two examples are cited here (Dewdney and Ross, 1994; Spribille, 1998). Though "usefulness of the answer" scored only between 38.2 and 47 %, between 59.7 and 64 % of users were willing to return to the same staff person another time. Satisfaction is apparently highly influenced by staff behaviour. In another study with unobtrusive testing (but without accuracy rating), satisfaction with the answer received reached 48 % (Gatten and Radcliff, 2001). In most studies trying to assess user satisfaction, user surveys or interviews have been applied, especially exit surveys when the user leaves the reference desk or the library.

Other studies have measured the **duration of the reference interview** in order to assess whether length of time has an influence on the accuracy of answers. Results differed. While in the Canadian study mentioned above the number of complete or partially complete answers increased with the amount of time spent on the interview (Dilevko, 2001, p.54), Hernon and McClure found no statistically significant relation (Hernon and McClure, 1986b, p.39), but experienced a sort of "internal clock" that seemed to impede staff to spend more than a certain time on a reference interview (Hernon and McClure, 1987).

Waiting time for access to reference staff has also been evaluated in the context of reference service quality, as it will certainly influence user satisfaction. A study in a Canadian university library recorded on average about two minutes of waiting time (Tillotson, Adlington and Holt, 1997). A study in Northampton (Martin, 1998) collected more differentiated data:

- 0 – 2 min   =   98%
- 2 – 5 min   =   7%
- 5 – 10 min =   1%

All in all, literature on reference quality is by now so extensive, that only a few studies can be named that have initiated new methods in assessing quality or that can be seen as typical examples.

ALA. American Library Association. Reference and User Services Association (2004), Guidelines for implementing and maintaining virtual reference services, available at: http://www.ala.org/ala/rusa/rusaprotools/referenceguide/virtrefguidelines.htm

ALA. American Library Association. Reference and User Services Association (2006), Guidelines for cooperative reference services, available at: http://www.ala.org/ala/rusa/rusaprotools/referenceguide/guidelinescooperative.htm

Benham, F. et al. (1995), The Reference assessment manual, American Library Association, Evaluation of Reference and Adult Services Committee, Pierian Press, Ann Arbor, Michigan

Booth, D., Dawes, E. and Kigbo, F. (2004), Performance indicators for digital research and information services, University of Newcastle, Australia, available at: http://www.caul.edu.au/best-practice/PerfInd.html

Childers, T. (1987), The quality of reference: still moot after 20 years, *Journal of Academic Librarianship* 13,2 , pp. 73-74

Christenson, J. O. et al. (1989), An evaluation of reference desk service, *College & Research Libraries* 50,4, pp. 468-483

Crowley, T. and Childers, T. (1971), Information service in public libraries: two studies, Scarecrow, Metuchen.

DBS. Deutsche Bibliotheksstatistik, Hochschulbibliothekszentrum, Köln, available at: http://www.hbz-nrw.de/angebote/dbs/

Dewdney, P. and Sheldrick Ross, C. (1994), Flying a light aircraft: reference service evaluation from a user's viewpoint, Reference Quarterly 34, pp. 217-230, available at: http://www.ala.org/ala/rusa/rusapubs/rusq/specialfeatures/rspawardwinning/1996/1996.ht m

Dilevko, J. (2000), Unobtrusive evaluation of reference service and individual responsibility, Ablex, Westport, Conn.

Elzy, C. et al. (1991), Evaluating reference service in a large academic library, *College & Research Libraries* 52, pp. 454-464

Gatten, J. N. and J. Radcliff, C. J. (2001), Assessing reference behaviours with unobtrusive testing, in Wallace, D. P. and Van Fleet, C., Library evaluation, a casebook and can-do guide, Libraries Unlimited , Englewood, Colo., pp. 105-115

Gers, R. and Seward, L. J. (1985), Improving reference performance: results of a statewide study, *Library Journal* 110, Nov.1, pp. 32-35

Havener, W. M. and Murfin, M. E. (1998), Cronbach revisited: a powerful enemy to validity in library services, *Proceedings of the 2ⁿᵈ Northumbria International Conference on Performance Measurement in Libraries and Information Services,* Newcastle upon Tyne, pp. 139-155

Hernon, P. and McClure, C.R. (1986a), Unobtrusive testing and library reference services, Ablex, Westport, Conn.

Hernon, P. and McClure, C.R. (1986b), Unobtrusive reference testing: the 55% rule, *Library Journal* 111,7 , pp. 37-41

Hernon, P. and McClure, C.R. (1987), Library reference service: an unrecognized crisis – a symposium, *Journal of Academic Librarianship* 13,2, pp. 69-71

Høivik, T. (2003), Why is quality control so hard? Reference studies and reference quality in public libraries: the case of Norway, *World Library and Information Congress: 69ᵗʰ IFLA General Conference and Council,* available at: http://www.ifla.org/IV/ifla69/papers/131e-Hoivik.pdf

IFLA (2005), Digital reference guidelines, available at: http://www.ifla.org/VII/s36/pubs/drg03.htm

Martin, A. (1998), Setting standards for enquiry desk operations: a case study, *Proceedings of the 2ⁿᵈ Northumbria International Conference on Performance Measurement in Libraries and Information Services,* Newcastle upon Tyne, pp. 165-171

McClure, C. R. et al. (2002), Statistics, measures, and quality standards for assessing digital reference library services, guidelines and procedures, School of Information Studies, Syracuse N.Y.

Meserve, H. (2006), Evolving reference, changing culture: the Dr. Martin Luther King, Jr. Library and reference challenges ahead, in Anderson, B. and Webb, P.T. (eds.), New directions in reference, Haworth Press, Binghamton, N.Y., pp. 23-40

Richardson, J. V. (2002), Reference is better than we thought, *Library Journal*, 127,7 , pp. 41-42, available at: http://www.libraryjournal.com/article/CA206407.html

Roesch, H. (2006), Digital reference services: state of the art in the focus on quality, *World Library and Information Congress: 72ndIFLA General Conference and Council,* available at: http://www.ifla.org/IV/ifla72/papers/098-Roesch-en.pdf

Rothstein, S. (1964), The measurement and evaluation of reference service, *Library Trends* 12, pp. 456-472

Roy, L. (1995), Reference accuracy, *The Reference Librarian* 49/50, pp. 217-227

Saxton, M. and Richardson, J.J. (2002a), Understanding reference transactions: transforming an art into science, Academic Press, Amsterdam

Saxton, M. and Richardson, J. J. (2002b), Understanding reference transactions: transforming an art into science. Suppl. (1.000 citations), available at: http://polaris.gseis.ucla.edu/jrichardson/dis220/urt.htm

Scholle, U. (2000), Kann ich Ihnen behilflich sein? Erhebung am zentralen Auskunftsplatz der ULB Münster, *Bibliotheksdienst* 34,1, pp. 39-48

Smith, J. (2002), The Reference Interview: connecting in-person and in cyberspace, a selective bibliography from the 2002 President's Program, available at: http://www.ala.org/ala/rusa/rusapubs/pastpresidentpro/20023/selectivebibliography.htm

Spribille, I. (1998), Die Wahrscheinlichkeit, in einer Bibliothek eine nützliche bzw. zufriedenstellende Antwort zu bekommen, ist „fifty-fifty", *Bibliothek* 22,1, pp. 106-110.

Stalker, J. C. and Murfin, M.E. (1996), Quality reference service: a preliminary case study, *Journal of Academic Librarianship* 22,6 , pp. 423-429

Tillotson, J., Adlington, J. and Holt, C. (1997), Benchmarking waiting time, *College & Research Libraries News* 58,10, pp. 693-694, 700

UNISON (2006), Digital reference key performance indicators, project report, available at: http://www.caul.edu.au/best-practice/reference.html

Wasik, J. M. (2005), Digital reference bibliography, available at:
http://www.webjunction.org/do/DisplayContent?id=11878

White, M. D., Abels, E.G. and Kaske, N. (2003), Evaluation of chat reference service quality:
pilot study, *D-Lib Magazine* 9,2, available at:
http://www.dlib.org/dlib/february03/white/02white.html

WOREP. Wisconsin Ohio Reference Evaluation Program, available at:
http://worep.library.kent.edu/

C.13 Shelving accuracy

Background

Though "shelving accuracy" may not be a fashionable performance indicator in times of growing electronic services, correct shelving remains essential for the availability of the library's physical collection. User satisfaction surveys show that the issue "materials in their proper place" ranks high in users' wishes (Harwood and Bydder, 1998).

Incorrect shelving will not only affect user satisfaction, but will also be the cause of much unnecessary effort in the library. "While a shelf-reading program requires an investment of work hours and funds that must compete with other needs for dollars and time, not shelf-reading costs the patrons access and costs the library time and money in conducting missing book searches, processing interlibrary loans, and purchasing duplicate copies ..." (Anderson, 1998, p.2).

Definition of the indicator

The percentage of documents that are in their correct place on the shelves at the time of investigation

Aims of the indicator

The indicator assesses the accuracy of the library's shelving and shelf monitoring procedures and therewith the availability of documents for the user. It does not measure the speed of shelving.

The indicator is applicable for all libraries with physical collections. It can be used for collections in free or closed access, for special parts of the collection or for branch libraries.

Comparisons between libraries are possible, if differences in storing (free or closed access) and in the frequency of use are taken into consideration.

Method

Check a sample of shelves with the help of a shelf-list. Usually, libraries will not check their whole collection, but will choose a certain part of the collection, e.g. the children's library, the collection of rare material, a subject collection like medicine or history.

Documents waiting for shelving should be reshelved before counting.

Record for each document in the list whether it is shelved correctly. It is advisable to search also behind the documents to detect items that have been pushed back. Documents found near their correct place are also counted as misplaced. For serials or monographs with several volumes, each physical unit counts as one document.

For missing documents, check in the library system whether the absence is accounted for (the document is on loan, sent to the bookbinder, noted as lost etc.). Missing documents accounted for are excluded from the sample. Missing documents not accounted for are counted as misplaced. The count thus includes the documents that have been misplaced as well as those that are lost (e.g. stolen), but not yet noted as lost. Thus, the indicator measures not only the accuracy of the shelving procedures, but also the effectiveness of shelf monitoring.

Shelves in free access areas should be checked outside opening times in order to include documents that have been used inside the library.

If all items in a collection are equipped with barcodes, scanning tools and wireless technology might be used instead of shelf-lists. This makes the checking process easier for staff. While the barcodes of the items on the shelves are scanned, a direct connection to the library's integrated system shows

- whether items are in the correct order,
- whether missing items are accounted for by the system.

The shelving accuracy is affected by open access for users and by the frequency of use. In free access collections or during peak times of use (e.g. end of the term in universities), more items may be misshelved. Collection parts in high use and/or in free access should therefore be checked separately from collection parts with low use and/or in closed magazines.

Journal collections should also be checked separately, as the volumes are less likely to be misshelved.

The time required for using the indicator will depend on

- the library's shelf-location system,
- the kind of collection surveyed,
- the expertise of the staff in the project,
- the number of missing documents that have to be followed up,
- the accuracy of the catalogue (shelf-list).

The shelving accuracy is the percentage of all documents in the sample that are in their correct place at the time of investigation.

Interpretation and use of results

High shelving accuracy will be considered as good.

Low shelving accuracy can be caused by
- careless or hasty shelving,
- a complicated shelf-location system,
- infrequent shelf-reading.

Actions taken in order to achieve higher accuracy could be
- better instruction of shelving staff (often part-time staff or student assistants),
- a higher number of shelving staff during peak times,
- a more transparent shelf-location system,
- regular shelf-reading procedures.

The results of the indicator do not only point to errors in shelving and failures in shelf-reading, but in following up missing items can also help to improve catalogue accuracy.

As shelving or shelf reading is tedious work, motivating shelving staff is important. It should be demonstrated that correct shelving is crucial for the accessibility of the collection, and that shelving errors can cause considerable additional workload.

Examples and further reading

Though probably most libraries use procedures for checking shelving accuracy, literature about practical experiences in this sector is not abundant. "Shelving is mundane, lacking the high-wire excitement of ... technical topics en vogue." (Kendrick, 1991, p.16). Apart from the indicator described above, the following methods have been used:
- Checking a sample of titles that have been actually ordered by users. This is usually done in the frame of an availability study.
- Checking only the sequence of documents on the shelves, without the help of a shelf-list. With this method, missing documents are not considered.
- Choosing a sample of documents waiting to be shelved and checking the shelving accuracy after shelving. This method measures only the accuracy of the shelving staff and disregards documents misshelved by users.
- Taking a random sample of titles out of a specified collection and checking them on the shelves.

The following table shows examples of shelf checking results that may help to find the "acceptable level of error" (Kendrick, 1991, p.17).

Library	Year of survey	Method of survey	Shelving accuracy
Wiesbaden Polytechnics Library (Poll, 1997, p.21)	1995	A sample of titles ordered by users; missing books included	94 %
Pretoria University of South Africa Library (Poll, 1997, p.21)	1995	Same method	98 %
Münster University Library (Poll, 1997, p.21)	1995	Same method	97,5 %
Dublin City University Library (EQLIPSE)	1996	A sample of 1.000 volumes (books and journals); checking the sequence of documents on the shelves; absent documents were not counted as misshelved	89,4 %
Copenhagen Business School Library (EQLIPSE)	1996	Same method	97 %
University of Central Lancashire Library (EQLIPSE)	1996	Same method	98 %
Münster University Library (EQLIPSE)	1996	Same method	98,6 %
Briscoe Library, University of Texas (Pedersen, 1989)	1988	Only the sequence of documents on the shelves was checked.	95,9 %
Leeds Metropolitan, Derby, Staffordshire and Huddersfield University Learning Centre (Everest, 2003)	200/01 and 2001/02	Only the sequence of documents on the shelves was checked.	between 95,4 and 98,4 %
University of Virginia Library (White, 1999)	1999	Shelf reading in 5 subject areas	between 91 and 96,7 %
Greenblatt Library, Medical College of Georgia (Rodgers, 1998)	1998	10-12 items on every truck ready for shelving were selected and checked after shelving.	98 %
Brigham Young University Library (Sharp, 1992)	1988/89	Each day in the sample period, 30 items were checked after shelving for each shelver.	90,8 % and 91,4 %
State University of New York Library (Kendrick,1991, p.17)	1988	5 items on every truck ready for shelving were selected and checked after shelving.	91 %
William Paterson College Library (Ciliberti, 1987)	1985	Includes missing books and books waiting to be reshelved.	74 %
University of Illinois Library (Weible, 2005)	2005	A random sample of 586 titles of 6.491 PhD dissertation titles was checked	93 %

Shelving accuracy will probably be higher if only the sequence on the shelves is checked and absent documents are not considered. If documents waiting to be shelved are included in the "misshelving" counts, shelving accuracy will appear much lower. Though of course backlogs in shelving can frustrate users, it would not be logical to count the waiting documents as misshelved.

Shelving errors could be differentiated as to:

- Minor errors (books out of place, but still on the correct shelf or the shelf immediately before or after)
- Major errors (all others)

Especially in collections with free access, the number of minor errors will be much higher than that of major errors. A study at the University of Illinois showed a ratio of 18.15 minor errors to one major error (Anderson, 1998, p.12). Minor errors would probably cause less trouble, as the documents could be found in a short search.

A recent study in the University of Illinois differentiated again between "slightly misshelved" and "not found" (Weible, 2005), but was conducted in a collection of PhD dissertations. 2.05 % were slightly misshelved, 4.95 % were not found at all. This study also reports about the time needed for checking shelf availability. One student spent 35 hours for the three phases: looking titles up in the OPAC, physically searching for materials, and entering the results into a spreadsheet. The example shows that checking correct shelving must not be time-consuming.

Eastern Illinois University Library uses a "Library Stacks Management System" that automatically generates and stores a shelf-list and a status-list for the collection part that is checked (Sung, Lanham and Sung, 2006). Staff members scan the barcodes using a scanner attached to a laptop that is wirelessly connected to the server. During the scanning process, the system alerts the operator if the items are out of order or not found and not accounted for in the system. The system also calculates the distance of misplacement. Scanning of 102.000 books showed a misshelving rate of 6.6%; over 72% of the misplaced books were found within a range of 1 to 10 books.

Speed of reshelving is a different issue and should be assessed separately. In a survey of 19 university libraries in 1999, University of Virginia Library found that the fastest "turnaround time" of documents from return desk to shelf was 4 hours (White, 1999). In a benchmarking project of four UK university learning centres, the site with the quickest reshelving times had reshelved 95 % within 14 hours (Everest, 2003, p. 44).

Some projects have also measured the average books shelved per hour per person. Brigham Young University Library had a shelving average of 230 to 253 books per hour; there was no relation between shelving average and level of accuracy (Sharp, 1992, p.187).

Generally, a shelving accuracy of 95% upwards seems to be attainable, depending on the storing and usage conditions of the collection part that is checked. The Copenhagen Business School Library reported a maximum rate of misshelved books fixed by the Library Board: 1-2 % in an UDC-based shelf arrangement system (Cotta-Schonberg and Line, 1994, p.61). This corresponds with the target value of 97% accuracy in the Hale Library, Kansas State University (Edwardy and Pontius, 2001).

Anderson, D. R. (1998), Method without madness: shelf-reading methods and project management, *College & Undergraduate Libraries* 5,1, pp .1-13

Ciliberti, A. C. et al. (1987), Material availability: a study of academic library performance, *College & Research Libraries* 48,6, pp. 513-527

Cotta-Schønberg, M. and Line, M. B. (1994), Evaluation of academic libraries: with special reference to the Copenhagen Business School Library, *Journal of Librarianship and Information Science* 26,2, p.55-69

Edwardy, J. M. and Pontius, J. S. (2001), Monitoring book reshelving in libraries using statistical sampling and control charts, *Library Resources & Technical Services* 45,2, pp. 90-94

EQLIPSE, Unpublished data collected within the Project EQLIPSE, project available at: http://www.cerlim.ac.uk/projects/eqlipse/

Everest, K. (2003), Benchmarking shelving processes 2000/01 and 2001/02, in Creaser, C. (Ed.), As others see us: benchmarking in practice, LISU, Loughborough University, *LISU Occasional Paper 33*, pp. 37-48, available at: http://www.lboro.ac.uk/departments/ls/lisu/downloads/OP33.pdf

Harwood, N. and Bydder, J. (1998), Student expectations of, and satisfaction with, the university library, *The Journal of Academic Librarianship* 24,2, pp. 161-171.

Kendrick, C. L (1991), Performance measures of shelving accuracy, *The Journal of Academic Librarianship* 17,1, pp. 16-18.

Pedersen, W. A. (1989), Statistical measures for shelf reading in an academic health science center library, *Bulletin of the Medical Library Association* 77,2, pp. 219-222.

Poll, R. (1997), Leistungsindikatoren für wissenschaftliche Bibliotheken, in Ressourcen nutzen für neue Aufgaben, *Zeitschrift für Bibliothekswesen und Bibliographie. Sonderheft* 66, Klostermann, Frankfurt a.M., pp. 15-22

Rodgers, J. (1998), The evaluation of correct shelving quality in the Robert B. Greenblatt, M.D. Library, available at: http://www.mcg.edu/Library/MLA/title.html

Sharp, S. C. (1992), A library shelver's performance evaluation as it relates to shelving accuracy, *Collection Management* 17, 1/2, pp. 177-192

Sung, J., Lanham, A. and Sung, N. (2006), Transforming data to build knowledge for healthy libraries, *World Library and Information Congress; 72nd IFLA General Conference and Council Seoul,* available at: http://www.ifla.org/IV/ifla72/papers/141-Sung_%20Lanham_Sung-en.pdf

Weible, C. L. (2005), Where have all the dissertations gone? Assessing the state of a unique collection's shelf (un)availability, *Collection Management* 30,1, pp. 55-62

White, L.S. (1999), Report on shelving process, University of Virginia Library Benchmarking Team, available at: http://www.lib.virginia.edu/mis/benchmarking/bench-shortrpt.html

D. Potentials and development

D.1 Percentage of acquisitions expenditure spent on the electronic collection

Background

Users today expect to have access to information resources from their workplace or home. They want not only to search for information in electronic sources, but to get the full view of a document that they think relevant on the screen.

Libraries worldwide are therefore offering a growing number of electronic resources in their collections, either by purchase or licensing agreements. This means that a considerable amount of funds is shifted from the traditional to the electronic collection. The hope of the funding institutions is generally that offering information resources in electronic form will save costs. Experience shows that acquisitions costs for electronic instead of print media will not be lower, and that possible savings in shelving and space will be made up by high IT equipment costs. But as electronic resources in most cases are more frequently used than traditional ones, higher usage can reduce the cost per use and thus improve the efficiency of the services.

The library's investment into its electronic collection is therefore seen as indicator not only for user-orientation, but also for efficiency and future-orientation.

Definition of the indicator

The percentage of acquisitions expenditure that is spent on the electronic collection.

Acquisitions expenditure in the sense of this indicator means the total expenditure for traditional and electronic media, including licenses and pay-per-view costs. Binding expenditure is excluded.

Expenditure on the electronic collection in the sense of this indicator comprises the library's acquisition, subscription and licensing costs for databases, electronic journals and digital documents, including pay-per-view costs.

Electronic document delivery costs are excluded.

Expenditure on infrastructure, such as hardware, software or networking, and on digitisation of documents is excluded.

Aims of the indicator

The indicator assesses the library's investment into electronic media and therewith the priority that the library gives to developing its electronic collection.

The indicator is relevant for all libraries with both print and electronic collections.

Comparison of results between libraries with similar mission, structure and clientele is possible, if differences in subjects and collection policies are taken into account and if the acquisitions expenditure is calculated in the same way.

Method

Determine the total acquisitions expenditure and as a subtotal the expenditure on the electronic collection during a year.

Where electronic versions of documents, especially journals, are acquired in a package with print versions, only the surplus payment for the electronic version should be counted.

If the library joins in consortia or other over-all contracts, only the library's own share in the contractual expenses should be counted.

Interpretation and use of results

A higher score will normally be considered as better, as it indicates high investment into new services. But what percentage of the library's acquisitions budget would be seen as appropriate for the electronic collection will be influenced by the library's collection subjects and clientele. In a medical library the percentage will be much higher than in a library of human sciences. In public libraries the percentage will generally be lower.

The indicator is influenced by

- the library's collection policies,
- the range of electronic publications available in the library's collection subjects,
- specialized needs of the population to be served,
- external means (e.g. special grants) for consortia.

If the percentage of acquisitions expenditure spent on the electronic collection seems too low, libraries could use the following methods to decide whether to invest more into electronic resources:

- Evaluate usage data for both print and electronic collections
- Evaluate interlibrary lending or document supply requests in order to adapt the acquisition policy to user needs
- Perform a user survey for assessing the market penetration of electronic services and the satisfaction with electronic resources

The indicator will be especially useful if applied consequently over years.

Examples and further reading

The German benchmarking project BIX (BIX. Der Bibliotheksindex) uses the indicator as described here for academic libraries. The results in 2005 were (BIX, 2006):

Percentage of expenditure for information provision spent on the electronic collection	mean	maximum	minimum
Universities of applied sciences	10,9	25,4	0,9
Universities: One-tier systems	19,3	43,8	8,8
Universities: Two-tier systems (only the central library considered)	26,9	72,7	4,5

The results show that the percentage can vary considerably, according to a library's subject collections and clientele.

The Finnish research library statistics for 2005 show for all research libraries "library material costs" of 28.964.900 €, of those for electronic resources 12.312.700 €, which is 42,5 %. For university libraries only, "library materials costs" are 20.996.500 €, of those for electronic material 10.790.200 €, which comes up to even 51,4 % (Finnish research libraries statistics database). Nearly the same percentage (50,64 %) was reported by the Netherlands university libraries in 2004 (UKB, 2004).

The statistics of the Association of Research Libraries show for 2003/04 the following percentages of expenditure for electronic materials of total library materials expenditure (Kyrillidou and Young, 2005):

- median = 37,53 %
- high = 76,89 %
- low = 9,71 %

In the Swiss university libraries 23,23 % of the acquisitions expenditure in 2005 were spent on electronic documents (Schweizerische Bibliothekenstatistik, 2005).

The Swedish research libraries show an extremely high percentage: In 2005, 58,4 % of acquisitions expenditure were spent on the electronic collection (Forskningsbiblioteken, 2005).

In public libraries the percentage is generally lower.

The UK public libraries had in 2003/04 a total acquisitions expenditure of 121.719.000 £ and 4.261.000 £ for electronic resources, which is 3,5 % for electronic resources (Creaser, 2006, p.37). Expenditure for electronic resources doubled since 1997/98 and increased by 63 % since 5 years.

The Swiss public library statistics show that in 2005 4,35 % of acquisitions expenditure were spent on electronic documents (Schweizerische Bibliothekenstatistik, 2005).

Public libraries in British Columbia, Canada, spent in 2003 6,72 % of acquisitions expenditure for "electronic information", that is for licensed online databases and subscriptions (British Columbia public library statistics, 2004).

When comparing the results of this indicator, it will be extremely important to compare only with libraries with similar collections and clientele and to calculate acquisitions expenditure in the same way.

BIX. Der Bibliotheksindex, available at: http://www.bix-bibliotheksindex.de/

BIX. Der Bibliotheksindex (2006), *B.I.T. online* Sonderheft 2006

British Columbia public library statistics (2004), Ministry of Education, Victoria, British Columbia, available at: http://www.bced.gov.bc.ca/pls/bcplstats_2004.pdf

Creaser, C., Maynard, S. and White, S. (2005), LISU annual library statistics 2005, featuring trend analysis of UK public and academic libraries 1994 – 2004, LISU, Loughborough University, available at: http://www.lboro.ac.uk/departments/dils/lisu/downloads/als05.pdf

Finnish research library statistics database, Helsinki University Library, available at: https://yhteistilasto.lib.helsinki.fi/language.do?action=change&choose_language=3

Forskningsbiblioteken 2005 (2005), KB/Bibsam och SCB, Sveriges officiella statistik, available at: http://www.scb.se/statistik/_publikationer/KU0102_2005A01_BR_KUFT0601.pdf

Schweizerische Bibliothekenstatistik (2005), Bundesamt für Statistik, available at:
http://www.bfs.admin.ch/bfs/portal/de/index/themen/kultur__medien__zeitverwendung/ku
ltur/blank/analysen__berichte/bibliotheken.html

UKB (2004), Benchmarking, Samenwerkingsverband van de Nederlandse
universiteitsbibliotheken en de Koninklijke Bibliotheek, results only available to
participants

D.2 Percentage of library staff providing and developing electronic services

Background

Libraries have to keep pace with the developments in information technology and information resources. They have to invest into new web-based services and products. The necessary investment will include equipment, hard- and software, space, and above all human resources.

There are no existing standards to tell what number or percentage of staff would be adequate for the task of providing end developing electronic services. It may be possible to calculate the "necessary" staff for regular tasks like media processing or lending services, based on the library's acquisitions and loan statistics and on average production times. The activities in providing end developing electronic services differ so widely between libraries and in each library over years, depending on projects and on the introduction of new services, that standards would be outdated as soon as formulated. But comparing the percentage of staff invested into electronic services over years and with other libraries can indicate whether the library's organisation and staff allocation consider the needs of continuous development.

Therefore, the allocation of staff resources to electronic services can be seen as an indicator of the library's ability to cope with future.

Definition of the indicator

The percentage of all library staff members in FTE (full-time equivalent) that are planning, maintaining, providing and developing IT services and technically developing and improving the library's electronic services.

Library staff for this indicator includes project staff, temporary staff, voluntaries, student assistants etc.

Staff is calculated as FTE (full-time equivalent). Figures for part-time employees are converted to the equivalent number of full-time workers.

Example:
If out of three persons employed as librarians, one works quarter-time, one works half-time, and one works full-time, then the FTE of these three persons would be 0,25+0,5+1,0=1,75 librarians (FTE).

In the sense of this indicator, providing electronic services means maintaining and developing the automated library system, the library's web server(s), a depository for electronic publications, the electronic reference system and all other software applications provided for users, and staff taking care of computer hardware (servers, computers, printers and scanners).

Staff in reference services, in acquisition/processing of electronic resources, in digitisation of material for the electronic collection, in user training dealing with electronic library services and in content-related work on the library's internet services (e.g. adding texts or data) is excluded.

Aims of the indicator

The indicator assesses the amount of staff time dedicated to the library's electronic services and therewith the priority that the library gives to developing and maintaining electronic services.

The indicator is relevant for all libraries providing electronic services with their own staff. It will be especially interesting for following the development in a library over years.

Comparison between libraries with similar mission and clientele is possible, if the same method of calculating staff has been used.

Method

Calculate the total library staff in FTE (full-time equivalent), including project staff, temporary staff, voluntaries, student assistants etc.

Calculate the number of library staff providing and developing electronic library services in FTE (full-time equivalent). Generally, staff in the library's IT department can be simply counted, as it may be assumed that their work time is spent on maintaining and developing electronic services. The time spent by other staff members on electronic services in the sense of this indicator will be best assessed by sampling. Staff members are asked to keep work diaries for several representative days, and the amount of time spent on electronic services can then be calculated in FTE for the year.

The indicator is calculated as percentage of FTE staff providing and developing electronic services of total FTE staff.

If the tasks of maintaining and developing the library's electronic services have been partly out-sourced to an IT department or other external institutions (in return for payment or not), this indicator should only be applied if the external workload can be quantified accordingly in FTE. This number should be added to both the total library staff and to the library staff providing and developing electronic services.

Interpretation and use of results

A higher score will normally be considered as better, as it indicates high investment into new services. But what percentage of staff would be seen as sufficient for the library's electronic services will depend on the library's mission and goals, that is on the definition of what services the library has to offer, and what range of electronic services is adequate to its clientele.

The indicator will be influenced by a high amount of staff being involved in special tasks of the library, e.g. preservation tasks.

The indicator should be compared with indicators measuring the use of electronic services (see Indicator B.3 "Library visits per capita" or B.5 "Number of content units downloaded per capita").

Examples and further reading

The indicator was developed in the project EQUINOX: Library performance measurement and quality management system (EQUINOX, 2000), where it included user training on electronic services.

The indicator as described here is used in the German benchmarking project BIX (BIX. Der Bibliotheksindex). In 2005, BIX showed the following results (BIX, 2006):

Percentage of staff developing and maintaining electronic services	mean	maximum	minimum
Universities of applied sciences	7.5	12.5	0.0
Universities: One-tier systems	7.5	17.8	3.1
Universities: Two-tier systems (only the central library considered)	7.9	12.4	1.1

The university libraries in North-Rhine Westphalia, Germany, assessed over years the allocation of staff resources to specified service areas (Poll, 2000). One of the background service areas was "central tasks", including electronic services, staff training, central services for branch libraries, and public relations.

Percentage of staff allocated to tasks	1995	1997	2001
Management/subject specialists	8.03	8.14	6.98
Administration	7.27	7.24	6.74

Central tasks	4.69	7.02	10.08
Media processing	31.49	28.92	23.05
Collection maintenance	5.24	5.80	5.41
User services	40.96	42.68	43.52
Special tasks	2.32	0.19	4.23

The results showed a continuous decrease of staff in management, administration and media processing, due to reorganisation of processes, and an increase in staff allocation to user services and especially to "central tasks", due to the growing importance of electronic services.

BIX. Der Bibliotheksindex, available at: http://www.bix-bibliotheksindex.de/

BIX. Der Bibliotheksindex (2006), *B.I.T. online* Sonderheft 2006

Equinox. Library performance measurement and quality management system (2000), available at: http://equinox.dcu.ie/index.html

Poll, R. (2000), Three years of operating ratios for university libraries, *Performance Measurement & Metrics* 1,1, pp. 3 - 8

D.3 Attendances at training lessons per staff member

Background

Library staff with high competences as well in traditional as in new web-based library services is the most important criterion for a library's ability to cope with rising user expectations and rapid developments in the information sector. Further education of staff has become a continuous task.

But developing and offering training courses for library staff will involve considerable effort and input of resources. Therefore, libraries should be able to show at least basic data about input and output of their training activities. Judging from national library statistics it seems that libraries are only recently starting to collect data about the number, duration, and costs of staff training lessons and the number of attendants. If possible, they should also try to assess the effect and impact of staff training activities by satisfaction surveys and by tests of the attendants' skills and competences before and after training.

The indicator described here concentrates on the amount of library training per staff member. It was chosen because of its practicality and its suitability for benchmarking purposes.

Definition of the indicator

The number of attendance hours of staff members at formal training lessons during one year divided by the total number of library staff at the end of the year.

Formal training lessons in the sense of this indicator are pre-planned lessons which can be held in-house or externally and can be hosted by library staff or external experts.

Online lessons by an expert from outside the library are included. Conference visits are excluded. Informal training, e.g. point-of-use training, is excluded.

Library staff includes all persons working in return for payment in the library. Volunteers are excluded. For this indicator, the number of library staff members is counted in persons, not in FTE (full-time equivalent).

As a subset, the indicator counts the number of attendances at training lessons per staff member.

The indicator does not measure the quality or the impact of the training.

Aims of the indicator

The indicator assesses the improvement of library staff skills by attending training lessons and the priority that the library gives to staff training and therewith to the library's ability to cope with new developments.

The indicator is relevant for all libraries.

Comparison of results between libraries with similar mission and structure is possible.

Method

Count the number of attendants at each training lesson and the duration of each training lesson. A training lesson of 3 hours with 12 staff attendants would be 36 attendance hours. The numbers are accumulated at the end of the year.

The total number of attendance hours is divided by the total number of library staff (persons). The total number of library staff includes part-time staff and project staff, temporary staff, student assistants etc., but excludes volunteers. The number of persons, not FTE (full-time equivalent), is chosen for this indicator, as training attendance will be important for all persons in the library, and as it is important to know how many persons attended training lessons. A high number of attendances at formal training lessons may, however, involve the same staff members.

As a subset, the number of attendance hours at training lessons on electronic services and information technology could be counted.

Interpretation and use of results

A high score will be generally seen as good; only an extremely high score might also be seen as affecting the time available for the library's services. A low score, especially in comparison with libraries of similar mission and structure, points to the need of intensifying staff training.

The indicator will be affected by the number of training lessons offered and by the quality of the training. The quality of the lessons should be monitored by satisfaction questionnaires and/or by tests that assess the learning outcome.

The indicator will also be influenced by the library's introducing new services during the reporting year, e.g. a new cataloguing system that requires more training.

In case of low attendance at training lessons, the library could
- promote the training lessons via its intranet or personal invitation,

- survey staff as to their need and preference of certain topics for training lessons,
- adapt the training to special target groups of staff members,
- improve the quality of training.

A high number of attendance hours at training lessons per staff member do not mean that every staff member attended the training to the same degree. The same persons may have attended many training lessons.

As the indicator does not include informal training, it may undervalue the amount of training attendance per staff member.

Examples and further reading

Libraries assess the amount of staff training in different ways:
- Hours of training per staff member
- Days of training per staff member (hours calculated in days)
- Percentage of staff members who received training during the year
- Number of training lessons per staff member

The German benchmarking project (BIX. Der Bibliotheksindex) uses the indicator "training days per staff member" for academic libraries, summing up the attendance hours to working days. The number of training days is divided by the number of regular staff (staff in the position chart) in FTE (full-time equivalent). The results in 2005 were (BIX, 2006):

Training days per staff member	mean	maximum	minimum
Universities of applied sciences	3,5	13,8	1,0
Universities: One-tier systems	2,7	9,5	0,9
Universities: Two-tier systems (only the central library considered)	2,8	5,4	1,1

The Finnish university libraries had in 2005 a total of 1.350 staff members (including all staff), of which 1.154 = 85.5 % received training during the year (Finnish research library statistics database). The libraries counted 5.889 "days of staff training", which would be 4,36 days per staff member.

The Bavarian libraries in universities of applied sciences use the indicator "number of training attendances per staff member" (Indikatoren für Fachhochschulbibliotheken, 2000). The number of training attendances is divided by the number of regular staff (staff in the position chart) in FTE (full-time equivalent). The mean result in 2000 was 6,6 attendances per staff member.

The number of training attendance hours might also be compared to the total staff working hours during the year in order to assess the percentage of work time devoted to staff training.

The German benchmarking project BIX has an indicator "ratio of staff training" for public libraries that calculates the percentage of training attendance hours of the total staff working hours during a year, including work hours of project staff and volunteers. Staff training in this indicator includes conference visits. The results in 2005 were (BIX, 2006):

Ratio of staff training (Percentage of training hours of the total working hours)	mean	maximum	minimum
Libraries in communities under 15.000 inhabitants	1,6	5,8	0,1
Libraries in communities from 15.000 to 30.000 inhabitants	0,9	2,3	0,0
Libraries in communities from 30.000 to 50.000 inhabitants	1,2	3,0	0,1
Libraries in communities from 50.000 to 100.000 inhabitants	1,0	2,7	0,2
Libraries in communities over 100.000 inhabitants	1,3	3,6	0,2

There seems to be no difference between libraries in smaller or larger communities.

The benchmarking project of the Netherlands university libraries does not measure attendances at training lessons, but the expenditure for staff training, excluding conference visits. In 2004 there was an average of 36.400 € of such expenditure for 12 reporting libraries (UKB, 2004).

BIX. Der Bibliotheksindex, available at: http://www.bix-bibliotheksindex.de/

BIX. Der Bibliotheksindex (2006), *B.I.T. online* Sonderheft 2006

Finnish research library statistics database, Helsinki University Library, available at: https://yhteistilasto.lib.helsinki.fi/language.do?action=change&choose_language=3

Indikatoren für Fachhochschulbibliotheken – Beispiel Bayern (2000), available at: http://www.fh-bibliotheken-bayern.de/projekte/indikatoren.shtml

UKB (2004), Benchmarking, Samenwerkingsverband van de Nederlandse universiteitsbibliotheken en de Koninklijke Bibliotheek, results only available to participants

D.4 Percentage of library means received by special grants or income generation

Background

In the last years, most library budgets have been stagnant and have not been adapted to rising prices and new tasks of the libraries. In addition, there is often no longer a fixed budget that the library can rely on in its planning. It will therefore be crucial for libraries to try for additional financial resources from institutions or private persons outside its financing authority. Such resources could be obtained via project grants, sponsoring, or income generated by the library.

The library's success in gaining additional funds can be seen as an indicator for the library's ability to cope with financial restraints and for enlarging its scope for development.

Definition of the indicator

The percentage of all library means in the reporting year received by special grants or income generated.

The overall library means include means from the funding institution and external means, also means for capital expenditure.

The means received by special grants or income generated include means for capital expenditure if they were not paid by the funding institution.

Special grants in the sense of this indicator are grants of a non-recurrent nature to fund major projects, e.g. a cost analysis project or the test of a chat reference service. Continuous funding by external bodies for special tasks of the library (e. g. maintaining a centre for library education) is not considered as special grant, but included in the overall library means.

Income generated by the library includes income from fees, charges, donations, and income generated by special activities like a library shop or advertisements.

Aims of the indicator

The indicator assesses the library's success in obtaining additional funding via projects or income generation and therewith its ability to gain scope for necessary developments.

The indicator is relevant for all libraries.

Comparison of results between libraries with similar mission and structure is possible, if differences in the funding institutions are taken into account, and if the income is calculated in the same way.

Method

Determine the overall means of the library, including means for capital expenditure. As a subtotal, determine the means obtained by income generation and special grants, including those means for capital expenditure that were not paid by the funding institutions.

Calculate the percentage of the total means obtained by special grants and income generation.

In order to get a more detailed view, the different groups of income could be assessed separately:

- Percentage of library means received by special grants
- Percentage of library means received by fees and charges
- Percentage of library means received by donations
- Percentage of library means received by income generated by special library activities

Interpretation and use of results

A higher score is usually considered as good, as it shows that the library is successful in obtaining additional means on its own initiative. The indicator can also show the extent to which the library is involved in tasks that go beyond its main mission and therefore qualify for extra means. But this interpretation is doubtful if the largest part of the additional income results from fixed fees and charges that do not indicate additional effort of the library.

The score will be greatly influenced by the financing conditions for libraries in the country or region, e. g.

- whether there are central institutions where libraries can apply for special grants,
- whether libraries can or must take fees for all services or for special services,
- whether libraries can use the total income from fees and charges for themselves or must deliver it to the funding institutions.

The indicator may also be influenced by the national tax laws concerning donations that make it more or less advantageous for sponsors to support a library.

If the library's normal budget decreases and the library's income from special grants and income generated keeps constant, this will lead to a higher score without additional initiatives of the library.

Because of the differing legal and political conditions, it will be problematic to compare the results of this indicator between libraries in different countries.

Examples and further reading

The German benchmarking project BIX (BIX. Der Bibliotheksindex) uses the indicator "percentage of library means received by external funding, special grants and income generation" for academic libraries. This includes continuous external funding for special tasks of the libraries. The results in 2005 were (BIX, 2006):

Percentage of library means received by external funding, special grants and income generation	mean	maximum	minimum
Universities of applied sciences	4,8	24,6	0,0
Universities: One-tier systems	5,8	17,2	0,8
Universities: Two-tier systems (only the central library considered)	8,8	36,9	0,8

The statistics of the UK academic libraries count the total library expenditure and the income generated, which includes special grants. The statistics of 2004/05 show for all academic libraries an expenditure of 500.005.000 £ and an income generated of 70.442.000 £, which is 14,09 % (Creaser, 2006, p.129).

The Swedish libraries in institutions of higher education had in 2005 a total income of 1.555.261 (in 1.000 SEK) and 78.414 (in 1.000 SEK) by special grants and income generated, which is 5,04 % (Forskningsbiblioteken, 2005, p.38).

The Netherlands university libraries use the indicator "percentage of own revenues of the total library expenditure" (UKB, 2004). The own revenues include fees and charges, special grants, donations, and income generated by special activities like document delivery. In 2004, the libraries had an average own revenue of 14,85 %.

The public libraries of British Columbia, Canada, had in 2003 a total revenue of 153.553.679 CAD, of which 7,42 % were project grants, donations, and income generated (Ministry of Education, British Columbia, 2004).

A report by OCLC showed the situation of public libraries' income in 2001 for 29 countries (Wilson, 2004): "For all countries covered, public funding is the primary source of library funding, comprising 87 percent of funding on average... User fees and charges represent 4 percent of library funding on average, with the remainder of resources coming from the miscellaneous 'other' sources."

The examples show that the calculation varies considerably in the library statistics and that it is difficult to compare results between countries or library types.

BIX. Der Bibliotheksindex, available at: http://www.bix-bibliotheksindex.de/

BIX. Der Bibliotheksindex (2006), *B.I.T. online* Sonderheft 2006

Creaser, C., Maynard, S. and White, S. (2005), LISU annual library statistics 2005, featuring trend analysis of UK public and academic libraries 1994 – 2004, LISU, Loughborough University, available at:
http://www.lboro.ac.uk/departments/dils/lisu/downloads/als05.pdf

Finnish research library statistics database, Helsinki University Library, available at:
https://yhteistilasto.lib.helsinki.fi/language.do?action=change&choose_language=3

Forskningsbiblioteken 2005 (2005), KB/Bibsam och SCB, Sveriges officiella statistik, available at:
http://www.scb.se/statistik/_publikationer/KU0102_2005A01_BR_KUFT0601.pdf

Ministry of education, British Columbia, Public Library Services Branch (2004), British Columbia public library statistics 2003, available at:
http://www.bced.gov.bc.ca/pls/bcplstats_2004.pdf

UKB (2004), Benchmarking, Samenwerkingsverband van de Nederlandse universiteitsbibliotheken en de Koninklijke Bibliotheek, results only available to participants

Wilson, A. ed. (2004), The OCLC 2003 environmental scan: pattern recognition, A report to the OCLC membership, available at: http://www.oclc.org/reports/escan/toc.htm

D.5 Percentage of institutional means allocated to the library

Background

For offering high quality services to their users, libraries need financial resources that are adequate to their mission, tasks and clientele. Without adequate funding, the quality of service delivery may diminish, and even if the library finds ways of coping with budget cuts and keeping up its service quality, it will not be able to invest into necessary developments. In a time of rapidly changing information channels and information types, it is especially important for libraries that their budgets allow introducing new web-based services and investing into electronic collections.

In the last years, most library budgets have been stagnant and have not been adapted to rising prices and new tasks of the libraries. In addition, there is often no longer a fixed budget that the library can rely on in its planning. The library must compete for resources with other claimants in its funding institution, e.g. in universities with the faculties or the computer centre, in communities with other cultural institutions like museums or theatres.

Therefore the library's success in gaining sufficient funding from its parent institution can be seen as an indicator for the importance of the library in the institution and for the library's ability to cope with emerging new services and future development.

Definition of the indicator

The percentage of institutional means allocated to the library.

The institutional means, in the sense of this indicator, include the total budget of the parent institution in the reporting year, but exclude third-party funds (external funds for special purposes) and possible rests of the previous year.

The means of the library, in the sense of this indicator, are all funds received from the institution during the reporting year, including funding for capital expenditure and one-time funding. External funding, e.g. from other public sources, or from corporate or private sources (including donations) is excluded. Income generated by the library, e.g. from fees, charges, or by a library shop, is excluded.

The indicator does not consider external funding and income generated, as its object is to set the library's budget in relation to the institution's budget.

Aims of the indicator

The indicator assesses what part of its budget the institution allocates to its library and therewith the priority the institution gives to the library.

The indicator is most valuable for libraries of an institution of higher education. Comparison between integrated library systems and two-tier systems with many departmental libraries may be difficult.

Public libraries may adapt this indicator to obtain the percentage of public means allocated to the library from the total budget of their funding authority.

Comparison of results between libraries with similar mission and structure is possible, if the institutional and library means are calculated in the same way.

Method

Define the total means of the library (including capital expenditure and one-time funds received from the institution, excluding external funding and income generated by the library) in the reporting year.

Define the total means of the institution (excluding third-party funds and rests of the previous year) for the same period.

Calculate the library means as percentage of the institutional means.

Interpretation and use of results

A higher percentage will be considered as good. It indicates that the funding institution acknowledges the library's value for the institution and its financial needs and may allow the library to offer better services to its users.

This indicator will be influenced by the existence of external funding bodies and structures (e.g. governmental means). It will also be influenced by special tasks of the library with a high amount of funding, e.g. special collections funded by an external institution..

Examples and further reading

The German benchmarking project BIX (BIX. Der Bibliotheksindex) uses the indicator in the sense described here for academic libraries. The results in 2005 were (BIX, 2006):

Library means as percentage of institutional means	mean	maximum	minimum
Universities of applied sciences	4.8	19.0	1.9

Universities: One-tier systems	6.0	10.9	1.2
Universities: Two-tier systems (only the central library considered)	4.2	7.3	1.7

The percentage seems to be lower for libraries in two-tier systems, but there the means of faculty and institute libraries are not considered.

The statistics of the UK academic libraries show the proportion of total institutional expenditure spent on the library (Creaser, Maynard and White, 2005, p.119). The results for 1993/94 and 2003/04 were:

	1993/94	2003/04
Old universities	2.9 %	2.8 %
New universities	3.8 %	3.5 %
Higher education colleges	3.3	3.2

In all UK academic libraries, the percentage decreased slightly during the 10 years.

The benchmarking project of the Netherlands university libraries calculates library expenditure as percentage of the university's expenditure (UKB, 2004). In 2004, 11 libraries delivered data for this indicator. The average was 3.09 %.

No example was found for public libraries. A report by OCLC showed the situation of public libraries' income in 2001 for 29 countries (Wilson, 2004): "For all countries covered, public funding is the primary source of library funding, comprising 87 percent of funding on average."

The examples show that the percentage differs between types of libraries and between methods of calculation (budget or expenditure).

BIX. Der Bibliotheksindex, available at: http://www.bix-bibliotheksindex.de/

BIX. Der Bibliotheksindex (2006), *B.I.T. online* Sonderheft 2006

Creaser, C., Maynard, S. and White, S. (2005), LISU annual library statistics 2005, featuring trend analysis of UK public and academic libraries 1994 – 2004, LISU, Loughborough University, available at:
http://www.lboro.ac.uk/departments/dils/lisu/downloads/als05.pdf

UKB (2004), Benchmarking, Samenwerkingsverband van de Nederlandse universiteitsbibliotheken en de Koninklijke Bibliotheek, results only available to participants

Wilson, A. ed. (2004), The OCLC 2003 environmental scan: pattern recognition, A report to the OCLC membership, available at: http://www.oclc.org/reports/escan/toc.htm

Annex 1: Calculating costs

This handbook includes several indicators that compare the use of library services to costs in order to show the cost-effectiveness or efficiency of the library.

"Costs" in the indicators can have different meanings: costs of an electronic resource, total cost of the library or unit costs (cost of a single product or service).

Costs of electronic resources

The indicator

- C.6 Cost per download

calculates the costs of the individual electronic resource (a database, an electronic journal, a digital document) and compares them to the number of downloads. These costs include the subscription or licensing costs paid by the library for that resource during a specified time, usually a year. Pay-per-view costs are excluded.

The calculation of such costs is comparably easy, but there may be some problems:

- Electronic versions of a document could be acquired in a package with the print version of the document. If the costs for each version cannot be clearly separated, such documents should be excluded in this indicator.
- Electronic documents are sometimes acquired in bundles (e.g. all serials of one publisher, subject bundles of e-books), especially in consortia agreements. In that case, the bundle price could be divided by the number of documents in the bundle

Total costs of the library

The following indicators compare the total costs of the library to the number of library users or the quantity of library use:

- C.1 Cost per user
- C.2 Cost per visit
- C.3 Cost per use

"Total costs" in the sense of these indicators means the total operating or recurrent expenditure of the library.

This includes expenditure on

- staff,
- collection building and maintenance,

- operations and maintenance of the computer network,
- library administration (e.g. maintenance and repair of equipment, materials, communication).

It is irrelevant for the calculation whether the expenditure was transacted out of means received from the parent institution or out of external funding or income generated by the library.

Capital expenditure - expenditure for new buildings, new computer systems, etc. - is not included in the calculation as such expenditure varies greatly over years. The intention of the indicators is to compare the yearly costs of running the library to the use of library services.

In reality, the total operating expenditure of a library would also include:
- utility costs like heating, electricity, water, sewage, cleaning, security,
- calculatory depreciations of assets (buildings, IT- and other equipment).

These costs are usually "hidden" costs, as they do not appear on the library's bills or payrolls. Utility costs are often paid by the library's parent institution, not by the library itself. They must be split up in order to define the library's part, and this might prove difficult.

Calculatory depreciation means that a minimum useful life-time is defined for groups of assets, e.g. 4 years for a computer or 20 years for a library building. The purchase price is then divided by the number of years of useful lifetime, and for each of these years the annual depreciation can thus be calculated. But depreciation costs are calculated differently in countries and even in many institutions, so that comparison of the indicator scores would be difficult.

Therefore, when "total costs" are used as dataset for the indicators in this handbook, only the operating or recurrent expenditure of the library is calculated, excluding utility costs and depreciations. This will in many cases be equivalent to the library's yearly budget and will be most interesting to the funding institution.

Unit costs of a product or service

For many reasons, libraries need data about the costs of their products. Especially financing authorities often ask for the cost of one loan, document delivery, or catalogue entry. This handbook offers one indicator for "unit costs":
- C.5 Cost per document processed

Calculating all costs associated with the production of a single product or service requires time cost analysis for the activities connected with the product or service.

The unit costs could be calculated in two different ways, both including time cost analysis.

1. Only the staff costs are considered.

   To obtain the number of hours spent on producing specified services or products (e.g. bibliographic records, loans, reference answers) staff involved in these services (cataloguing, lending, reference) note the time they spend on this task during a sample period. Thus, the proportion of time that every employee dedicates to this special service (cataloguing, lending, and reference) can be calculated in hours. If time logging is not possible, this proportion could, instead, be estimated.

   The hours are then multiplied with the cost per hour of labour (wages divided by the regular working time of the relevant staff), and the result is divided by the number of "units" produced (titles catalogued, loans transacted, reference questions answered) during the sampling period. Thus, the unit costs for one title catalogued, one loan or one reference answer can be calculated.

2. If the library wants to assess not only staff costs, but all costs directly associated with a product or service, all operating cost as shown before must be included.

   The total operating costs of the library are assigned to "cost centres" or working areas of the library, in these examples to the cataloguing or processing department, the lending department or the reference service. Some costs can be assigned directly to each cost centre, for instance the staff costs in media processing. Other indirect costs like the costs of information technology must be assigned by using keys. Information technology costs could be calculated according to the number of computers in the cost centre.

   As in method 1, the proportion of time that every employee spends on the specified service (cataloguing, lending, reference) is calculated by time-logging. The total operating costs of the cost centre are then allocated to cataloguing, lending, or reference according to the percentage of staff time spent on these services. The result is divided by the number of "units" produced (titles catalogued, loans transacted, reference questions answered) to obtain the unit costs.

Example

Costs of the cost centre "media processing"	188.000,00 €
Costs of the activity "cataloguing"	67.716,00 €
Number of titles catalogued	5.232
Total costs of one title catalogued	12,94 €

Further information as to cost analysis in libraries is given in:

Ceynowa, K., Coners, A. (2003), Cost management for university libraries, *IFLA Publications* 104, Saur, München

Heaney, M. (2004), Do users get what they pay for? A resource allocation model for Oxford University library services, *World Library and Information Congress: 70th IFLA General Conference and Council,* available at: http://www.ifla.org/IV/ifla70/papers/179e-Heaney.pdf

Poll, R. (2000), The costs of quality: cost analysis and cost management as counterpart to performance measurement, *Proceedings of the 3rd Northumbria International Conference on Performance Measurement in Libraries and Information Services*, Newcastle upon Tyne, Information North, pp. 43-52

Roberts, S. A. (1998), Financial and cost management for libraries and information services, 2nd ed., Bowker-Saur, London.

Snyder, H. and Davenport, E. (1997), Costing and pricing in the digital age, a practical guide for information services, Library Association, London

Annex 2: Main sources of the indicators

A. Resources, infrastructure: What services does the library offer?

	IFLA 1st ed. (1996)	ISO 11620 (1998)	EQLIPSE (1995-98)	EQUI-NOX (1998-2000)	ISO TR 20983 (2003)	BIX (2002)	ISO 11620 (2006)
1. User area per capita						1.1	B.1.3.3
2. Seats per capita							B.1.3.4
3. Opening hours compared to demand	No.2		Nr.43				
4. Expenditure on information provision per capita						1.3	
5. Availability of required titles	No.11	B.2.2.2	Nr. 7				B.1.1.1 B.1.1.2
6. Percentage of rejected sessions				No.10	B.1.3.4		B.1.1.4
7. Ratio of requests received to requests sent out in interlibrary lending (taken from the Netherlands benchmarking project)							
8. Immediate availability						2.3	
9. Staff per capita			Nr.51			1.2	B.1.4.1
10. Direct access from the homepage (new)							

B. Use: How are the services accepted?

	IFLA 1st ed. (1996)	ISO 11620 (1998)	EQLIPSE (1995-98)	EQUI-NOX (1998-2000)	ISO TR 20983 (2003)	BIX (2002)	ISO 11620 (2006)
1. Market penetration	No.1	B.2.1.1	Nr.2				B.2.4.1
2. User satisfaction	No.16	B.1.1.1	Nr.1			in test	B.2.4.2
3. Library visits per capita		B.2.1.3	Nr.4			2.1	B.2.2.1
4. Seat occupancy rate		B.2.9.3	Nr.42				B.2.3.1
5. Number of content units downloaded per capita				No.4			B.2.1.4
6. Collection use (turnover)	No.4	B.2.4.1	Nr.24				B.2.1.1
7. Percentage of stock not used	No.6		Nr.29				B.2.1.3
8. Loans per capita		B.2.4.2	Nr.25			Public libraries 2.2	B.2.1.2
9. Percentage of loans to external users							B.2.2.4
10. Attendances at training lessons per capita				No.12	B.1.5.1		B.2.2.6
11. Reference questions per capita			Nr.36				
12. Attendances at events per capita			Nr.50				B.2.2.5

C. Efficiency: Are the services offered cost-effectively?

	IFLA 1st ed. (1996)	ISO 11620 (1998)	EQLIPSE (1995-98)	EQUI-NOX (1998-2000)	ISO TR 20983 (2003)	BIX (2002)	ISO 11620 (2006)
1. Cost per user		B.2.1.2	Nr.3			3.1	B.3.4.1
2. Cost per visit		B.2.1.4	Nr.5				B.3.1.4
3. Cost per use (new)							
4. Ratio of acquisitions costs to staff costs						3.2	B.3.3.3
5. Cost per document processed		B.3.3.1					
6. Cost per download				No.6	B.1.3.3		B.3.1.3
7. Acquisition speed	No.9	B.3.1.1	Nr.47				B.3.2.1
8. Media processing speed	No.10	B.3.2.1	Nr.48				B.3.2.2
9. Employee productivity in media processing						3.3	B.3.3.4
10. Lending speed	No.12	B.2.3.1	Nr.21				B.1.2.2
11. Interlibrary loan speed	No.13	B.2.5.1	Nr.34				B.1.2.3
12. Reference fill rate	No.14	B.2.6.1	Nr.37				B.3.3.2
13. Shelving accuracy			Nr.23				B.1.2.1

D. Potentials and development: Are there sufficient potentials for future development?

No indicators in IFLA (1996), ISO 11620 (1998) and EQLIPSE

	EQUINOX (1998-2000)	ISO TR 20983 (2003)	BIX (2002)	ISO 11620 (2006)	Comments
1. Percentage of acquisitions expenditure spent on the electronic collection	No.11	B.1.2.1	1.4	B.4.1.1	
2. Percentage of library staff providing and developing electronic services	No.13	B.2.2.1	4.4.	B.4.2.1	
3. Attendances at training lessons per staff member		B.2.1.1	4.1	B.4.2.2	ISO TR = attendances at IT training BIX = days of training per staff member
4. Percentage of library means received by special grants or income generation			4.3	B.4.3.1	
5. Percentage of institutional means allocated to the library			4.2	B.4.3.2	

Selective bibliography

Handbooks and standards

Barton, J. and Blagden, J. (1998), Academic library effectiveness: a comparative approach, *British Library Research and Innovation Report* 120, British Library Research and Innovation Centre, Boston Spa

Bertot, J. C., McClure, C. R. and Ryan, J. (2001), Statistics and performance measures for public library networked services, American Library Association, Chicago

Bertot, J. C., Ed. (2004), Planning and evaluating library networked services and resources, Libraries Unlimited, Westport, Conn.

Bloor, I. G. (1991), Performance indicators and decision support systems for libraries: a practical application of "Keys to success", *Library Research Paper* 93, British Library Research and Development Department, London

Brophy, P. (2006), Measuring library performance, Facet, London

Brophy, P. and Coulling, K. (1996), Quality management for information and library managers, Aslib Gower, Aldershot

Ceynowa, K. and Coners, A. (2002), Balanced Scorecard für wissenschaftliche Bibliotheken, *Zeitschrift für Bibliothekswesen und Bibliographie, Sonderheft 82,* Klostermann, Frankfurt a.M.

Edgren, J. et al. (2005), Quality handbook, performance indicators for library activities, The Swedish Library Association's Special Interest Group for Quality Management and Statistics, available at: http://www.biblioteksforeningen.org/sg/kvalitet/handbook_eng.html

Hernon, P. and Altman, E. (1996), Service quality in academic libraries, Ablex Publ., Norwood, NJ

Hernon, P. and Whitman, J. R. (2001), Delivering satisfaction and service quality: a customer based approach for libraries, American Library Association, Chicago

ISO 2789 (2006), Information and documentation – International library statistics, 4th ed., International Organization for Standardization, Geneva

ISO DIS 11620 (2006), Information and documentation – Library performance indicators, 2nd ed., International Organization for Standardization, Geneva

Kantor, P. B. (1984), Objective performance measures for academic and research libraries, Association of Research Libraries, Washington, DC

Keys to success: performance indicators for public libraries; a manual of performance measures and indicators developed by King Research Ltd. (1990), *Library Information Series* 18, HMSO, London

Lancaster, F. W. (1993), If you want to evaluate your library…, 2nd ed., University of Illinois, Graduate School for Library and Information Science, Champaign, Ill.

The effective academic library: a framework for evaluating the performance of UK academic libraries; a consultative report to the HEFCE, SHEFC, HEFCW and DENI (1995), HEFCE, Bristol

VanHouse, N. A. et al. (1987), Output measures for public libraries: a manual of standardized procedures, 2nd ed., American Library Association, Chicago

VanHouse, N. A., Weil, B. T. and McClure, C. R. (1990), Measuring academic library performance: a practical approach, American Library Association, Chicago

VanHouse, N. A. and Childers, T. (1993), The public library effectiveness study, the complete report, American Library Association, Chicago

Ward, S. et al. (1995), Library performance indicators and library management tools, Office for Official Publications of the European Communities, Luxemburg

Projects and conferences

Australian public libraries comparative report 1998 – 2004, available at: http://www.nsla.org.au/publications/statistics/2004/pdf/NSLA.Statistics-20040701-Australian.Public.Library.Comparative.Report.1998.2004.pdf

BIX. Der Bibliotheksindex, available at: http://www.bix-bibliotheksindex.de/

EQLIPSE. Evaluation and Quality in Library Performance: System for Europe (1995-1997), available at: http://www.cerlim.ac.uk/projects/eqlipse/

EQUINOX. Library performance measurement and quality management system (1998-2000), available at: http://equinox.dcu.ie/index.html

Forslag til indikatorer for fag- og folkebibliotek (2007), ABM-utvikling, Oslo, available at: http://www.abm-utvikling.no/bibliotek/statistikk-for-bibliotek/indikatorer-for-fag-og-folkebibliotek

Indikatoren für Fachhochschulbibliotheken – Beispiel Bayern (2000), available at: http://www.fh-bibliotheken-bayern.de/projekte/indikatoren.shtml

Proceedings of the Northumbria International Conference on Performance Measurement in Libraries and Information Services, 1 (1995) ff.

Report on the 1992 evaluation study of the Copenhagen Business School Library (1993), Copenhagen Business School Library

UK higher education library management statistics 2003-2004 (2005), Sconul, London

UKB, Benchmarking, Samenwerkingsverband van de Nederlandse universiteitsbibliotheken en de Koninklijke Bibliotheek, available at: http://www.ukb.nl/benchmark.htm

Articles

Brophy, P. (2002), Performance measures for 21st century libraries, *Proceedings of the 4th Northumbria International Conference on Performance Measurement in Libraries and Information Services,* Association of Research Libraries, Washington DC, pp. 1-7

Calvert, P. (2000), Integrated performance measures in New Zealand, *Proceedings of the 3rd Northumbria International Conference on Performance Measurement in Libraries and Information Services*, University of Northumbria, Newcastle upon Tyne, pp. 11-17

Cram, J. (2000), "Six impossible things before breakfast": a multidimensional approach to measuring the value of libraries, *Proceedings of the 3rd Northumbria International Conference on Performance Measurement in Libraries and Information Services*, University of Northumbria, Newcastle upon Tyne, pp. 19-29

Crawford, J., Pickering, H. and McLelland, D. (1998), The stakeholder approach to the construction of performance measures, *Journal of Librarianship and Information Science* 30,2, pp. 87-112

Cullen, R. J. (1998), Measure for measure: a post modern critique of performance measurement in libraries and information services, *IATUL Proceedings* 8, available at: http://iatul.org/conferences/pastconferences/1998proceedings.asp

Cullen, R. J., Calvert, P. J. (1995), Stakeholder perceptions of university library effectiveness, *Journal of Academic Librarianship* 21,6, pp. 438-448

Derfert-Wolf, L., Górski, M. and Marcinek, M. (2005), Quality of academic libraries – funding bodies, librarians and users, *World Library and Information Congress, 71st IFLA General Conference and Council,* available at: http://www.ifla.org/IV/ifla71/papers/080e-Derfert-Wolf.pdf#search=%22Derfert-Wolf%22

Ford, G. (2002), Strategic uses of evaluation and performance measurement, *Proceedings of the 4th Northumbria International Conference on Performance Measurement in Libraries and Information Services,* Association of Research Libraries, Washington DC, pp. 19-30

Harer, J. B. and Cole, B. R. (2005), The importance of the stakeholder in performance measurement: critical processes and performance measures for assessing and improving academic library services and programs, *College & Research Libraries* 66, 2, pp. 149-170

Hernon, P. and Dugan, R. E. (2004), Different perspectives on assessment and evaluation: the need to refine and link them, *Proceedings of the 5th Northumbria International Conference on Performance Measurement in Libraries and Information Services,* Emerald, Bradford, England, pp. 23-30

Laeven, H. and Smit, A. (2003), A project to benchmark university libraries in the Netherlands, *Library Management* 24, 6/7, pp. 291-304

Lambert, S., Willson, J. and Oulton, T. (1998), Use and interest in performance measures: differences between library sectors, *Proceedings of the 2nd Northumbria International Conference on Performance Measurement in Libraries and Information Services,* Information North, Newcastle upon Tyne, pp. 67-76

Pienaar, H. and Penzhorn, C. (2000), Using the balanced scorecard to facilitate strategic management at an academic information service, *Libri* 50,3, pp. 202-209, available at: http://www.librijournal.org/pdf/2000-3pp202-209.pdf

Poll, R. (1998), The house that Jack built: the consequences of measuring, *Proceedings of the 2nd Northumbria International Conference on Performance Measurement in Libraries and Information Services,* Information North, Newcastle upon Tyne, pp. 39-45

Poll, R. (2001), Performance, processes and costs: managing service quality with the balanced scorecard, *Library Trends* 49,4, pp. 709-718

Poll, R. (2007), Benchmarking with quality indicators: national projects, *Performance Measurement and Metrics* 8,1, pp. 41-53

Pors, N. O., Dixon, P. and Robson, H. (2004), The employment of quality measures in libraries: cultural differences, institutional imperatives and managerial profiles, *Performance Measurement and Metrics* 5,1, pp. 20-27

Poustie, K. (1995), A climate of change: performance measurement in Australian public libraries, *Proceedings of the 1st Northumbria International Conference on Performance Measurement in Libraries and Information Services,* Information North, Newcastle upon Tyne, pp. 43-49

Revill, D. (1983), Some examples and types of performance measures, in Blagden, J. (ed.), Do we really need libraries: Proceedings of the first joint Library Association Cranfield Institute of Technology conference on performance assessment, Cranfield Press, Cranfield, pp. 59-66

Revill, D. (1990), Performance measures for academic libraries, in Kent, E. (ed.), Encyclopedia of Library and Information Science, Vol.45, Suppl.10, Dekker, New York, Basel, pp. 294 – 333

Revill, D. (2000), A polemic: what we still don't know about performance, *Performance Measurement and Metrics* 1,1, pp. 9-14

Self, J. (2003), From values to metrics: implementation of the balanced scorecard at a university library, *Performance Measurement and Metrics* 4,2, pp. 57-63

Sumsion, J. (1999), Popularity ratings, core sets and classification of performance indicators, *Proceedings of the 3rd Northumbria International Conference on Performance Measurement in Libraries and Information Services*, University of Northumbria, Newcastle upon Tyne, pp. 247-252

Town, S. (1998), Performance or measurement? *Performance Measurement and Metrics* 1,1, pp. 43-54

Willemse, J. (1995), The impact of performance measurement on library and information services, *Proceedings of the 1st Northumbria International Conference on Performance Measurement in Libraries and Information Services,* Information North, Newcastle upon Tyne, pp. 11-32

Winkworth, I. (1998), Making performance measurement influential, *Proceedings of the 2nd Northumbria International Conference on Performance Measurement in Libraries and Information Services,* Information North, Newcastle upon Tyne, pp. 93-97

Winkworth, I. and Gannon-Leary, P. (2000), Library performance measures: government perspectives, *Proceedings of the 3rd Northumbria International Conference on Performance Measurement in Libraries and Information Services*, University of Northumbria, Newcastle upon Tyne, pp. 61-65

Young, P. R. (2002), Electronic services and library performance: a definitional challenge, *Proceedings of the 4th Northumbria International Conference on Performance Measurement in Libraries and Information Services,* Association of Research Libraries, Washington DC, pp. 51-66

Index to the Indicators

As the structure of the Balanced Scorecard for the indicators might be confusing to readers not familiar with it and as the names of indicators do not always clearly explain what services are concerned, a short index was added, considering only the main contents of the indicators. It should be seen as possible help for a quick search.

Essentials for Library and Information Professionals

■ IFLA Library Building Guidelines: Developments & Reflections

Edited on behalf of IFLA by Karen Latimer and Hellen Niegaard

2007. xxxii, 266 pp. Hc.
€ 58.00 / *US$ 81.00
ISBN 978-3-598-11768-8

The information society and the information age are changing library services as well as library premises. This raises questions about what needs to be considered when planning and designing new library buildings in order to achieve attractive, efficient and future-oriented new library spaces.

■ Marketing Library and Information Services: International Perspectives

Edited on behalf of IFLA by Dinesh K. Gupta, Christie Koontz, Ángels Massísimo and Réjean Savard

2006. xvi, 419 pp. Hc.
€ 68.00 / *US$ 95.00
ISBN 978-3-598-11753-4

This book offers a userful tool for both working librarians and future librarians to understand vital issues relating to marketing of library and information services at the local, national, and international level.

■ Handbook on the International Exchange of Publications

Edited on behalf of IFLA by Kirsti Ekonen, Päivi Papoloski and Pentti Vattulainen

5th completely revised edition
2006. 158 pp. Hc.
€ 54.00 / *US$ 76.00
ISBN 978-3-598-11752-7

The international exchange of publications continues to be an important mode of collection building. This handbook addresses the changes which have taken place and provides practices, history, current examples, as well as a directory.

de Gruyter
Berlin · New York

www.saur.de

Journals for Library and Information Professionals

■ LIBER QUARTERLY

The Journal of European Research Libraries

Edited by Trix Bakker on behalf of the Ligue des Bibliothèques
Européennes de Recherche (LIBER)

1 print volume p. a. Online quarterly. ISSN 1435-5205

LIBER Quarterly offers in-depth reports on the practical aspects of library management
and expert analysis of current developments within the information world. It helps library managers to improve services, to understand new developments and to keep their
professional skills right up to date.

■ Libri

International Journal of Libraries and Information Services

Edited by Nancy R. John, Ian M. Johnson and Svend Larsen

4 issues p. a. Print and Online. ISSN 0024-2667

Libri examines the many functions of libraries and information services from a histori-
cal, cultural and political angle and looks at the role of information in cultural, organi-
zational, national and international developments. For information specialists who want
to see the larger picture, *Libri* opens up a wealth of new perspectives.

■ Microform & Imaging Review

Edited by Ken Middleton

4 issues p. a. Print and Online. ISSN 0949-5770

This quarterly publication deals with practical and theoretical aspects of microform and
digital imaging. Each issue also contains critical reviews of new microform and imaging
projects, valuable resources when making acquisition decisions.

■ Restaurator

International Journal for the Preservation of Library and Archival Material

Edited by Helmut Bansa

4 print issues p. a. ISSN 0034-5806

Restaurator reports on the latest advances in restoration technique from around the
world. The journal keeps its focus firmly on specifics, favouring articles which give a
clear and detailed presentation of technical procedures.

W
DE
G de Gruyter
Berlin · New York

www.saur.de   *Please ask for our current journals pricelist.*